NO MORE SECRETS

NO MORE SECRETS
violence in lesbian relationships

JANICE L. RISTOCK

ROUTLEDGE
New York London

Published in 2002 by

Routledge
29 West 35th Street
New York, NY 10001

Published in Great Britain by

Routledge
11 New Fetter Lane
London EC4P 4EE

Routledge is an imprint of the Taylor & Francis Group.

Copyright © 2002 by Routledge

Printed in the United States of America on acid-free paper.

10   9   8   7   6   5   4   3   2   1

Library of Congress Cataloging-in-Publication Data

Ristock, Janice L. (Janice Lynn)
  No more secrets : violence in lesbian relationships / Janice L. Ristock.
    p. cm.
  Includes bibliographical references and index.
  ISBN 0-415-92945-8 — ISBN 0-415-92946-6 (Pbk.)
    1. Abused lesbians. 2. Lesbian couples. 3. Conjugal violence.
  4. Family violence. I. Title

HQ75.5 .R574 2002
305.48'96643—dc21   2001041840

This book is dedicated
to the courageous and generous women
who trusted me with their stories.

CONTENTS

PREFACE
Bearing Witness

Telling secrets is never easy. Going naked in public is more dangerous for some of us than others, and the fear is always there.[1]

Dorothy Allison

Testimony is always directed towards, indeed requires witnesses: those prepared to accept the obligation of reading, viewing, listening, and subsequently responding to an embodied singular experience not recognizable as one's own.[2]

Roger Simon

"NO MORE SECRETS" is likely a familiar phrase for feminists who have been active in the movement to end violence against women. It is most strongly connected to the public discussion of childhood sexual abuse, where women turned their personal experiences into courageous testimonials that exposed their father's secrets.[3] Secrecy is often part of relationship violence, where a victim is expected to continue with "life as usual," never revealing her private hell for fear of repercussions. For lesbians, keeping secrets about abuse in our relationships is also linked to homophobia and heterosexism: it is still risky for some of us to be out, and it can be dangerous to reveal abuse within an already oppressive context. Secrets are sometimes kept for strategic reasons within liberatory movements such as feminism that are trying to eradicate the globally pervasive phenomenon of male violence against women. As Dorothy Allison says, telling secrets is never easy. But ultimately, we know the human cost of maintaining them is too great, and so we acknowledge that sometimes mothers sexually abuse their children, and we admit that violence of all kinds—racial, sexual, physical, emotional, workplace, domestic, public, private—does happen between women.

This book bears witness to dangerous stories that are often suppressed in lesbian and feminist communities. The suppression seldom results from a deliberate effort to deny unpalatable facts; more often, it is the reflexive outcome of our beliefs about the nature of lesbians and domestic violence and, by extension, of domestic violence in lesbian relationships. I felt its effects myself when I was volunteering at the Toronto Counseling Center for Lesbians and Gays in the mid-1980s, and first began to hear about abuse in lesbian relationships. I felt confused; I had worked in rape crisis centers and shelters in large cities; in fact, I had come out in the supportive feminist environment of a rape crisis center where issues such as sexual identities were freely discussed. I knew of the extent of violence against women, but I had never encountered or received training about violence between women. My confusion was not owing to simple naiveté. I had known of "bad relationships," had seen lesbians physically fighting at bars, for example. But these incidents were never named as a community or social issue; they were seen as individual problems. I had many conversations about domestic violence with my colleagues, Laurie Chesley and Donna McAulay, what we knew about it as feminists, and what did not seem to fit lesbian experiences. We felt we needed to do something to respond to lesbians who had been abused. As a first step we got funding from the Ontario Women's Directorate to obtain more information on how large an issue this was within our communities. We put together a questionnaire and surveyed lesbians in Toronto. One significant finding from that survey, for us, was that 66 percent of the 189 respondents knew of lesbians who had been in abusive relationships. We learned from this that abuse in lesbian relationships was something that we could not ignore. We then wrote a booklet on lesbian abuse that provided information and resources, and we ran two support groups for survivors through the Center. My experience in cowriting the booklet and cofacilitating the support group was that we often felt unsure and conflicted about how best to respond, and that we were often worried about causing more harm to lesbians and to feminism by speaking about the issue too publicly.

When I moved to Winnipeg, I joined the Coalition of Lesbians on Support and Education (CLOSE), and we received funding to do a needs assessment and then design antihomophobia trainings and education on lesbian relationship violence for all shelters in the province. It was, by then, the early 1990s and there was slightly more information on lesbian partner abuse to inform our work, but we encountered not only a lack of information about lesbians in shelters, but a lack of awareness of how the very language and policies of domestic violence made lesbian experiences hard to hear or articulate; all attempts were immediately encased in established thinking based on heterosexual women's experiences. Ten years later, lesbians remain barely visible in some places, but in many others there has been more focus on responding to our needs. I have been asked to do workshops in organizations ranging from nurses associations to law conferences. Such experiences of working in lesbian communities and in feminist services, along with my awareness of the need to give voice to experiences while remaining aware of how those voices are taken up and heard, have informed this current project. I share other lesbians' concerns with how easily "lesbian abuse" can be sensationalized in a homophobic culture, and conversely, how within our own lesbian communities we have used terms like abuse and violence so loosely that they lose their meaning. These sorts of distortions do a terrible disservice to women who are experiencing abuse and need our support. Further, I am aware of the limits of the category "lesbian" and that many women involved in relationships with women identify as queer, bisexual, two-spirited, or transgendered. I use the term "lesbian relationship" to denote any intimate relationship between women, not to restrict our focus to women who identify as lesbian.

What I have hoped for in writing this book is an accounting of the specificity of lesbian relationship violence and an examination of how this category is being defined, responded to, and institutionalized. From women's stories, I offer new insights into the power dynamics in abusive lesbian relationships, and the categories victim and perpetrator. From discussions with feminist service providers, I critically examine the theories and practices of social service agencies and counselors that work to respond to domestic violence, and to gay and lesbian communities. I draw on feminist and postmodernist perspectives to show that work in this area needs to address both the material realities of violence and the language that informs, shapes, and limits how we talk and know about violence. I do not offer a new model for understanding lesbian relationship violence, even though that may be what many people want. The whole book is a refusal of the social science/social service drive to create all-explanatory models. My point is that all such models, all monolithic understandings of abuse, are flawed. "Mutual abuse" is wrong, "power and control" is wrong, "effects of patriarchy" is wrong when indiscriminately applied. When looking at specific situations, there is no simple pattern of x or y— we need a much more adaptive, context-sensitive analysis to figure out what is going on. This makes life harder for service providers, and challenges some feminist theorizing, but it offers a much better chance of seeing what is there and responding appropriately. In troubling this terrain, I think about the sticker in my office that says, "there is no excuse for do-mestic abuse." And although I agree that abuse is always inexcusable, the research in this book shows there are many different kinds of abusive relationships and many reasons for why it happens. I think we need to un-derstand those differences so that we can respond in more helpful ways. The same responses are not appropriate for someone who has experienced abuse her whole life and occupied both the perpetrator and victim posi-tions, someone else who has been terrorized by her first lesbian lover, some-one else who uses violence to retaliate against an abusive partner, and someone else who has experienced shifting power dynamics where both she and her partner have been verbally and emotionally abusive. The violence still has to stop: in looking at these contexts, I am not saying that women are not responsible for abuse, but I do think we need different ways of re-sponding that attend to the complexities of these differing power dynamics.

I write this book as a lesbian and a feminist; as someone who has a stake in both identities. In showing that women are violent, I do not want to thwart efforts to end the huge problem of male violence against women; I want those efforts to continue as they must. Nor, in describing the dam-ages done by lesbian violence, by each other and society, do I want to undo our sexuality. On the contrary, I want to claim the identity space we need to acknowledge the realities of abuse in our relationships. However, in describing some of my experiences, I am not claiming an authoritative voice. I have been lucky. I have experienced neither violence in my family nor relationship violence. I have had the privilege of being able to do this research as a feminist academic, an out lesbian within a university setting without any apparent negative repercussions, aside from an occasional anonymous threatening letter. I occupy the space of both insider and out-sider in doing this work, and have struggled to remain aware of the limita-tions inherent in my social positionings. Overall, my challenge has been "to risk the necessary invasions and misuses of other people's stories in order to bear witness with fierce but unsentimental conviction that such stories can transfix, overwhelm, linger and compel" us to action.[4] I alone am responsible for how I have heard, the filters that I have listened through, and ultimately what I have written in this volume.

In spite of my own limitations, women were willing to talk to me about very personal and emotionally difficult aspects of their lives. I have been deeply touched by their openness and generosity of time and spirit. Most often they did the interviews with the hope that retelling their story would help other women. I owe thanks as well to the feminist services providers who participated in focus groups or interviews. I deeply value the work that they do and am grateful for the time they took from that work to engage in a critically reflexive process.

Some acquaintances have not liked the fact that I continue to do work on this issue. Friends sometimes ask why I do not move on to something else, a more cheerful topic, perhaps one that is more celebratory of lesbians. Others have offered encouragement, support, and very welcome advice. When Laurie, Donna, and I first offered the group for survivors, we placed an ad in the local queer newspaper that said, rather sensationally, "Believe it or not, abuse can happen in lesbian relationships." A lesbian that I went to graduate school with generously pulled me aside and told me that she had been abused in her relationship, and although she was glad that I was doing this work, thought the ad would make abused lesbians feel like they were seen as freakish. I have learned so much from conversations like that one, from women I have talked with on committees, at conferences, and in informal exchanges.

My research was supported by a grant from the Lesbian Health Fund of the Gay and Lesbian Medical Association, and from the Social Sciences and Humanities Research Council of Canada. I was able to hire a number of research assistants who helped me with organizing focus groups in various cities, advertising the research, and transcribing interviews. Many thanks to Vycki Anastasiadis, Caroline Fusco, Lois Grieger, Natasha Hurley, Beth Jackson, Kavita Joshi, Kristi Kemp, Jan Mitchell, and Betsy Szilock for their work and their feedback. I was often enriched and sustained by conversations with Cindy Holmes who worked as a research assistant on this project while also engaging in her own research in this area. I thank her for her insights and friendship and most recently for her astute feedback on the guidelines presented in chapter 7. I also thank Sherri McConnell and Sharon Taylor of The Fort Garry Women's Resource Center for their helpful comments on the guidelines. Many community organizations provided me with space for conducting interviews and focus groups, gave me names of service providers to contact, and more generally advertised and supported my work. Thanks to the Rainbow Resource Center in Winnipeg; the FREDA Center for Research on Violence Against Women and Children, Battered Women's Support Services, and the Center for GLBTs and Allies in Vancouver; The David Kelley GLBT Counseling Program and Women's Health in Women's Hands in Toronto; the Sexual Assault Center in London, Ontario; Peer Support Services for Battered Women in Calgary; the Avalon Sexual Assault Center in Halifax, Nova Scotia; the New York City Gay and Lesbian Anti-Violence Project, and the Fenway Community Health Center in Boston. Special thanks to Myrna

Carlsen, Laurie Chesley, Diane Dolan-Soto, Karlene Faith, Donna Huen, Yasmin Jiwani, Donna McAulay, Louise MacPherson, Marg McGill, Kathleen O'Connell, Jane Oxenbury, Emily Pitt, Donna Wilson, and Rae-Ann Woods, and Beth Zemsky for their help. I am grateful to Kristi Kemp, who carefully and skillfully worked with me on the final stages of this manuscript to get all of the footnotes and references to conform with the Chicago Manual of Style. I thank my editor Ilene Kalish for her enthusiastic support of the project and many good ideas that I have incorporated into the final manuscript. Thanks as well to the anonymous reviewer for her comments. Finally, I thank my parents for their encouragement; and most of all, I thank my partner Catherine for her never-ending support, patience, humor and intellect, and her gifts for editing and writing.

ONE
The Emergence of Lesbian Partner Abuse
Creating a New Category

Publicly addressing the issue of lesbian battering, while necessary, is done with the recognition that we live in increasingly repressive times. The hard-won gains of the civil rights movement, women's movement and gay and lesbian rights movement over the past twenty-five years have been met by increasing resistance and setbacks. Many lesbians are understandably reluctant to air issues related to lesbian battering, for fear of triggering homophobic attacks on our communities. In a society where there has been no acceptance of lesbian relationships, the fears are legitimate. By discussing these issues openly we risk further repression. Yet our only alternative is one of silence, a silence that traps battered lesbians into believing that they are alone and that there are no resources available to them.

Kerry Lobel, 1986[1]

THIS QUOTATION is from *Naming the Violence: Speaking Out About Lesbian Battering*, the first published book to address the issue of abuse in lesbian relationships. In many ways, we have moved beyond the silence and secretiveness that once surrounded this issue. There have now been very public education campaigns in Boston, New York, and San Francisco that include billboards and posters in subway stations with slogans stating that one in four gay and lesbian couples will experience domestic violence.[2] There have been public stories that refer to same-sex partner abuse in popular magazines such as *People* where, for example, gay Olympic diver Greg Louganis and lesbian actress Amanda Bearse both spoke openly about having experienced physical abuse at the hands of their same-sex partner. In many major cities in the United States, Canada, the United Kingdom, and Australia, there are programs within gay and lesbian organizations and within women's organizations to specifically respond to lesbian partner abuse. Over the past fifteen years, then, there has been a great deal of response since a few brave lesbians in the early 1980s began talking about lesbian battering within the domestic violence movement.[3] Yet the words of Kerry Lobel that suggest "we risk further repression" in openly discussing lesbian battering still have relevance. Intense debates about the dangers of publicly acknowledging this issue continue as they did in the 1980s within feminist, lesbian, and queer communities. Surrounding these debates are urgent discussions about how we can best respond to lesbians who have been victimized, and lesbians who have engaged in abusive behaviors. I begin this book by providing an extensive overview of the information that we currently have on lesbian partner violence and exploring why the stakes remain so high in naming and responding to this form of abuse.

The Emergence of a New Category

Breaking silences, sharing secrets, and naming forms of violence are the acts women have undertaken as ways to address male violence. As our knowledge has increased, we have insisted that our language be more precise, moving from generic terms such as domestic violence and family violence to specific terms rooted in women's experiences, such as wife assault, woman abuse, child sexual abuse, and date rape. Naming forms of violence within feminism is a political act of high stakes, not just semantic quibbling: it frames the way we see and understand the issues and therefore how we respond to them—whether we focus on rehabilitation of the abuser or challenge the power structures of dominant culture as causing or worsening the abuse, for example.[4] There is often resistance from dominant culture to these feminist framings. For example, resistance can take the forms of not believing women when they speak of being sexually abused as children, seeing women as teasing men sexually rather than really saying no to date rape, and viewing women as vindictive liars rather than as battered wives. Yet resistance to naming abuse in lesbian relationships has occurred not only in the mainstream, but within the women's movement.

Within the women's movement, there have been two main forms of resistance to examining abuse in lesbian relationships: one stems from the desire to keep a focus on male violence, thereby minimizing women's violence; the other arises from the fear that this issue will create a backlash against feminism and lesbians. The ideology that only men were violent was adopted by the radical lesbian feminist culture of the 1970s as one way of validating lesbian relationships and working against dominant constructions of lesbians as sick, perverted, or deviant. However, accepting this ideology also created the conditions to make violence in lesbian relationships into a secret or private issue. In their historical study of working-class lesbians in Buffalo, Elizabeth Kennedy and Madeline Davis show that violence in lesbian relationships used to be observed and talked about in public places such as the bars. Many fights happened in lesbian spaces, allowing other women to see the violence, intervene, and put a stop to abusive behavior. When a new ideology of violence took hold as something that men did to women, violence between lesbians became a private issue and left women who were being battered without protection from other women in the community.[5] More recently, Ellen Faulkner describes a cultural feminist perspective that continues to see violence as a male biological trait, and that argues for the development of lesbian communities and ethics as a way to prevent male violence from infecting women's culture; according to this view, women would not have this violent tendency on their own.[6] This tidy logic completely sidesteps the issue of lesbian abuse that happens in this world. Because of the utopian view of lesbian relationships still presented in some strains of feminism, many lesbians feel they will not be believed.[7] Another form of disavowal happens outside the women's movement, where there is a tendency to trivialize violence between two women as a "cat-fight." Of course this dominant cultural view does not see lesbian relationships as utopian, but rather sees "the fight" as trivial either because women are incapable of inflicting harm or because lesbians are trying to act in "mannish" ways. In either case, the context of the violence as occurring within an intimate relationship is most often ignored.[8]

A larger form of resistance emerges from the well-founded fear that public discussion of abuse in lesbian relationships will contribute to negative stereotypes that exist about lesbians and will hurt the battered women's movement by fueling a backlash against feminism. There is still a concern among some lesbians that we need to have more conversations about violence in relationships within lesbian communities, refraining from speaking with heterosexual women until we develop our own accurate—but politically strategic—analysis. In practice, though, a common

starting place for addressing abuse in lesbian relationships has been to educate mainstream services by correcting heterosexist misconceptions that
understand lesbian relationships as mimicking heterosexual relationships.
For example, efforts go into dispelling assumptions that abuse occurs
mainly in "butch/femme" relationships in which the butch is the batterer
and the femme is the victim, as well as more subtle misconceptions that
suggest that abuse occurs only in nonfeminist lesbian relationships.[9] In
other communities there is a concern that the category "lesbian partner
abuse," should be broadened to "woman-to-woman abuse" which would
take the limiting emphasis off lesbians, be more inclusive of bisexual and
queer women,[10] and force all women to look at their own propensity for
violence. These kinds of debates remain grounded in the concern about
the dangers of acknowledging this issue *and* grounded in the discursive
opportunity to construct a "new" category of abuse that is at once accurate, meaningful, and politically astute.

Perhaps the biggest source of resistance from feminist communities in
general is that acknowledging lesbian abuse will threaten a dominant feminist analysis of violence against women in intimate relationships, which
most often assumes a male perpetrator and sees the roots of violence in
patriarchy and misogyny.[11] Gender and power are the main components of
this perspective. With this analysis lesbian abuse is either seen as an impossible contradiction in terms, or lesbian violence is explained within a
theory of male domination and internalized misogyny and homophobia,
where a lesbian has to be seen as tainted by male cultural influences for
the analysis to fit. Preserving a gender-based analysis has been a central
concern of the women's movement as we have tried to confront the over-
whelming level of male violence against women. To avoid disturbing this
analysis, when we acknowledge lesbian abuse we keep our focus primarily
on the victims and plug lesbian abuse into the theories we have developed
to explain heterosexual abuse. This additive approach does allow for a
recognition of different categories of abuse: lesbian abuse/heterosexual
abuse/woman of color abuse/women with disabilities abuse. Yet it falsely
compartmentalizes women's experiences while leaving in place a homogenizing foundation that all forms and causes of abuse are the same.[12] The
primacy of a gender-based analysis in feminism does not mean we are se-
lectively keeping secrets, as the title of this volume might suggest, but it
has meant we can be reticent about revealing things that disrupt our efforts to create seamless, unitary understandings of violence. Although my
work in this volume offers a critique of this tendency within feminism (a
movement I am a part of), I understand the fortitude at work and the de-

sire to create a sturdy "regime of truth" in the face of both male violence against women and antifeminist backlash efforts.

Backlash against Feminism

Within Canada and the United States there has been a specific backlash against feminist research and activism on male violence against women.[13] This countermovement defines itself as "pro-family," idealizing traditional, patriarchal, heterosexual normative models of the family. Feminists are accused of exaggerating the rates of men's violence against women[14] and of promoting the false view of woman as innocent victims.[15] A key tactic in challenging feminist research is to say that "women do it too" or that "women are just as bad as men."[16] In the 1990s, several popular texts by backlash writers focused on examples of women as perpetrators of violence as a way to expose a gender bias in feminist scholarship, claiming we cannot use gender as part of our analysis to understand the dynamics of battering relationships because it presents a limited view in which women are seen only as good/victims and men are seen only as bad/perpetrators. Several of these texts use the example of abuse in lesbian relationships to support their arguments against feminist research and analyses of violence.

In the book *Who Stole Feminism*, Christina Hoff Sommers mentions lesbian abuse studies as an example of scholarship that could help shed light on the dynamics of battering relationships but claims it is ignored by gender feminists (her term for feminists who believe women are oppressed by a male hegemony). She refers specifically to the research of Claire Renzetti,[17] which she says suggests that violence in lesbian relationships occurs with about the same frequency as violence in heterosexual relationships. Sommers then concludes that "once again, it appears battery may have very little to do with patriarchy or gender bias. Where noncriminals are involved, battery seems to be a pathology of intimacy, as frequent among gays as among straight people."[18]

Similar to the view of Sommers is the work of Canadian Donna Laframboise in *The Princess at the Window*, which is particularly critical of the report prepared by the Canadian Panel on Violence Against Women. Laframboise feels this government-sanctioned panel constructed a politically biased report that claims that men's violence is always an example of "deliberately carrying out a political agenda of oppression whenever they mistreat female persons."[19] She argues that women who are violent are held to a different standard and using the example of lesbian abuse, raises the question, "why do lesbians who batter other lesbians get to blame it on the stress that a society hostile to lesbians places them under? What is so unique about this sort of pressure that nothing remotely approximates it?"[20] To support her argument of double standards for men and women, she quotes directly from the report:

> Although research into the incidence and prevalence of lesbian battering is virtually non-existent in Canada, women who spoke to the panel contend that it is the result of institutionalized heterosexism which isolates lesbians and adds pressure to their relationships.[21]

Laframboise acknowledges that this is one form of women's violence that the report discusses, but is critical of the fact that the Panel ignores research done in the United States, which she says suggests that lesbian abuse is just as prevalent as heterosexual abuse. Laframboise concludes that lesbian battering is excused as an example of women being doubly oppressed by patriarchy and homophobia; and lesbian batterers are not held accountable in the same way that men are. (She also applies this discourse of "double standards" to people of color who have used violence.) In her view, oppression is used as an excuse for violent behavior. She cannot imagine an analysis of violence that would include both individual accountability and systemic oppression, and seems to want to jettison any political analysis altogether.

Finally, Patricia Pearson, a journalist who is critical of second wave feminism for ignoring examples of women's violence and insisting on women's stance as victims, also raises the issue of lesbian abuse to make her case. She even shows concern for gay and lesbian communities in bringing forward this example of violence:

> Feminists who refuse to admit that heterosexual women can be violent leave the gay community by itself out on a limb, vulnerable to further slander by self-appointed keepers of public morals. There is a long tradition in our culture of depicting aggressive or criminal women as sexually perverse. That link can only be fortified if feminists refuse to concede straight women's violence, forcing lesbians to appear as the only ones who abuse.[22]

Her review of research on lesbian abuse is far more extensive than that of Sommers or Laframboise, and she presents some of the findings that challenge a feminist analysis of violence. For example, she says relationship violence cannot be understood in terms of male social and economic power because in many abusive lesbian partnerships it is the woman with the higher earning power and self-esteem who gets assaulted (again based on Claire Renzetti's work). She also reports on the pattern of some abused lesbians becoming abusers in other relationships (something my research has also confirmed[23]) as another example that goes against the gender-power theory of violence. Pearson's critique, then, raises some interesting questions about the nature of power, and the meaning of the discrete categories, perpetrator and victim. Yet, she too, like Sommers and Laframboise, relies on Renzetti's work to make a definitive claim that violence in lesbian relationships occurs with the same frequency as violence in heterosexual relationships, and adds "with the smaller, more conventionally feminine partner often being the one to strike" to emphasize her point that feminine female abusers exist.[24]

Although some of these writings may be provocative as challenges to a dominant feminist analysis of violence, they remain intent on using lesbian abuse to show that "women are just as bad as men" rather than to actually work on the problem of lesbian relationship violence (with the momentary exception of Pearson). Nor are they interested in widening the analysis from gender to include, race, class, or sexuality in any way. These are depoliticized perspectives that focus on gender only to neutralize it as a category for understanding relationship violence. Further, these authors are very selective in the research they use to support their claims. They all refer to Renzetti who did indeed write in 1992, "it appears that violence in lesbian relationships occurs at about the same frequency as violence in heterosexual relationships."[25] But they ignore the tentativeness of that statement and other more recent writings by Renzetti in which she makes it clear that the research that she conducted was not a study of prevalence and cannot be used to support the claim that abuse in lesbian relationships happens with the same frequency as heterosexual abuse.[26]

As many feminists feared it would be, the issue of abuse in lesbian relationships has been used to fortify claims that are meant to discredit and harm the battered women's movement. Yet their criticisms also offer a reflective occasion for us to ask: Do our current discourses on violence let us speak about women who abuse their children or their elderly relatives, or lesbians who have experienced abuse within their relationships, or gay men who have been sexually assaulted by straight men? How does a will to ignorance and the pursuit not only of safety but of respectability operate in our discourses on relationship violence?[27]

There is now a substantial body of material addressing lesbian abuse so we cannot say the issue has been ignored by feminists as the writers that I reviewed would have us believe. There are, in fact, more studies on abuse in lesbian relationships than on abuse in gay male relationships, which suggests that feminists and lesbians have not shied away from the issue. The topic has been discussed in most lesbian communities with statements being issued about it through organizations connected to the battered women's movement and through lesbian groups.[28] But there has been no groundswell of attention to this topic which one might expect feminists interested in theorizing domestic abuse to want to understand. As Claire Renzetti states, "Unfortunately what we know about lesbian partner abuse is less than what we don't know."[29] Lesbian relationship violence remains an albatross for the battered women's movement—recognized as something we must deal with eventually, but not fully embraced in research, theorizing, and action. The issue remains a source of guilt, because battered lesbians are not fully attended to, and of vulnerability, because our theorizing in the larger areas of relationship violence and women as perpetrators remains underdeveloped.

What We Know about Lesbian Partner Abuse

The body of literature on lesbian partner abuse includes personal testimonies, writings about advocacy work, writings by clinicians and other professionals on providing services and developing theoretical models, and research studies by academics. Some of the research is specifically on lesbian partner abuse whereas other articles, particularly the more recent ones, are written more broadly on same-sex partner abuse to include the experiences of gay men, bisexuals, and transgendered people. Overall, the literature comes from diverse sources and remains very consistent. The most commonly used definition of lesbian partner abuse is the one offered by Barbara Hart, who defines it as "a pattern of violent [or] coercive behaviors whereby a lesbian seeks to control the thoughts, beliefs or conduct of [an] intimate partner or to punish the intimate for resisting the perpetrator's control."[30] Like that of heterosexual domestic violence, this definition includes physical abuse, destruction of property, psychological/emotional abuse, sexual abuse, economic control, and threats of violence. Lesbian partner violence is acknowledged as being different from heterosexual domestic violence, though mainly because it includes homophobia as a controlling tactic: most often the threat to reveal a person's sexual orientation to others (e.g., parents, employers). What is stressed as unique to lesbian (and gay) relationships is the cumulative effect of living in a homophobic and heterosexist world.[31] For someone in an abusive relationship, social marginalization can mean being more isolated and experiencing denial or minimization of the abuse from straight and lesbian friends. Living in a heteronormative society also means that mainstream institutions can be hostile or insensitive to lesbians, which can prevent abused lesbians from seeking help or getting the help that they need.[32]

The research by Claire Renzetti, which is cited by so many other writers, both feminist and backlash, was one of the first empirical studies to explore both the similarities and differences between heterosexual and lesbian partner abuse.[33] Her research included distributing a questionnaire to 100 women who self-identified as lesbian abuse victims and then conducting forty follow-up interviews. Her findings are important to describe in some detail not only because her work is widely cited, but because it remains one of the most comprehensive studies yet done in the area. Renzetti's study provided empirical evidence that lesbian abuse includes the same range of abusive behaviors that we see in abusive heterosexual relationships. The most common forms of physical abuse reported by lesbians in her sample were being pushed and shoved; being hit with fists or open hand; being scratched or hit in the face, breasts, or genitals; and having objects thrown at them. Some of the most severe forms of violence, such as being stabbed, or shot, or having weapons/objects inserted into one's vagina, were rare, but nonetheless, they were reported. Seventy-one percent of her sample indicated that the severity and frequency of the physical abuse increased over time. Although psychological abuse was more frequent than physical abuse, 87 percent reported experiencing both physical and psychological abuse. The most common forms of psychological/emotional abuse experienced were threats, being humiliated or demeaned in front of others, interruptions to sleeping and eating, and having possessions destroyed. Renzetti also reports that women mentioned other forms of abuse that were not included as items on the questionnaire: being physically restrained, abusers hurting themselves or threatening to hurt themselves as a way to control their partners, and "tailoring the abuse to the specific vulnerabilities of their partners (e.g., a diabetic was forced to eat sugar as 'punishment' for 'misbehavior')."[34] Examples of homophobic control were also reported with 21 percent of respondents indicating their abusive partners threatened to out them.

Renzetti concludes that in addition to the various forms of abuse we must look at the motivations underlying the coercive tactics in order to fully understand abusive relationships, whether lesbian or heterosexual.

Her study suggests that the abusive partner's dependency, most often manifested as jealousy and sometimes through alcohol abuse, is the strongest factor associated with abusive behaviors. One other factor that she explored is how a personal history of family violence can facilitate lesbian abuse. In her study, she found that batterers and victims were not any more likely to have experienced violence growing up but those who had (both victims and perpetrators) tended to excuse the batterer's behavior as being the result of a history of abuse. Overall, Renzetti's research engages with the literature on heterosexual abuse and offers some important information on the context of homophobia that makes lesbian abuse different.

Rates of Lesbian Partner Abuse

It is perhaps not surprising that the largest body of research on abuse among lesbian couples has primarily tried to determine prevalence. (Fewer studies exist that document the rates of gay male relationship violence.) Determining the incidence of lesbian partner violence is an important way to legitimize the issue, secure funding for social services, and begin to provide an overall picture of who and how many are affected.[35] Several survey studies report widely varying rates of domestic violence amongst lesbian couples ranging from 17 percent to 52 percent. For example, Pamela Brand and Aline Kidd[36] report that 25 percent of their sample of fifty-five self-identified lesbians said that they had been physically abused by a lesbian partner in the past. Joanne Loulan, in her study of 1,566 lesbians, found that 17 percent had been involved in violent relationships.[37] Valerie Coleman found that of the ninety couples she surveyed, 46 percent experienced acts of violence in their relationships.[38] Gwat-Yong Lie and Sabrina Gentlewarrier, in a survey of 1,099 lesbians at the Michigan Womyn's music festival, found 52 percent of their sample reported being abused (this included physical, verbal, and/or sexual aggression) by a former female lover.[39] More recently, Lettie Lockhart, Barbara White, Vickie Causby, and Alicia Isaac found victimization rates of 31 percent in their survey of 284 lesbians who reported physical abuse in the past year or in a current relationship.[40] The numbers vary too widely to be useful, but this research has been establishing that lesbian abuse does, indeed, exist and is a form of violence that we need to attend to.

However, based on these studies, many academic researchers and practitioners, such as the backlash writers, have also concluded that lesbian battering occurs at the same or at even a higher rate than heterosexual violence. Susan Turell, for example, states that we are experiencing an "epidemic" in which "physical abuse in relationships can conservatively be estimated to happen for one in three same-sex couples, and sexual abuse occurs in at least 12 percent of homosexual relationships."[41] Yet we have to interpret the results of survey research carefully as none of the aforementioned studies used random sampling techniques; therefore the rates of victimization they report do not reliably represent true prevalence.[42] In addition, each of the studies relies on different definitions of abuse, with some restricting the definition to physical abuse and others not differentiating between the different forms of abuse.

Recently, Lisa Waldner-Haugrud, Linda Vaden Gratch, and Brian Magruder reviewed the studies that report rates of violence within lesbian and gay relationships to show that the range can be accounted for by the different ways violence is operationalized in each survey:[43] those reporting lower rates of victimization simply ask respondents whether they were physically abused or had experienced abuse, whereas those studies reporting higher rates of victimization rely on the Conflict Tactics Scale, which is a quantitative instrument that lists items describing physical and nonphysical conflict and asks respondents how many times they have engaged in a tactic and how many times they have been on the receiving end of the tactic.[44] In an attempt to clarify some of the discrepancies in the literature, Waldner-Haugrud, Vaden Gratch, and Magruder undertook their own study that surveyed 283 gays and lesbians (165 and 118, respectively) using a modified version of the Conflict Tactics Scale. They found that 47.5 percent of lesbians and 29.7 percent of gay men reported having been the victim of relationship violence, with pushing, threats, and slapping being the most frequent tactics experienced by lesbians. They also report 38 percent of lesbians and 21.8 percent of gay men indicated using violence against their partners with pushing, slapping, and making threats being the most frequent tactics directed toward their partner. These results fall within the range of victimization rates reported by previous research but provide more information on the nature of the violent tactics used. Their research also supports other findings in the heterosexual partner abuse literature that has found women reporting higher levels of perpetration than men. But the data generated from this scale cannot tell us what these higher levels mean—are women hitting back in an act of self-defense? Are women self-reporting their actions differently than men do on these surveys? There remain many criticisms about the assumptions on which these studies are based.

The Conflict Tactics Scale, for example, has been criticized primarily by feminist researchers who are concerned with the failure of the scale to provide a context in which to understand the violence that is reported. The scale is most often used in research on heterosexual relationship violence, where several studies have concluded that heterosexual women initiate violence as frequently as heterosexual men.[45] Yet Murray Straus, one of the researchers who developed the scale, acknowledges that in heterosexual relationships, men tend to underestimate their use of severe violence and women tend to normalize men's use of violence, making both more likely to underreport male violence.[46] Both lesbians and heterosexual women may also self-report higher levels of violence than men do because they see given behaviors by women as more violent than the same behaviors by men, and this is the case whether they are reporting themselves to be victims or perpetrators.[47] Further, lesbians as a group may be more likely to recognize and name abuse than gay men because many lesbians have been politically active in the antiviolence movement. Therefore we have to be careful in how we understand the gender differences of lesbians using more violence than gay men as reported by Waldner-Haugrud and others. They too acknowledge that "researchers need more insight into the dynamics of lesbian relationships in order to account for any differences between lesbians and gay men."[48] Further we have to ask whether a scale that was developed to capture the dynamics of interpersonal conflict in marital relationships[49] is, in fact, transferable to the experiences of gay and lesbians. In other words, is the psychological and social meaning of "violence" in a relationship the same for lesbians and heterosexuals;[50] gay men and lesbians? Are we counting the same things? The dynamics of intimate relationships can further vary by the race, ethnicity, and social class of the partners,[51] yet the scale assumes a universal model of conflict in which both parties are seen as equal participants and in which choices of conflict tactics are personal.[52] Teresa Scherzer modified the Conflict Tactics Scale in her study to emphasize emotional abuse and include behaviors "having particular relevance for lesbians (e.g., threats to 'out' a partner)."[53] In her sample of 256 lesbians, 17 percent reported physical abuse at some time during their current or most recent relationship while 31 percent reported experiencing emotional abuse. These percentages are much lower than the findings of Waldner-Haugrud et al.[54]

Obviously, many discrepancies still exist in the rates of victimization in lesbian relationships. Scherzer herself suggests that qualitative research is needed to study power dynamics and move us beyond basic incidence reporting of abusive behaviors.[55] The surveys using the Conflict Tactics Scale cannot answer questions about basic incidence, let alone about meaning, motive, or outcome of the tactics reported,[56] whereas other quantitative methods cannot capture the context of the abuse. In addition, most studies continue to use heterosexuality as the norm through which to understand abusive same-sex relationship dynamics.[57] Comparing abuse in lesbian relationships to abuse in heterosexual relationships recenters heterosexuality and keeps the context in which the relationship violence occurs invisible. This is in part a function of positivist social science methodology, where we work to build on previous research by replicating findings that make certain lines of inquiry authoritative. Rather than asking new questions to widen the scope or work for social change, the existing literature becomes a normative framework for future work in the area.[58] The proliferation of positivist empirical research in the area is not surprising given that it is the most sanctioned form of research by funding agencies and academic institutions and becomes a way of legitimizing this research area.[59]

Theories to Explain Same-Sex Partner Abuse

In addition to these empirical studies, though, efforts have been focused on developing theories or models to explain and account for abuse. As the research and attention to abuse in lesbian relationships have increased, many opposing views on how to understand this form of domestic violence have emerged. These include psychological explanations, social psychological models, feminist gender-based theories, and lesbian-specific theories. Tensions exists between individual-based explanations and societal explanations, just as they do in the larger field of "family" violence.

Some theorists seem more intent than others on debunking feminism in their efforts to create new theories or understandings of domestic violence. David Island and Patrick Letellier argue that same-sex spousal abuse exposes the limitations of feminist theory (which they denounce) and argue instead for a psychological, gender-neutral theory.[60] Their views are consistent with those of Donald Dutton, who uses information on same-sex battering to prove that feminist theories of domestic violence are "wrong" and to suggest that the psychopathology of batterers must be explored.[61] Unlike Island and Letellier, and more like backlash writers, Dutton is more interested in showing that patriarchy is not a cause of wife assault than he is interested in exploring the issue of same-sex domestic violence. Island and Letellier theorize same-sex partner abuse from an individual-based framework.[62] Like Dutton, they emphasize that abuse occurs

because of a personality disorder of the perpetrator. Using a limited definition of gender as biology or anatomy, they reject gender as a factor worthy of consideration, since both men and women can be perpetrators.[63]
They suggest that batterers learn to be violent "evidencing a disorder
which is both correctable through treatment and punishable by law."[64]
Their view is also supported by Valerie Coleman, who feels there has been
too much attention given to sociopolitical factors, and not enough to individual personality dynamics of batterers. Her clinical work with lesbian
batterers suggests that they often exhibit borderline and narcissistic personality disorders. However, she maintains that a multidimensional view
of partner abuse is needed and that we still have to determine the extent
to which misogyny, homophobia and child abuse influence lesbian battering.[65] This preference for a multidimensional view is the most predominant in the area.

   Gregory Merrill builds on the work of Gilbert, Poorman and Simmons,
and Beth Zemsky to offer a social psychological model of same-sex domestic violence that can be used to explain gay, lesbian, and heterosexual abusive relationships.[66] He argues against the individual pathology model by
showing that it cannot account for the fact that more heterosexual men
than women are abusive. He also suggests that feminist theories alone
with their emphasis on sociopolitical factors like misogyny and patriarchy
are inadequate because they treat same-sex partner abuse as an exception.
For him, feminist theory "does not and cannot fully or adequately explain
why the same dynamics of abuse in heterosexual relationships occurs with
as much frequency and severity as same-sex relationships."[67] Therefore
Merrill accepts, uncritically, the results of the studies that have been done
to determine the frequency of abuse and concludes that partner abuse
happens at the same rates for gays, lesbians, and heterosexuals. His model
draws on social learning theory to explain the causes of abuse as arising
from three categories: "learning to abuse, having the opportunity to abuse,
and choosing to abuse."[68] Learning to abuse involves the psychological
processes of modeling, learning by reinforcement or by direct instruction,
whereas the opportunity to abuse reflects a sociopolitical context (what
feminists stress when acknowledging the impact of misogyny, racism, homophobia, etc.) that creates environments that support violent acts without consequence. Finally, by suggesting that abusers ultimately make the
choice to abuse or not to abuse, his model nevertheless places the responsibility for violence on the abuser. Merrill also emphasizes that we need to
assess the severity of the abuse as another dimension of the personal or
psychological power of the abuser that has to be considered when explain-

ing domestic violence. Recently, Joan McClennen endorsed Merrill's model as the one most likely to account for same-sex abuse. Yet she suggests an amendment to differentiate between lesbian and gay partner abuse: practitioners who provide interventions need to understand lesbian and gay partner abuse slightly differently to account for sexism that lesbians experience and that gay men do not.[69]

A social psychological model that includes attention to personality characteristics, feminist/sociopolitical analyses, and social learning theories is seen by many as the kind of theorizing that is needed because dominant gender-based feminist analyses of domestic violence have only emphasized men's violent behavior against women. It is a theorizing that builds directly on many of the empirical studies that have been done to show that abuse happens in the same forms and frequency to gay men, lesbians, and heterosexuals, and yet it can also show that gay and lesbian abuse is different because of a context of homophobia and heterosexism.

However, for others, lesbian battering can be explained within the dominant gender-based feminist theory of domestic violence when gender is understood as a patriarchal social construct rather than as a biological fact. Mary Eaton gives the following example of this gendered analysis applied to a lesbian battering situation: "When a lesbian abuses her lover, she is behaving in socially masculine ways; when a lesbian is victimized through her lover's violence she is behaving in socially feminine ways and therefore the battering is a gender-based activity . . . women batter other women because they have internalized interconnected norms of heterosexism/homophobia and misogyny which lie at the core of the sex-role system."[70] This understanding, although more political and social in focus, ends up asserting a view that all forms of violence are ultimately the same: abuse is abuse. A gender-based analysis that shows the effects of patriarchy has been important for many antiviolence women's organizations who want to respond to lesbian partner abuse. With such a universalizing analysis, they can carry on with their established programs and practices and simply open up spaces for lesbians—although this is never simple in practice, as shelters often struggle with how to assess who the perpetrator is and who the victim is when both women may feel victimized and seek their services.[71] This type of analysis can easily assert the ways in which heterosexual abuse and lesbian abuse are the same, for example, the similarities in the types of abuse experienced, the similarities in the psychological impact, and therefore the similarities in responses that are needed. Even differences in lesbian partner violence such as homophobic control can be accounted for within gender-based theory as another example of internalized patriarchal oppression. Lesbian partner abuse within this kind of feminist theorizing is seen as a function of gender-based oppression.[72] By continually returning to a focus on the similarities between lesbian and heterosexual abuse, gender-based theory supports the desire to steer the discussion away from what is happening between women, and back toward the issue of male violence.

Some writers who have been exploring the specificity of lesbian abuse argue for the need to consider the context in which violence occurs, as well as the need to acknowledge that explanations and theories of violence will always be partial and limited.[73] This line of theorizing dissents both from the dominant social psychological model and totalizing gender-based theory and, daring to ask new questions. For example, Melanie Kaye/Kantrowitz acknowledges that lesbian abuse is a serious problem, but not the same problem. She writes,

> Discussions of lesbian violence have ignored what seems to me a significant difference. Male violence and male sexuality are practically synonymous under patriarchy. . . . Lesbians do not go out on to the street and attack women, nor do they climb into windows or assault them on dates. How often do you hear of a lesbian serial rapist or killer? Some of us—lesbian and heterosexual—remember as children making smaller children take their clothes off, playing sexual games, exercising the small power we had over smaller ones who had less. But even as sexual abuse explodes in the media and women figure as abusers in several of these cases, most people of whatever age and gender victimized by sexual abuse are victimized by men.[74]

I quote Kaye/Kantrowitz at length because her clear examples show why we need to analyze the context of violence when developing explanatory theories. She is not simplistically saying men are abusive and lesbians are not, but her writings do pay attention to constructions/expectations of gender and provoke the question, "can our current theories of domestic violence account for differences that may suggest that lesbians are far less likely than men to rape or kill their partners, but are more likely to push them?" The research to date has not closely examined these areas of difference and has instead been urgently trying to document the problem of same-sex domestic violence in order to have it acknowledged by the mainstream. Women who are interested in exploring the specificity of lesbian violence are no less concerned with interrupting violence, but they also priorize the need for "making sense of the particularities."[75]

Mary Eaton, for example, sees the enforced invisibility of lesbians as a factor that must be considered when accounting for abuse. For her, the erasure of lesbians from society's cultural imagination is a unique feature of lesbian oppression that makes it different from other forms of social inequalities. Research, theories, and action on partner abuse need to take this particular context into account. Further, Liz Kelly as well as Joelle Taylor and Tracey Chandler suggest that we need a theory that examines both gender and sexuality as well as constructions of lesbianism that individuals either integrate into their sense of self or challenge.[76] Claire Renzetti has been critical of her own early work as having had a heterosexual bias.[77] She now calls for research that is both contextualized and that takes intersectionality into account.[78] By this, she means we must consider how people are differently located and examine how racism, classism, heterosexism, and sexism affect the causes and consequences of violence. She writes,

> The goal is not to fit "others" into the dominant mould, but rather to come to a better understanding of the diversity of domestic violence experiences, the significance and meaning this violence has in the lives of different groups of people, and how this intersectionality affects outcomes, particularly institutional responses to domestic violence.[79]

Valli Kanuha and Charlene Waldron have shown not only that the writings in the area of same-sex abuse have been based on heteronormative assumptions, they have been centered on white women's experiences, thereby ignoring the effects of systemic power relations such as racism, homophobia, and heterosexism on abusive relationships.[80] Similarly, Rhea Almeida and others challenge the public and private dichotomy we make when addressing forms of violence and suggest that we must look at violence enacted on gays and lesbians and people of color from different sites and multiple sources. They explain that white heterosexual women may benefit from the public illumination of their private life of intimate violence, but heterosexuals of color and gays and lesbians do not because the public world is a more ambiguous space filled with various oppressions and privileges.[81]

However, writings such as these that emphasize an understanding of the social context as well as the specificity and heterogeneity of lesbian abuse (and other forms of violence against marginalized people) remain in the minority. My review of the literature suggests that the overarching conceptualization of lesbian abuse has emphasized either its comparability to gay men's partner violence and hence to assert the gender-blended category "same-sex domestic violence," or to emphasize its similarity to heterosexual women's abuse through gender-based theory and thereby keep the focus on female victimization. The difference in conceptualization leads to different responses. When same-sex partner abuse becomes the focus, we see work that emphasizes the need for new services, new programs, and interventions that can address sexual identities as a primary focus. When lesbian abuse remains within a feminist gender-based analysis, we see writings that focus on women's shared experiences of victimization and a reassertion (with minor adjustments) of the tools, categories, and constructs we have in place to respond to gender-based intimate violence. Neither approach is wrong and both are invested in their positions because of a concern first and foremost with ending relationship violence and intervening in supportive ways. Yet both focus on the thesis that violence and the threat of violence always function to maintain power and control over another person, regardless of the particular forms that violence may take; therefore neither is raising new questions about the meanings of intimate violence in different contexts.[82] Both approaches risk losing any focus on liberation/social transformation (whether that be dismantling homophobia and heterosexism or patriarchy and misogyny) and being obscured instead by a social control/problem management focus (that preserves gender, race, and class hierarchies) if we look at what has been happening in the area of heterosexual domestic violence as an indication of what lies ahead.[83] We need, therefore, to examine the consequences of our conceptualization of partner violence and how our responses to it become institutionalized.

Within these conceptualizations of partner abuse, Renzetti's call for intersectionality has not been totally ignored. Many important articles have been written exploring different contexts of experiences. For example, Patrick Letellier explores the impact of HIV/AIDS on gay male violence;[84] Lola Butler looks at the experiences of African-American lesbians in abusive relationships;[85] and Michael De Vidas discusses a support group for Latino gay men and lesbians that address both childhood sexual abuse and domestic violence.[86] Yet despite these efforts what often remains is a shared and unchallenged assumption that we can find one universalizing explanation or "grand narrative" to account for relationship violence, no matter what the social context. I am troubled by this assumption because of its homogenizing effect on people's experiences. Making fixed "truth claims" about lesbian violence allows us, on the one hand, to move forward and respond to abuse, yet on the other hand, our urgency to respond may mask other motivations (conscious and unconscious) for the claims we make about this form of violence. We are, in fact, creating discourses about lesbian abuse/same-sex partner abuse that determine, produce, and limit what can be seen, heard, thought, known, and done. Ellen Faulkner sums up the research in the area: "[It] generates an understanding of lesbian battery from a white, middle-class, heterosexist, Western standpoint."[87] Further, Cindy Holmes' analysis of the construction of lesbian abuse in educational materials and research shows that "with few exceptions it has largely relied on modernist discourses and constructs: such as a positivist approach to research, the construction of a universal woman or lesbian, and an additive approach to analyzing and theorizing violence."[88] Research that acknowledges the larger social context, that is qualitative, or that is critical in perspective remains rare.

I am reminded of my experience at the Scientific Workshop on Lesbian Health sponsored by the U.S. Department of Health and Human Services in Washington DC, March 2000. I was invited as one of 200 researchers to make recommendations that would inform policy and research in this newly acknowledged area called "lesbian health." On one level, it was very exciting to have lesbian health on the agenda of the government, yet they were only willing to recognize, fund, and legitimize information that came from "science": that is, quantitative, positivist-empirical studies that offer cause-and-effect explanations for complex "lesbian health issues." Within the scientific model, the larger social context surrounding issues is something that must be controlled for, not understood. In our quest for legitimization, then, we need to ask, "whose interests are being served by our theorizing; what are we missing; what are we leaving out when we follow dominant, depoliticizing lines of inquiry?" These have been central epistemological questions for feminist, anticolonialist, and postmodern theories on the production of knowledge.[89] Forging ahead in a relatively new area such as lesbian partner abuse means that we need to retain some awareness of the constructedness of the category we are studying. In saying we are constructing an area, I am not suggesting that we are making it up; rather I am pointing to lesbian relationship violence as a cultural construct, where, depending on the historical period and the cultural and social context, the meaning of the category will be different as it will change over time. We therefore need to think carefully about what we are creating in naming this form of violence.

I remain convinced of the need to focus on the social context, on the specificity and heterogeneity of relationships as the way to encourage openness to seeing the complexities and dynamics because of variously gendered, racialized, sexualized, and personal relations between two women, or two men, or a man and a woman. To do this, feminism along with postmodern insights remains the strongest theoretical framework for understanding lesbian relationship violence while retaining a necessary analysis of the pervasiveness of male violence against women.[90]

Feminist Postmodern Theorizing

Much of the literature in the area of violence against women has relied on either empirical approaches such as the survey research discussed earlier, or standpoint approaches. Standpoint approaches have been very important to the feminist production of knowledge because they are grounded in an awareness of the material conditions of women's lives and seek to bring forward a diversity of women's experiences of violence in differing social contexts. But both standpoint and empirical research assume that there is a single social world and reality to be discovered. Experiences of the material realities of violence alone, however, cannot explain the complex dynamics of abuse. What I think needs to happen in the field of same-sex partner abuse has been happening within some other feminist writings on violence. What gets defined as "the feminist explanation of violence" is in fact just one view, albeit a dominant one, within a much larger area of feminist theorizing. Many feminists are exploring the complexity of violence between women and between men and women without solely relying on a material, gender-based explanation. It is not that we have needed to learn that patriarchy is not all-explanatory: for years feminists have been working at understanding the role of other forms of socially mobilized differences in women's lives. But as Bat-Ami Bar On writes, we need a "nuanced feminist rethinking of the relationship between women and violence . . . in a manner that necessarily problematizes the neat, clean distinctions, the feminist paradigmatic understandings of violence and their paradigmatic critiques generally assume, such as those between bad (aggressive or oppressive) and good (defensive or resistant) violence and between passive (silenced or erased) victimhood and active (speaking or vital) agency."[91] For some feminists, this has meant a turn to attend to the discursive terrain of violence in addition to understanding the material conditions of violence. In paying attention to discourse, many feminist postmodernists are relying on the work of Michel Foucault, who argued that the language systems available to us shape and limit the very ways we can experience and define ourselves.[92] They use an analytical framework that seeks to disrupt universalizing and essentializing constructs while exploring taken-for-granted assumptions and questioning the belief that there is "innocent knowledge to be had."[93] Such a framework emphasizes the social construction of reality and asserts that what is knowable is constructed through culture, language, and social processes.[94]

Many feminists have been examining the "discourses" we have available to us to talk about violence against women: the sets of assumptions, socially shared, and often unconscious, reflected in language that produces meanings, constructs knowledge, and organizes social relations.[95] In this way we can scrutinize the categories and subject positions that are created through discourses while also exploring their investments and exclusions. For example, Linda Alcoff and Laura Gray have explored the differing effects of "survivor speech," and found it to be both transgressive (speaking out about violence has had an empowering effect for women) and also quite easily absorbed, despite its liberatory intentions, within dominant discourses (for example, testimonials about violence can be subsumed into discourses about women having victim personalities). Their work is important in helping us to recognize how women's subjectivities, including our sense of self, have been constructed as a result of this speech.[96] Similarly, a collection edited by Sharon Lamb explores, through a number of essays, the category "victim" that has been developed within feminist work on violence. By interrogating the meanings that get produced by the categories "victim" and "abuse" as well as by examining the power relations involved in labeling, they are able to acknowledge different kinds of victimization and of women's agency in order to move beyond simplistic assertions of who and what a victim is.[97] Further, the work of Sharon Marcus reveals the ways in which a rape script exists to help create a rapist's power. In identifying a rape narrative or a story of rape, she shows how the known script produces a sense of futility in women—by having women living in fear of rape, by seeing all men as potential rapists, by constructing the act of rape as something that takes away dignity, and by seeing interventions as occurring after the rape. She suggests that we rewrite the script to shift our focus from female vulnerability to the male bodies that are doing the rape. Her work, like the others, strives to disrupt or deconstruct limiting categories and discourses.[98]

Other feminists have focused on the exclusions created in the discourses through which we talk about violence, particularly how assumptions of race operate in language practices to keep whiteness at the center, in a dominant place of privilege when it remains unnoticed and un-marked.[99] For example, Sherene Razack has examined the treatment of sexual assault cases involving Indigenous communities in Canadian courts and describes that colonization, if it is mentioned as a factor, is understood as a cultural characteristic, something that affects only First Nations peoples and not something that has affected white colonizers.[100] Further, it is not understood by white judges how this history has an impact on the victim for whom her community is the only safe place against racism. Anannya Bhattacharjee focuses on South Asian immigrant women's experiences of domestic violence in the United States as a way of exposing Western feminists' assumptions in the concepts "home," "private," and "public" that are often used to understand violence. Her work suggests that Western feminists have to be willing to rethink and overturn oppressive definitions because for immigrant women there are multiple experiences of "home" (domestic sphere, ethnic community, country of origin), which in turn changes the conventional understandings of "public" and "private" as separate, distinct spheres.[101] Conventional understandings have ignored or deemphasized certain kinds of violence such as genocide, immigration laws, and globalization. These scholars extend the notion of intersectionality[102] to an analysis of interlocking sites of oppression,[103] which examines how the categories race, class, gender, and sexuality in systems of domination rely on each other to function.

These writings, and many others,[104] seek to disrupt any "grand narrative of violence" that asserts a universal position[105] and emphasize the importance of constantly interrogating the boundaries of categories we use in discourses of violence to see how they exclude some experiences while naturalizing others.[106] Feminist postmodern perspectives deconstruct assumptions found in discourses and further challenge the "either/or" binaries that we often work within and have us consider "both/and" or "neither/nor" constructions of social reality.[107]

This is the theoretical framework that I bring to my exploration and understanding of violence in lesbian relationships. I seek to focus on the social context and heterogeneity of lesbian relationship violence while also exposing the assumptions and limitations of the language practices that structure our thinking about this form of abuse. I base the remaining chapters on interviews with women who have been in abusive lesbian relationships and with feminist service providers who have been responding to this form of violence. The feminist analysis that I develop in this volume attempts to rise to the challenges raised by third wave feminisms that seek to open up spaces for subjugated voices, while seeing the situational, local, and particular conditions that shape women's experiences, and that expose the limitations of mainstream dualities for defining our subjectivities.

Why Focus on Lesbians?

In using a feminist postmodern framework that stresses multiplicity, contradictions, and diversity, I open myself to criticism of my use of the term "lesbian." Queer theory, for example, has emerged in postmodern theorizing to interrupt the production of the heterosexist binary straight/gay that assumes we define ourselves against another. Queer is a term used to shift the focus from essentialist categories such as gay and lesbian to something more fluid that works against establishing authentic, normative sexual identity positions.[108] At the same time, lesbian is a term in which lives are lived, including my own. I am not using the term lesbian to suggest a fixed, stable core identity that is part of an essentialist understanding. I use it as a convenient, albeit inadequate, umbrella term to signify someone in an intimate relationship with another woman. I am also aware that people covered by the term prefer many others such as bisexual, gay, dyke, boyz, butch, femme, transgendered, two-spirited, queer. Further, I am aware that for many other women their sexual identity is not their primary identity. I am interested, however, in what is contained in the category lesbian relationships (and what is not) and how women who have been abused by other women feel the impact of discourses about lesbians and discourses about abuse when they become victims and seek services regardless of how they self-identify. I agree that we need to disrupt the foundational assumptions contained within sexual identity categories and remain attentive to how heteronormative conditions, not just homophobia, regulate the lives associated with sexual categories. At the same time, I insist on retaining a focus on lesbians (as a category distinct from gay men and more specific than queer) to resist the historic marginalization and invisibility of lesbians in society and in academic scholarship.

Summary

In reviewing the emergence of the category "abuse in lesbian relationship," I have ended by making strong claims about the need for new kinds of theorizing and for new questions to be asked as we further the work in this area. I do not mean to discount all the work that has been done to

date on same-sex partner violence. We all share a strong concern for responding to and preventing same-sex relationship violence. This shared
focus is evident when so much of the work has addressed the barriers to
gays and lesbians in accessing mainstream services, strategies in conducting antioppressive education and training, and creating coalitions to orga-
nize against lesbian, gay, bisexual, and transgendered domestic
violence.[109] As long as queer people remain marginalized within societies,
as long as women continue to experience alarming rates of male violence,
as long as we live within systems of domination based on race, class, ability,
gender, and sexuality, work on lesbian partner abuse risks being used in
dangerous ways. Yet doing work in this area requires us all to bear witness,
which Nancy Ziegenmeyer defines as "to speak out, to name the unname-
able, to turn and face it down."[110] The stakes are high. My hope in writing
this book is both to witness the stories that women told me and to help create new discursive forms and spaces so that we can speak about relationship violence in ways that are less likely to be misused, defused, or ignored.

Overview of the Volume

In Chapter 2, I describe the methodological approach developed for the
research project on which much of the content of this book is based. The
methodology and analysis emphasize an attempt to make both "feminist
links and postmodern interruptions": affirming marginalized voices that
have been ignored or silenced while disrupting dichotomous and rigidified
thinking about domestic violence and sexual identities. The research
process involves three strategic components: material, discursive, and reflexive "tales." The structure of the remaining sections of the book is
based on these three troubling tales.

Chapter 3 brings forward the violence that women report having experienced in their intimate relationships with other women. It explores the
ranges and forms of abuse women experienced, and the differing contexts
and power dynamics of intimate violence. The chapter reveals the heterogeneity of women's experiences and presents findings that do not fit current theories of same-sex domestic violence. Chapter 4 continues to bring
forward women's accounts, presenting their emotional responses to violence while also revealing their actions in trying to get support from
friends, family members, and formal services. The chapter concludes by
shifting the focus to the experiences of feminist service providers in responding to this form of violence. In their capacity as counselors, they re-

port many patterns and dynamics often not reflected in other research that relies strictly on self-report methods. They are often in the position of naming a relationship as abusive because abused women seeking services often present something else as the issue for which they need support. Service providers speak of seeing complicated relationship dynamics and of their difficulties in making assessments.

Chapters 5 and 6 move to the discursive terrain as a way of exposing discourses about violence and their effects on social relations and practices. Chapter 5 raises some of the controversies service providers grapple with, such as how they work within dominant feminist understandings of relationship violence, how they assess power dynamics, whether consensual sadomasochistic practices are inherently abusive, the existence of "mutual abuse," and whether services should be provided to batterers. By interrogating the concepts and constructs that are used in domestic violence work, such as power and control, trauma, and victim/perpetrator, we can begin to see their normative and regulating effects on how we understand abuse. We also begin to expose our investments (conscious and unconscious) in maintaining dominant discourses, even when they interfere with our struggles to respond appropriately to particular situations and develop more complex understandings of abusive dynamics.

Chapter 6 describes how dominant understandings of lesbian abuse have become institutionalized within social service organizations, including women's, gay and lesbian, and lesbian-only services, deeply entrenching and reinforcing a decontexualized regime of truth about power and control. This happens through social service mandates, policies, and established practices related to lesbian abuse, such as victim-only mandates, survivor-only support groups, and educational materials that reinforce simplistic binary understandings of abuse. I examine both the material and discursive regulation of lesbians' experiences of violence that is evident in such practices, a regulation that obscures, delegitimizes, or subjugates certain knowledges or subjects, and normalizes others. I also bring forward some examples of innovative responses that resist the homogenizing tendencies of institutional practices. The chapter ends by raising ethical questions for us to consider when developing responses to lesbian relationship violence.

Finally, Chapter 7 offers a reflexive tale, arguing for self-critical theorizing, research, and social service provision that attend to the specificity and heterogeneity of lesbian domestic violence. I then suggest some ways in which we might work to develop new initiatives within communities and social services that would allow us to address the complexities of abusive relationships. Having argued throughout this volume for a far more contexualized and situation-specific analysis of lesbian abuse (sometimes in rather abstract terms), I realize that the analysis is not useful if it cannot be mobilized into a helpful response. I therefore end by offering some advice for lesbians who are in abusive relationships together with guidelines for friends and feminist service providers who want to help.

TWO
Troubling Tales
Telling Stories, Exposing Language, Raising Questions

THIS CHAPTER DESCRIBES the approach I have taken to research and to understand lesbian partner abuse. I detail the processes I went through both to interview lesbians about their experiences in abusive relationships and to speak with feminist service providers who are responding to this form of violence. In addition to describing the interviews and focus groups that I conducted, I outline my method for analyzing the content of websites and other educational resources that provide information on lesbian partner abuse. Each method that I rely on illuminates different aspects of the issue of violence in lesbian relationships.[1] Drawing on these multiple sources to describe common experiences and unpack discourses is necessary as this issue is as much about the effects of the language we use to talk about violence (including the ubiquitous use of such polarized categories as innocence/guilt, us/them, lesbian/straight, inside/outside) as it is about the consequences of the violence itself and the need for caring responses.[2] Researching lesbian relationship violence also requires that a strong ethical stance be taken in order to remain conscious of the divisive and sometimes dangerous terrain described in Chapter 1. In doing this work, I always have to be aware of the larger social context and ask: what does a focus on giving voice to battered lesbians tell us—about lesbians and about battering? What are we constructing in creating a category called "lesbian partner abuse"? Given this terrain, it makes sense to use more participatory and emancipatory approaches to research where issues of accountability, ethics, and responsibility remain central to a goal of social action while also draw-ing on discursive and reflexive components that require thinking con-sciously about power relations and social, historical, and cultural contexts.[3]

Troubling Tales

My work on lesbian abuse seeks to tell troubling tales, not pretending that lesbians are unified where we are not, while at the same time pro-viding solid information that can be acted upon to change conditions for the better and respond to lesbians who have experienced abuse. This book is based on an approach to research that uses a double gesture of "feminist links and postmodern interruptions."[4] The focus on feminist links keeps the research firmly aligned with participants and with efforts to overcome intersecting forms of oppression, while attention to post-modern interruptions keeps the research open and responsive to cultural context, dismantling as need be, both what we are studying and how we are studying it. This study involves three strategic moves in this double play of affirmation and disruption: (1) researching material conditions by bringing forward the voices and subjective experiences of abuse and of service provision reported by participants; (2) researching discursive conditions as a way to disrupt rigidified thinking and break down false dichotomies by examining language to see how our current categories and constructs in the field of violence shape and limit the way we can re-spond to violence; (3) and engaging in reflexivity for critical analysis and accountability by critically examining what is being produced and who is producing it. This includes being aware of my own subjectivity as a white, middle-class lesbian who has not experienced relationship vio-lence and who has worked in feminist social service settings that respond to relationship violence.

I use the term *tale* to foreground the fictive dimensions of all research and research findings.[5] In this study, for example, I interviewed women who had been in abusive relationships and who told me their stories. They often came with stories composed in their head after weeks or sometimes years of working at making sense of their experiences of abuse. Most often they were anxious to share their stories as a cathartic opportunity, wanting their story to help others who were in similar situ-ations. Sometimes I was the first person they had ever spoken to about their experiences. There are complex social processes involved in such tellings of stories. For example: How do women choose what to tell? What enables them to find a voice? How do they choose the words? What happens to them after they tell their story? What gets left out? How do I hear the story ? What do I do when I hear it?[6] These kinds of questions reveal that research is not simply about the findings but is also about the production of the accounts themselves and the power that circulates between researcher and researched, teller and listener, reader and writer. Rather than present a hygienic, tidy description of research, in this chapter I try to make transparent what has gone into the making of the three tales that I tell.

A Material Tale: Telling Stories

I have been researching abuse in lesbian relationships for a number of years now, relying on a variety of approaches including interviews, surveys, and a training/education project with shelter workers.[7] A primary objective in my work has been to document the material conditions that lesbians and feminist social service providers face, and to give voice to their subjective experiences. Bringing forward women's experiences has been important in areas in which experiences have been hidden or minimized or ignored. My approach in this "story" is consistent with the goals of feminist standpoint research, which seeks to build theory from women's subjective experiences while recognizing the limitations of any situated knowledge.[8] In this tale, the voices of women provide important evidence of the experience of violence in lesbian relationships. Bearing witness to violence involves listening to the women who have experienced it, and in several chapters, we can listen to and learn directly from the testimonies of many lesbians who provide us with perspectives often missing from research that has been done on this issue. At the same time, in focusing on women's subjective experiences I am aware that I am constructing a story or an account in order to raise consciousness and encourage action. I view experience not as a foundational, static truth, but see it as "at once always already an interpretation and [as] in need of interpretation."[9] This does not in any way mean that I do not see violence as "real" but rather recognize that our experiences are inevitably socially constituted and discursively regulated.[10] The experience of a lesbian who is abused by her lover is not only a matter of physical pain and material consequences, but those things compounded by social context and experienced through various discourses about sexuality, about violence, and about gender.

Interviewing Lesbians about Relationship Violence

The interview component of this research was designed to hear from women who self-defined as having experienced lesbian relationship violence and included those who defined as victims, and as perpetrators, and those who felt they fit neither category. I was able to conduct interviews in six Canadian cities of different sizes, covering a range of geographic regions: Winnipeg, Manitoba; Vancouver, British Columbia; Calgary, Alberta; Toronto and London, Ontario; and Halifax, Nova Scotia. The abusive relationships that women spoke of were not limited to the cities in which I did the interviews but took place in urban, rural, and northern locations across Canada, in the United States, and in a few cases, other countries. In each city, I worked with a research assistant from the area who was knowledgeable about lesbian communities and feminist service providers. They placed notices about the research in gay and lesbian community newspapers and organizations, ethnic and cultural community newspapers, women's bookstores, women's bars, and in a variety of gay/lesbian/ bisexual/transgender (glbt) and feminist organizations in each city. We had to be creative, at times, and sensitive to the fact that women might be afraid to be seen tearing off a phone number from a poster that described a project on lesbian abuse. We placed some posters, for example, in bathroom cubicles of lesbian bars, restaurants, and resource centers. This proved to be an effective strategy, giving women time and privacy to read the poster. The posters and advertisements used inclusive language inviting women to participate who identify as gay, bisexual, queer, heterosexual, and transgendered to account for the fact that not all women who are involved in intimate relationships with other women identify as lesbian. I relied on the research assistants' insider knowledge of lesbian communities in the cities in which I was doing the interviews to ensure that I used wording that was most appropriate for that geographic region. One of the first interviews that I conducted was with a woman who was married to a man, involved in a sexually intimate relationship with a woman (who was abusive), and identified as "gay." She saw one of my first posters, which used the term "lesbian" exclusively. When she came for the interview she immediately stated that she was not sure if she qualified for my study.[11] This encounter reinforced the need to be reflexive in the research process and in this case caused me to change the wording of my posters and to challenge some of my own assumptions of what appropriate language for recruiting participants should be.

I conducted the majority of the interviews in person, and some over the telephone. I would generally meet women for one to two hours, although in some cases the interviews lasted several hours. I was very aware of the need for confidentiality and anonymity given the smallness and insularity of lesbian communities. To protect their anonymity all names and initials used in this book are pseudonyms. Because of safety concerns, I rarely met women in their homes and instead used office space in gay/lesbian/queer resource centers, women' s services, universities, and counseling services. Where I could, I offered women different options for places where we could meet to conduct the interviews. In each interview I addressed similar topics covering information about the relationship (length of time, commitment, dynamics); when the abuse started; the types of abuse experienced; patterns in relationship dynamics; the responses of friends, family, co-workers, professionals (e.g., police, shelters, counselors, doctors); the impact of the violence (long-term, short-term effects); the background of the participant and their partner including previous histories of abuse, use of drugs, and use of alcohol. Most often, women came with a story that they wanted to tell, so once we began our discussion I rarely had to ask many questions as they covered the topics that I too wanted to explore. Some came to be interviewed to affirm their experiences whereas others wanted confirmation that what they had gone through was indeed abuse. A few women who identified as perpetrators of violence spoke of doing the interview as a form of restitution to the community and their partner. One woman who identified as abusive gave the following reason for doing the interview:

> I came here in part to make amends, to sort of make amends with—
> I want to contribute my part to your research. I am not quite sure as
> far as my ex-partner is concerned. I will probably have to do more,
> somewhere along the way.
>
> (Lola, interview #16)

Most hoped that their interview would help someone else in a similar situation and many spoke of the need for a witness. The following excerpt from an interview is an example of this:

> Telling my story is about being witnessed and that changes my story
> again for me and helps me in some way. When I tell my story it is
> not just about re-living the pain that I went through. It [retelling the
> story] makes me think about it differently. . . . I came here for some
> altruistic reasons and very selfish reasons at the same time.
>
> (Daphne, interview #43)

My approach to conducting interviews reflects that used by many other feminist researchers where interviews are interactive conversations and researchers are not detached and "objective" listeners.[12] When I turned the tape recorder off and the "official interview" was over, we would continue talking, often discussing different aspects of the interview, clarifying how we were feeling, what they would do next given the intensity of the time we had spent together, and what we would do if we saw each other in public places. Sometimes, I provided more information about the preliminary findings of the research, other times I offered women resources and referrals to services, and in some cases, we exchanged e-mail addresses so that we could keep in touch. Consistent with developing a reciprocal relationship in feminist participatory research approaches, I asked women for input on the research, getting their feedback on how I might better recruit participants, add to the questions I was asking, or refine the interview process.[13] I offered to send those who were interested copies of a final report and/or copies of their transcript.

In Chapters 3 and 4 I report on the many themes that emerged from the 102 interviews that I completed. Overall, I was able to speak with a diverse group of women whose ages ranged from 18 to 66 with most being in their twenties (31 percent), thirties (35 percent), or forties (23 percent). Most identified as lesbian (including preference for the terms gay, queer, dyke, butch, femme). Five identified as bisexual, two as two-spirited (a term preferred by many First Nations peoples to describe their sexual and/or gender identity), two as heterosexual, and two rejected any label. None of the women that I interviewed identified as transgendered. A majority of the women were white; 14 percent were women of color and included First Nations, Metis, South Asian, Asian, Black, and Latina women. Six women identified as recent immigrants from South Africa, Germany, Sweden, Nicaragua, Argentina, and England. Six women further identified as Jewish or French (this number may be higher as I did not specifically ask about this). Most were middle class (55 percent) and working class (38 percent), 3 percent were living in extreme poverty, and 5 percent identified as upper class. Fourteen percent of women reported disabilities that included hearing impairment, physical disabilities, chronic illness, and mental illness. Eighteen percent of the interviewees were women who had children and 28 percent spoke of relationships in which children were involved. Finally, I had originally interviewed 106 women, but had to exclude four women's interviews from this sample: two women were simply unable to remember and recount their experiences in enough detail because of medication they were taking for mental health is-

sues, and two women described experiences of woman-to woman abuse
that did not involve sexually intimate partnerships. The contexts of
teacher–student abuse and abuse between friends was beyond the scope of
this study.

This sample is limited in several ways and cannot represent the full
range of women who are involved in intimate relationships with other
women. One strong limitation of this purposive sample is that women who
come forward to be interviewed may differ in significant ways from those
individuals who did not volunteer to participate in this study. Therefore, it
is important to be cautious when interpreting the data and generalizing
the findings of this research. I am also aware that no transgendered
women came forward to be interviewed, and that I interviewed far more
white women than women of color for this study. In retrospect, I could
have done more intensive outreach to both transgendered and lesbian of
color communities beyond placing ads in a variety of newsletters, and
making contacts with specific community groups and organizations. Yet
several lesbians of color spoke to me directly about the risks they took and
conflicts they felt in coming forward to be interviewed by me, a white
woman and an outsider to their communities and most often an outsider
to their city. For example, an Asian woman spoke to me about her concerns over confidentiality along with her feelings of being disloyal when
speaking about the abuse that she experienced in her relationship:

> The confidentiality thing, I'm telling you is huge for me . . . huge,
> huge. I know from the inside that confidentiality isn't always that
> confidential and the community is small. And then the Asian com-
> munity is even smaller and there's extended families involved who
> are connected with other families and then it all subdivides
> again. . . . The Japanese community is teeny tiny and the Chinese
> community is huge in comparison. . . . That's why I think it is so
> hard to talk anywhere about anything. . . . But that's not all, I
> mean in the Asian community even if there is two stories, it doesn't
> matter because there is this loyalty thing. This is how friendships,
> relationships, even government in Asia, in Asian communities is
> conducted.
>
>   (Amy, Interview #49)

Although it is important to examine the limitations and exclusions produced by the research design, simply adding more lesbians of color is not
sufficient for making the research less white and informed by feminist

antiracist analyses. I do seek to address the intersectionality of race, class, gender, and sexuality when analyzing the interviews.

Discussing Lesbian Relationship Violence with Feminist Service Providers

In each city in which I conducted interviews with lesbians, research assistants worked with me to contact various organizations that either worked on issues of domestic violence or with glbt communities to get names of individual feminist service providers who had a reputation for doing work on this issue. Feminist service providers were called by the research assistants to answer further questions about their background and willingness to participate in the focus group, and to get names of other individuals who could be invited to participate. Feminist service providers (counselors, shelter workers, therapists, social workers, etc.) were sought because they have been at the forefront of grass-roots responses to abuse in lesbian relationships despite some of the contradictions this issue presents for gender-based theories that often inform their practices. In addition, several studies have reported that if lesbians access formal services, it is counselors, not police or lawyers, who they are most likely to seek.[14] I also had a more personal connection with this component of the research because I had cofacilitated a support group in Toronto for lesbians who had experienced relationship violence, and had my own experience-based perspectives and questions when thinking about issues of intervention and service delivery. Many women with whom I spoke would, of course, also define themselves as advocates for social change and activists in the struggle against violence against women: I refer to them as service providers in this study because I was primarily interviewing them about their work in that capacity. Not all service providers identified as feminist in the same way. Some wanted to ensure that I included an analysis of all forms of opression (not just sexist) while others were less comfortable with calling their analysis feminist because they did not see it as fitting their work on same-sex partner abuse.

I facilitated eight focus groups (with a total of seventy feminist service providers) with each discussion lasting three to three-and-a-half hours. The focus group questions served as a framework to encourage lively conversation and to allow for different viewpoints to be expressed rather than seeking consensus on a single answer. The questions included topics such as the patterns and dynamics they have noticed when addressing lesbian relationship violence; how they define abuse (including their views of issues such as consensual sadomasochism); how clients come to them; how they work with women (groups, couple counseling, individual, work with perpetrators etc.); questions that they have when doing this work; their own analysis/understanding of this form of violence and how it fits or does not fit within feminist understandings of violence; and what work needs to be done to best respond to this form of violence. Service providers were also encouraged to come with their own questions and to add to the discussion framework that I had provided them with in advance of our meeting.

I used focus groups as a method because they offer social contexts for meaning making and allow for "collective consciousness work"[15] to be undertaken by participants rather than simply gathering data from them. In this case, discussions allowed for information to be gathered on their observations about lesbian partner abuse and at the same time encouraged them to engage in critical reflexivity and to network with one another since service providers who are addressing lesbian partner violence often work in isolation. After holding two focus groups I became more aware that it was very important for me to explain again (not just in a letter or telephone call) who I was and why I was doing this research, as some of the questions that I was raising were focused on heated debates within lesbian feminist communities. For example, two of the more contentious topics were whether they viewed consensual sadomasochistic sex as abuse and whether they had ever seen examples of "mutual abuse." There was great concern among service providers that information from our discussions could be used against feminists and lesbians. Further, I found that in my opening remarks to the group discussion it was necessary to address the fact that although I was speaking to them as service providers I was aware that they too may have experienced abuse. I did not want to create a false dichotomy between service providers on the one hand and women who experience abuse on the other hand. This acknowledgment opened up a whole other dimension to the discussion, with several service providers sharing their experiences of being in abusive relationships, as well as talking about friends they knew who had experienced abuse in addition to speaking about the women that they saw as clients. This was a powerful shift because it broke down any remaining assumptions that might have left the issue of abuse in lesbian relationships as something external to all of us in the room.

Each focus group discussion was distinct as differing dynamics emerged that affected who would speak and what could be said. In one city, for example, two focus group participants organized a second focus group because they felt some feminists who were doing important work had been missing from the first one and also felt that they were unable to speak freely given a history of political difference between them and some of the other participants. As with my interview research, I tried to be flexible and responsive to the women who were participating, greatly valuing their commitment to my project. The conversations we engaged in were just a beginning step in "collective consciousness work" with some areas opening up and others shutting down. Many feminist service providers welcomed the opportunity to speak with others about the work they were doing, the dilemmas that they encountered, and their shared concern for developing effective responses and interventions to this form of violence. At the end of the discussion I provided a bibliography of resources and other handouts. Participants also requested that they be part of a directory that I would create based on my contacts in other cities, so they could share information and resources and continue conversations.

In most cities, feminist responses to lesbian relationship violence occur within mainstream (mostly heterosexual) service organizations where individual service providers (often lesbian themselves) work with individual lesbian clients or offer support groups for lesbian domestic violence. In this sample, most of the women worked in agencies including shelters, battered women's services, glbt organizations, family services, sexual assault centers, women and community resource centers, drug and alcohol addiction programs, and university/college counseling services, whereas several of the participants worked solely as counselors in private practice. In larger urban centers with big and visible gay and lesbian communities in Canada, and even more so in the United States, some services have emerged that focus solely on lesbian, queer, or same-sex domestic violence or some services offer specific, well-defined streams of programs that focus on this issue. I conducted individual interviews with seven women who worked in these settings in San Francisco, Boston, New York, Albany, Minneapolis, and Toronto. I also interviewed three other individual service providers in Canada who had been unable to make the focus group meetings and who had important experience working with specific lesbian constituencies: South Asian lesbians, Filipina women who were recent immigrants, and lesbians with childhood histories of extreme abuse. A total of eighty service providers were interviewed either individually or in focus groups for this component of the study. To protect the anonymity of service providers I use pseudonyms or initials that I have made up when reporting conversations from focus groups.

The women that I spoke with ranged in age from 20 to 63 with 78 percent being in their thirties to fifties. The majority have a university degree (39 percent undergraduate degree, 45 percent master's level, 3 percent doctorates) with a few having college diplomas. Most participants identified as lesbian, a few as heterosexual and bisexual, and some chose not to identify. The participants were mainly white and 20 percent were women of color who identified as First Nations, South Asian, Asian, and Black (two participants did not provide this information). They bring a range of experience in the area of domestic violence (one to thirty years) with an average of fourteen years. Most have worked more with heterosexual domestic violence clients than lesbians and they have seen far fewer gay men. (One man participated in one of the focus groups but I do not reveal his background information because of issues of confidentiality and anonymity.)

Analyzing Accounts

All interviews and all focus group discussions with both lesbians and service providers were tape-recorded and then transcribed by research assistants. I reviewed them all, reading each one over several times and writing summary notes for each. I analyzed the transcripts for content to identify common themes and used discourse analysis to examine the assumptions that underlie the language used to talk about relationship violence. The voices of the participants and their constructions of their experiences were placed at the center of the analysis. I read each transcript three or four times. My first reading of the transcript focused on the material content of the narrative and asked, "What are the participants telling me?" Several themes were identified within each transcript following approaches similar in concept to "grounded theory" and "local integration."[16] Addressing the material conditions in this way acknowledges the experiences of lesbians and feminist service providers. As a researcher listening to and reading these accounts I find this focus on generating themes can open up new insights into areas that I had not considered. For example, in a preliminary analysis of the interviews I identified a pattern of women being abused within their first lesbian relationships, often by someone older and "out" as a lesbian longer.[17] This was not something I had expected to find, nor had I ever read about this theme in other research; but more than half the women that I interviewed spoke of this context. For example:

It was my first relationship, first long-term relationship. But you know I was—I was head over heels madly in love and thought this is the relationship for life. And it started out really good. This woman was nine years older than myself. It was verbally abusive to start off with and then physically, I was, quite often had black eyes and she

tried—she almost killed me once. Strangled me and this went on for
three years. . . . I was too young and insecure about the whole relationships—gay relationships, whatever. Anybody could have walked
all over me.

(Ellen, interview #17)

Identifying "new" stories based on the patterns that emerged from what
women told me better acknowledges lesbians' experiences and responds to
their needs. This "material tale" troubles the sea of heteronormativity because it makes it possible to hear normally subjugated voices. Although
my role as researcher will certainly have affected the production of the
"material tale" (I invited participants to do this, I set the framework of
questions and then identified common themes for my analysis), my attempt is to be faithful to their stories so that they can recognize themselves
when they see my rendering of their contributions. Of course, tales such as
these also leave much undisturbed and were my research to end here it
might drift to seeing experiences as foundational, fixed, and final rather
than providing a starting place for seeing how experiences are socially
constructed and reflecting on the effects of those constructions.

A Discursive Tale: Exposing Language

Another telling tale in this research can be told, however, through a critical, deconstructive lens where I can consider the discursive conditions in
the work that I am doing. I do not see the discursive turn as inconsistent
with the principle of respecting participants' voices. In fact, many women
(both service providers and lesbians who have been in abusive relationship) that I interviewed are themselves skeptical about some of the concepts available for considering lesbian abuse. In this kind of research the
participants themselves point to the need to be willing to ask, "What assumptions about the causes and effects of violence, the perpetrators and
victims of it, can be seen in the way we talk about, respond to, and research violence?" Here, I once again listen to the voices of the participants
and treat them as authoritative, as part of the material tale that I learn
and tell. But I also treat the interviews and focus group discussions as accounts—constructions that reveal their subjectivities as a way of understanding the participants' sense of self and their ways of understanding
their relation to the world. This is where it is important to take a critical
analysis, to ask, "Who is speaking, from what subject location and in what

historical and cultural contexts?" My second reading of interview transcripts shifted to the discursive content and asked, "What does the participant's language suggest about the ways in which their experiences have been produced by the available discourses and their social positionings within those discourses?" Language is seen as something that not only describes experience, but also as something that constructs it. Analyzing the discursive content of focus group discussions and interviews included looking at the dichotomies that are created and that relate to sexual identities and roles in abusive relationships (lesbian/heterosexual; abuser/abused; white/nonwhite; male violent/female victim). This level of analysis examines systems of oppositions that produce identities and meanings.[18] The third reading was done to make comparisons with themes found across the transcripts as a way of identifying patterns and counter-patterns.[19]

I continue to look at these texts with a deconstructive emphasis that also looks at what is not being said; for example, "How are these subjectivities racialized?" Looking at the transcripts as representing a predominately white group of participants, I can explore how whiteness is assumed and constructed in the discourses available to us to describe experiences of domestic violence. We have to ask, "What isn't being said by participants?" to see evidence of how we are constituted partially within dominant discourses that perpetuate the asymmetry of race relations as a central organizing feature of our society. Exposing the limitations of binaries that are at work in the discourses we have available to us is important for questioning the foundations of our knowledge. I do this kind of analysis not to devalue the content of what women have told me, but to gain insights into how agency and positioning are wrapped up in these discourses in a complex way. For example, in focus group discussions and individual interviews, I include looking at silences, deflections of discourse, and not naming, as part of the work of researching the power dynamics that are reflected in personal accounts such as these.

Discourse analysis is also helpful in understanding how various ideological constructions shape people's thinking. I am concerned with analyzing discourses as social practices that construct particular truths, particular realities and subjectivities, and therefore reproduce certain dominant power relations and normative frameworks.[20] For example, I explore both dominant and marginal feminist discourses (and the spaces in between) that emerge in focus group discussions and in websites that have been constructed to provide information on lesbian partner violence. My analysis reveals the difficulties of bringing forward complexities or counterdiscourses in our understandings around lesbian relationship violence.[21]

My analysis of focus groups reveals (as I discuss in Chapter 5) in part that feminist service providers often rely on"trauma talk" and articulate "necessary speech." In so doing they focus on the similarities of the effects of relationship violence and recenter the issue of male violence against women, making it hard to see lesbian violence clearly.[22]

In examining struggles with language and the politics of responding to abuse in lesbian relationships, I bring forward in Chapter 6 my analysis of several websites that have been created to talk about lesbian relationship violence. I examined five sites, all produced in the United States by non-profit agencies that exist to provide support, advocacy, and education on the issue of abuse in same-sex relationships. The organizations that produced the sites include Advocates for Abused and Battered Lesbians (AABL), Seattle, Washington; The Los Angeles Gay and Lesbian Center (LAGLC), Los Angeles, CA; The Network for Battered Lesbians and Bisexual Women (NBLBW), Boston, MA; The New York Gay and Lesbian Anti-Violence Program (AVP), New York, NY; and the Women Organized to Make Abuse Non-existent (W.O.M.A.N., INC.), San Francisco, CA. I recognize that groups produce these websites within a context of limited resources for lesbian or queer-specific projects and that these sites are important because they are accessible to a wide range of people. It is also striking that there are fewer comparable websites in Canada, the United Kingdom, or Australia, so that these are likely the main sites to be accessed by English-speaking people around the world. I also include an examination of a resource booklet that I helped produce for Health Canada, as well as an Australian publication of the Domestic Violence Resource Center in Melbourne, which produced a booklet on domestic violence in lesbian communities to further show the predominant views that are being put forward.

These sources are meant to educate, offer resources, and dispel misconceptions. At the same time they have to contend with the rhetorical limitations of many such educational forums (i.e., pamphlets, "fact sheets," booklets, etc.). They can reinscribe, legitimize, and normalize certain experiences of violence while obscuring or subjugating other experiences to present a homogeneous representation of the topic. Exploring the discourses that operate in websites reveals the processes of institutionalization by which our mental blueprints are produced and reveals the strategic investments we have in maintaining certain "truths." I am interested in exploring what kind of person can identify with or see themselves in these website discourses on lesbian abuse as well as what kind of subjectivity is produced through them. For example, I considered the following questions in my analysis: What is being said publicly on websites by organizations about lesbian partner violence? Is it consistent with what service providers spoke to me about in focus groups or what women I interviewed revealed in their accounts? What ideas, concepts, discourses are circulating, are being reproduced? What information is being left out, left unsaid? What necessary simplifications are committed and with what effects?

Cindy Holmes recently analyzed the educational discourses in three pamphlets that have been produced by community groups on lesbian abuse (including the booklet that I co-authored and include in my own analysis).[23] She notes the similarity in the topics that they cover discussing myths and facts about lesbian abuse, forms of abuse, and similarities and differences from heterosexual abuse and suggests that they rely on a simple conceptual framework that has the effect of promoting a dominant narrative or regime of truth that privileges white, middle-class, able-bodied women's experiences. She concludes: "I am not saying we should stop producing concise, short, educational pamphlets or that past and present educational materials are useless. But I want to suggest that many of the 'assumptions have led to some predictable cul-de-sacs' and that in order to respond to and end violence in its various forms and locations, we must examine what they produce and limit."[24] Similarly, Joshua Price has traced the travelings of the Power and Control Wheel, a visual diagram that was developed by the Domestic Abuse Intervention Project of Duluth, Minnesota in the early 1980s as a pedagogical tool to raise consciousness about domestic violence. Price found that the Wheel has become institutionalized, used in every shelter and program for batterers in the United States and Canada, including several versions in Spanish. Yet it is no longer used to develop critical consciousness about violence, as was the intent, but instead has become a model with the effect of treating violence everywhere the same. He writes, "As space is homogenized, the particularity of the forms that violence takes—whether lesbian battering, police brutalization of prostitutes, or the terrorizing of undocumented immigrants—is erased."[25] Exploring the content of websites allows me to trace the institutionalization of information on lesbian battering and ask what is being produced and what is being limited, erased, and excluded.

Always interesting and challenging, deconstructive thinking becomes almost a practical necessity when we are studying the lives of people who are marginalized within dominant discourses, and particularly when we are trying not to reproduce the systemic exclusion of heteronormative cultures. A material-discursive approach is one that pays attention to language, subjective experiences, and the material realities of how violence is embodied, felt, and lived.[26] Such an approach is necessary to situate knowledge and provide a more complex understanding of lesbian relationship violence. Yet the material and discursive tales leave out who I am in my research efforts. Ignoring the impact of my own psychic and social location can leave my voice as inappropriately authoritative, ignoring how research and writing are "a self-reflecting construction of others."[27] I engage in reflexivity then as a way of being "answerable for what [I] learn how to see."[28]

A Reflexive Tale: Raising Questions

In conducting research on lesbian relationship violence it has been important for me to locate myself as a white, able-bodied, middle-class lesbian. Yet, in declaring my identity what am I revealing? That I have a right to do this work? That I can be trusted? I am aware that so much more of my subjectivity than my sexual identity goes into the research process. Exploring some of the negotiations involved in the performance of our particular situated selves in the research process is one way of seeing how power operates in the production of knowledge. I use reflexivity in the spirit of Shoshana Felman's "self-subversive self-reflection,"[29] not to stake claim on the problem at hand but to interrupt my own storytelling by reserving time to look behind the veil at my own meaning-making processes. Throughout the research, I continually ask questions: Who am I in doing this work? How am I constituted? How am I relating to the person that I am interviewing? How am I positioned within the focus group discussion? How do these positionings change? How does my personal history show up in the trajectories of my own will to knowledge about lesbian abuse, and to ignorance about it? The experience of listening to women for hours and hours at times left me numb, and often overwhelmed. I knew that this research would affect me emotionally but I was not always prepared for my own reactions. I found myself thinking about every relationship I had been in, the times when I had misused power or was controlling as well as the times when I had been hurt deeply by a partner's words or actions. Remaining aware of these responses has helped me to notice and understand certain aspects of women's experiences and the limits of dichotomous categories such as perpetrator–victim that cannot fully account for a range of experiences. In this level of reflection I try to understand the personal grounds of my understandings and how they might be shaping the production of knowledge.

I also scrutinize the process that I have engaged in and acknowledge the many limitations to this work. For example, at the same time that I have been critical of creating a homogenized understanding of violence, my work at times contributes to that tendency. The interviews and focus group discussions remain focused on "lesbian intimate relationship domestic violence," perpetuating a public/private dichotomy that many women do not experience, something that stood out for me in the interviews. Many women described their experiences of other forms of violence including violent hate crimes, the effects of colonization, being raped by men, sexually abused in childhood, being harassed by a boss at work, being tortured in another country because of political beliefs, being homeless, and experiencing abuse in addition to abuse at the hand of an intimate partner. I was aware of how my focus on domestic violence was often enlarging a small slice of their lives where they had experienced far more violence than I was asking about and that they experienced domestic violence as something connected to and affected by and affecting those other parts. In addition, even though I use the category "lesbian" as an umbrella term to include bisexual, two-spirited, and transgendered women involved in same-sex relationships, my insistence on using the term lesbian can reinscribe the heterosexual/homosexual binary. In focusing on lesbian relationships I had to exclude two interviews from my sample: one woman spoke of abuse by a female teacher and another by a close friend. As I have said above, since neither was speaking about a sexually intimate relationship with another woman, I made the choice that these cases did not fit within the scope of this study. Many scholars are arguing for a spatial analysis of violence that looks at all the forms of violence enacted on women's bodies at different sites and from multiple sources as a way to break down dichotomies and normalize discourses.[30] I am encouraged by this line of inquiry. Yet, despite the limitations in my own work, I am very aware of the many women who took the risk of telling me their stories and who were convinced that this research focus was necessary and could perhaps make a difference in women's lives.

Accounts change, understandings change, meanings change. I use a reflexive approach to bring forward my own subjectivity for my own self-awareness and to reveal my meaning-making process so I can remain accountable to participants for what I am making of their stories as I produce my own. I have also shared my research with glbt and feminist community groups at workshops, forums, and academic conferences in order to get feedback and remain accountable.[31] A reflexive process is risky but necessary to the goal of working past personal and collective obstacles—it

requires that we become aware of our investments (conscious and unconscious) in remaining ignorant about some knowledge and our investments
in asserting other knowledge.

The three tales that I have presented here frame the remaining chapters where I keep the strands of material, discursive, and reflexive analyses
firmly woven into the fabric of the book. These tales are troubled, risky,
and reveal the dangers of knowledge. Still, focusing on their interplay is
my way of being able to respond to social issues such as violence, which is
useful in the here and now, which acknowledges lesbian existence, and
which is responsible. I hope to deepen our understandings and push at the
boundaries of what we know. Gloria Anzaldua, a Chicana lesbian, has
written about mestiza consciousness that she argues needs to be part of
our theorizing and research. She writes:

> As a mestiza I have no country, my homeland cast me out; yet all
> countries are mine because I am every woman's sister or potential
> lover. (As a lesbian I have no race, my own people disclaim me; but
> I am all races because there is the queer of me in all races). I am an
> act of kneading, of uniting and joining that not only has produced
> both a creature of darkness and a creature of light, but also a crea-
> ture that questions the definitions of light and dark and gives them
> new meanings.[32]

Doing this work calls for some such act of kneading the material, the discursive, and the reflexive to produce new meanings; an approach that ac-
commodates the lived experiences of women living our lives as lesbians
and a queered analysis of the socially constructed dimensions of experience. I find in the material tale a way of recognizing participants' valuable
contributions to the production of knowledge about lesbian relationship
violence, in the discursive tale a way of pushing the limits of understandings available to us, and in the reflexive tale a much-needed check on the
subjectivity behind this project and behind all of our efforts to know and
respond to lesbian relationship violence. Indeed the materials that I present from the interviews and focus groups are not simply testaments that
reveal static answers to questions about abuse in lesbian relationships—
they are, rather, richly various in their offerings. As James Baldwin put it
so well,

> While the tale of how we suffer, and how we are delighted, and how
> we may triumph is never new, it always must be heard. There isn't

any other to tell, it's the only light we've got in all this dark-
ness . . . and this tale according to that face, that body, those strong
hands on those strings, has another aspect in every country, and a
new depth in every generation.[33]

A MATERIAL TALE

telling stories

THREE
What the Body Remembers
Lesbians' Experiences of Relationship Violence

IT IS OBVIOUS that to define and name violence one must know that it has happened. Yet we have learned that forgetting and minimizing abusive experiences are common coping strategies that women may employ.[1] For many of the women who agreed to participate in my study, the interview was the first time they had told anyone their stories; for many others the retelling of their stories served to confirm their experience as real. In subsequent chapters, I will be exploring the ways that various discourses of abuse, gender, and sexuality affect the ways violence is represented, understood, and even experienced. In this chapter, though, I focus on the material aspects of violence, how it is experienced at the time and how it is recollected later: what the body remembers does not constitute the whole story of abuse in lesbian relationships, but the story does begin there.

The stories of women who have experienced abuse in lesbian relationships are at the same time strikingly similar and notably different in terms of the interactions and dynamics between partners and the context in which the abuse emerged. It can, therefore, be difficult to sustain a sense of the diversity of women's experiences while organizing those experiences into the common themes that can be found in their stories. Their accounts cannot simply be placed into neat and distinct categories. For example, of the 102 women interviewed for this study the majority identified themselves as being victims of abuse, although four women defined themselves as perpetrators, three explained that they were initially victimized but that they became perpetrators of abuse later on in the relationship, and one women felt she fit neither category but said her partner had engaged in abusive behaviors. (Are these four women anomalous or do their self-assessments reveal thinking outside the box of victim/perpetrator into which most of us categorize our experiences of violence?) Again, there was a range in terms of the length of relationships that women described, from four months to seventeen years. For the most part, women spoke about abuse occurring within committed relationships where they had lived together from two to six years. Not all couples lived together in this sample; some kept separate residences because of children, for example, and a few women had no permanent residences and described relationship violence that occurred in hostels or on the street. (Are the experiences of these homeless women or separately domiciled women understood to be part of the category "domestic" abuse in research surveys?) The women that I spoke with are a group as diverse and varied as are their experiences of relationship violence.

Forms of Violence

The forms of abuse that women spoke about are consistent with our now common understanding of violence as including emotional, verbal, physical, and sexual attacks ranging from mild to lethal.[2] Most often the effect of these attacks is to deny the will and autonomy of the victim and to hurt, humiliate, punish, manipulate, coerce, or degrade her.[3] In feminist explanations of heterosexual domestic violence, men's power over women in abusive relationships is seen as an extension of their power in a patriarchal society. Yet greater social power and physical strength do not seem to be indicators of who will be violent in lesbian or gay relationships.[4] Several women who identified as butch in this study reported being victimized by their smaller femme partner. They spoke of the added difficulties they face of not being believed or being shamed because of the assumption made on the basis of their butch identity or appearance that they must be the one who is abusive. Other women spoke of being victimized in spite of the fact that they had more money and resources (higher education, more prestigious jobs), or were healthier, or were taller or stronger than their abusive partners. This underlies the need to further explore the context in which abuse occurs, as well as to reassess how we have understood social location as linked to power and control in motivating abusive behavior.

Most of the women that I interviewed reported a combination of emotional, verbal, and physical abuse. Yet within the sample there is a broad range of experiences. As in Claire Renzetti's survey research with 100 lesbians,[5] the most common form of violence reported was emotional abuse.

In my study, all but one woman reported experiencing emotional abuse and nineteen women stated that this was the main or only form of abuse that they had encountered in their relationship. Most often the emotional abuse consisted of manipulation, lies, jealousy, isolation from friends and family, homophobic threats, not being allowed to sleep or having sleep interrupted—all ways of limiting or controlling their actions. Women described feeling as if they were "walking on eggshells," always worried about what might make their abusive partner angry or upset. For other women, emotional abuse also included threats to kill them, driving recklessly to frighten them, locking them out of the house, leaving for days without any contact, making threats to harm their pets, making harassing phone calls, threatening suicide or hurting themselves; in one case a woman actually hanged herself, having arranged to have her partner find her dead body as a final traumatizing act. Eight women spoke in chilling detail about being stalked by their abusive partners, some even after the relationship ended and the fear and terror that this created. Four women told of partners who had lied to them about having an illness such as cancer or AIDS as a way to control their behavior. When they found out about the elaborate lie, they had to look back at their whole relationship as a prolonged betrayal of trust, a second stage that itself caused great pain. Although the diversity of emotional abuse reported is clear, what stands out is the effectiveness of this form of violence in creating pain and in causing women to change their behaviors and doubt themselves. So much is submerged within the category "emotional abuse," and often this is the form of abuse that has women questioning whether they have really been abused.

Along with emotional abuse, ninety-four women reported experiencing verbal abuse most often consisting of yelling rages, frightening in private places and humiliating in public ones, name calling, insults, and in a few cases racist attacks. Eighteen women reported that financial abuse (creating debt, stealing money, running up credit cards, controlling all finances) was part of the damaging behaviors that they experienced. The physical abuse described by many women includes a wide range of behaviors. Eighty-five women reported physical abuse that was directed at objects and included hitting/punching walls, throwing things at them or around the room, destroying property, ripping up clothing or throwing belongings out, and in a few cases kicking pets. Eighty-eight women described physical abuse that was directed at them. Most often, this was behavior that occurred many times over the course of the relationship, sometimes increasing in frequency and in severity. The most common physically abusive tactics were restraining, grabbing, shoving, pushing, punching, kick-

ing, slapping, and biting. Ten women reported that the physical abuse occurred only one or two times in the relationship, often at or near the end of
their partnership. Nineteen women reported severe physical violence in
which they received broken bones, head injuries, knife wounds, or bruises.
Severe violence often involved weapons such as guns or knives and included being strangled or choked and beaten so badly that the women believed they were going to die.

Perhaps most striking, given the relative absence of this category in
other studies of lesbian partner violence, was the number of women who
reported sexual assault. This form of violence has been referred to as "the
most understudied topic in same-sex domestic violence."[6] Although male
rapists are by far the greater danger for women, it is important to acknowledge that women can injure another woman sexually.[7] For example,
Renzetti's research shows that 48 percent of women in her study stated
that they had been forced to have sex at some point in their abusive relationship, while Caroline Waterman, Lori Dawson, and Michael Bologna
found that 26 percent of lesbians in their sample were victims of at least
one act of sexual violence by a female partner.[8] In my study, women who
spoke of being sexually assaulted understandably had great difficulty
talking about this in the interview. Some women felt uncomfortable with
the term sexual abuse or assault being applied to their experiences, even
though they felt they had been sexually violated by their partners. They
associated the language of sexual assault with heterosexuals. For example,
one woman described how her partner would come home at night and
wake her up to sexually assault her. Yet she had never really classified her
abusive partner's behavior as rape:

> **W:** She'd come home, wake me up and say "I want to do this or
> that" and it's like "no," you know. And she used to give me bruises
> all over my arms when she'd come on the waterbed and hold my
> arms down . . . and stuff like that.
> **JR:** Would she be forcing you to have sex?
> **W:** Yeah, now there's something new, I hadn't really saw that.
>   (Wanda, interview #5)

The category sexual assault, like all categories of violence that I have been
using, covers a wide range of experiences. It is important to break down
women's experiences of sexual assault into different areas in order to be
clear about what women are describing. Unfortunately, other research has
tended to use questionnaires where interpretations of the question may

vary. For this study, I was able to classify women's responses into three categories: forced sex or rape (when women describe being sexually violated, and forced against their will; the perpetrator might use an object, weapon, hand, or finger to penetrate a woman's vagina, anus, or mouth, and/or may restrain women with their physical strength while assaulting their body); sexual coercion (which involves engaging in sex as a result of pressure when you do not want to); and finally emotional sexual abuse (which involves what a few interviewees identified as "emotional rape"; this can include partners acting in sexually controlling ways that are not consensual: for example, not letting their partners touch them sexually, rejecting partners sexually in ways meant to hurt or humiliate, or making demeaning comments about their sexual behavior or body parts). Twenty of the 102 women that I interviewed spoke of a rape or sexual assault occurring within their relationship. This was most often a one-time occurrence. Three women reported attempted sexual assaults that they were able to stop by fighting off their abusive partner. Nineteen women spoke of sexual coercion, and thirty-two women talked about emotional sexual abuse. Rarely is the scene of sexual abuse simple in these stories. For example, here is how one woman described how she began to feel emotionally sexually violated:

> When we were really intimate and we felt a lot for each other, that is when she felt she was losing control or whatever . . . she had this compulsive or obsessive behavior where she would scratch herself [her vagina] and she'd scratch and scratch like to the point she'd bleed and I would take her hands and say "stop it you're gonna bleed" and she'd pull away and go "no, no I have to do it" and she'd push me away. We had just been intimate and I'm feeling totally rejected and vulnerable. I didn't know what was going on. Then she'd say, "give me a hug, a cuddle" and I would be like, "two seconds ago you pushed me away, this is really hard for me to understand." And then she would swear at me and say, "Well what was this to you? Just some kinda fuck?". . . it made being intimate very difficult. That was the start of the breakdown because I couldn't feel intimate with her without feeling violated.
>
> (Anita, interview #14)

It is evident that abusive dynamics in relationships often include various kinds of sexually motivated violence. Women that I interviewed expressed a great deal of shame over being sexually assaulted by another woman—if you feel that as a lesbian your sexual identity is already viewed negatively by mainstream society, having your intimate partner humiliate or violate you sexually can have a tremendous impact on your sexuality. This is evident in the following excerpt:

> I am still healing or coming to terms with the sexual abuse, the sexual assault. It affected me so significantly. The main thing is that I feel marked by it. I feel somehow that that incident specifically marks me as being different from other people and somehow different from other lesbians. . . . I have really internalized the idea that it was somehow because I was a lesbian that this happened.
>
> (Samantha, interview #29)

Further, a few women described experiencing confusing sexually coercive behaviors, which occurred in the context of consensual sadomasochistic (s/m) relationships. There has been a great deal of controversy within feminist and queer communities about the relationship between s/m sex and sexual violence.[9] (It should also be noted that this practice is not limited to queer communities, but heterosexual s/m sex does not seem to be publicly discussed to the same degree.) I interviewed seven women who identified as engaging in s/m sex within their relationship with another woman, and of those, three women felt the abusive dynamics included crossing the line from consensual s/m sex into nonconsensual acts. They were confused by the dynamics because in these three cases their partners were introducing them to s/m, and they had no context within which to assess their own desires and limits, and the actions of their partners. This is evident in the following example:

> **B:** And during sex she was pushing some of my boundaries. Initially it was just kind of like trying to get me to try things, sort of light things, light s/m things and it was all stuff that I was okay with. But then she started saying things like "oh I think you can take it harder. I think you can take more." That kind of thing and I was thinking "no, I don't think so"; even that was too much. And you know she just started doing it anyway.
>
> **JR:** It didn't matter what you said?
>
> **B:** Yeah and then you know in certain situations you can't exactly do anything about it. . . . It was something that was really, like, very new to me. . . . It was very frightening and I think that was the hardest thing afterwards to work through on my own be-

cause, I mean, it is so easy to get hang-ups and have issues about
sex anyway. . . . That kind of put me back at a place I was never
even at before, you know?

(Bonita, interview #80)

Clearly not all s/m relationships are abusive. The three women I spoke
with, however, in addition to feeling shame and experiencing an impact on
their sexuality, blamed themselves for getting into an s/m relationship and
felt they would be judged negatively if they told anyone about what had
happened. From these examples of the forms of abuse that women have
encountered, it has become evident that it is necessary to understand the
context surrounding the experiences of abuse in order to fully grasp
women's experiences and appreciate the impact.

Context of Relationship Violence

Beyond identifying the various forms of violence that women experience,
feminist theories of intimate violence have stressed examining the social
context in which we live as necessary to understand what gives rise to violence. Male violence against women arises, in part, within a context of patriarchal traditions that include the belief in men's right to control women.
This is reinforced through societal constructions of masculinity and femininity.[10] Similarly, researchers have looked at internalized homophobia
and a context of heterosexism as factors in same-sex abuse. James Shat-
tuck,[11] for example, raised the question, "How might the experience of being gay or lesbian (oppressed and alienated by heterosexual society, being
forced to 'live outside the rules') affect one's relational abilities with an intimate partner?" Recent writings on the high incidence of abuse within
First Nations communities examine a context of colonization that displays
the extreme dynamics of domination and subordination, which then can
translate into the more intimate relations of abuser and abused.[12] These
conditions of patriarchy, misogyny, heterosexism, racism, and colonization
are overwhelmingly present in the lives of lesbians and all marginalized
peoples. They are the main constituents of our discursive environment,
and are propped up by countless institutional practices. They are like the
air we breathe, but there is more to understanding violence than can be
accounted for by identifying the influences of these particular systems of
oppression in the lives of women. These social forces do give permission
for abuse, provide its logic, and may even encourage it, but they are not

sufficient to explain why abuse happens in some relationships and not in others. This does not mean that I dismiss an analysis of the social forces of oppression and domination; far from it. Rather, I acknowledge their impact but do not see them as providing the complete explanatory framework for intimate violence in all cases. Further, interlocking layers of oppression operate in many different ways, with many of us having the experience of being simultaneously in a position of social privilege and power (for example, being white), while also being in a subordinate position (being lesbian, female). These social positionings, in turn, affect how we speak about, experience, and define relationship violence.[13]

The accounts of women that I interviewed suggest that there are different patterns of intimate violence that arise from different societal roots and interpersonal dynamics, indicating that not all violence is the same. I have tried to look more closely at the specific contextual features that women spoke about as mattering. Elaine Leeder has looked at more specific contexts within lesbian battering relationships and has distinguished between three types: situational, which occurs once or twice as the result of some event that throws a couple into crisis; chronic battering, in which physical abuse occurs two or more times, escalating over time; and emotional battering, which is similar to chronic except that the abuse is psychological or verbal rather than physical. Her classification is interesting to consider, because in my study, three women did describe physical abuse as arising from a specific situation, never recurring: two were breaking up with partners when physical abuse occurred and one woman who had been involved with a woman for six months revealed that she was physically attacked twice in her sleep by her partner. The majority of the interviews (as in Renzetti's 1992 study) can be placed within chronic and emotional battering situations. However, these categories are still not sufficient to capture the diversity of abusive relationships that women have experienced. For example, in some cases, the violence did not escalate, but remained constant in terms of the forms of violence used and the frequency with which it occurred.[14] These cases do not seem to fit within Leeder's classification system. Michael Johnson has also proposed categories for abusive relationships and suggests that there may be two distinct forms of couple violence. He proposes that some couples suffer from occasional outbursts of violence, which he calls "common couple violence," whereas others are terrorized by frequent, escalating incidents that he calls "patriarchal terrorism." Johnson, however, wrongly assumes that lesbian violence would fall only into the "common couple violence" category, because, he says, it has little to do with the taking on of patriarchal family values.[15] Yet, in creating this either/or classification, he ignores the potential for severe, extreme, controlling abuse within lesbian couples, something that this research has found does indeed occur. Renzetti's survey research identified seven factors that were strongly correlated with the occurrence of lesbian partner abuse. They included the following: power imbalance, dependency, jealousy, intergenerational transmission of violence, substance abuse, internalized homophobia, and personality disorders.[16] These are important variables to consider, but, as Claire Renzetti points out, these variables were chosen for exploration in the first place because they have been used in research with heterosexual couples.[17] We need to know more than whether there is a statistical correlation between them and lesbian partner abuse. We need to ask what these factors mean in the lives of women, and explore how, when, and if they are related to abusive behaviors.

As Ann Duffy and Julianne Momirov suggest, violence within lesbian relationships takes shape and has meaning within a specific context, which is very different from the context for heterosexual women. For example, as women, a lesbian couple (if from the same ethnic and class backgrounds) is most often equally marginalized by mainstream society, so there are not the patterns of inequality that are legitimated between a man and a woman. Further, when a woman beats her partner she does so within the context of a homophobic society that sees lesbianism as deviant. Both partners are aware of this context, and know that people will likely dismiss or be hostile to their situation. Duffy and Momirov argue that actions have such different meanings depending on the intention, the actor, and the history, that we should not see violence in lesbian relationships as parallel to that of male violence against women.[18]

Rather than creating typologies or correlates of lesbian partner violence, I have found it more helpful to consider a range of contextual factors that surround abusive relationships. For instance, there are social contexts that create isolation and invisibility for lesbians and that in turn may contribute to the risk of violence. These include contexts of first relationships, contexts of the closet and homophobia, and contexts of dislocation such as recent immigration. There are also contexts in which violence is normalized. These can include using drugs and alcohol, having a history of previous abuse, and experiencing a lifetime of abuse in a context of poverty and racism. Each of these contextual factors may increase the probability of experiencing or committing violence; however, this does not mean that they cause violence or that individual women in such contexts make risky partners. For some women that I interviewed, the context of their abusive relationship did not include any of the aforementioned factors. Given this diversity of women's accounts, it is important to closely examine the specific contexts and spaces in which violence occurs so that we can make distinctions between situations that will help us in our efforts to eradicate violence. Efforts to understand violence in lesbian relationships that ignore these contexts run the risk of treating all cases of relationship violence as equivalent and interchangeable, when that does not seem to be the case. Further, ignoring social contexts depoliticizes our analysis of violence by glossing over the social inequities that put people at risk.

Invisibility and Isolation: A Context of First Relationships

A strong pattern has emerged in this research of women being abused within their first relationships.[19] More than half (sixty-one) of the participants described their first relationship as abusive; often this was with someone who had been "out" for a longer period of time and sometimes the woman was older. The following extracts support this theme:

> I lived with two gay men and I always knew that I was a lesbian but there was no community that I was aware of. Gay men, boy there seemed like there was lots of them, but I didn't know any women and one of these guys knew this lesbian from another city. I didn't get a good impression when I met her the first time, but then she kind of won me over and I guess I was impressionable because I hadn't really met, you know, a real live lesbian. She was about four years older, a former school teacher. . . . I was really taken by her, you know this was sort of the first affection that I'd gotten from a woman which I had longed for. . . .
>
> (Melissa, interview #8)

> OK so probably the physically abusive relationship was my first relationship with a woman. . . . It would have been really nice if someone at the very beginning had—had told me, like when I first met her, said, "Na, na, na stay away from her." But because I was also very new to the community too, that's probably a big part of it. And she wasn't, I mean she was really firmly established and a lot of people know her. Well you know how the community is, everybody knows everybody. So she was an insider and I was an outsider and I

looked straight and I had a child. Having a child in the lesbian community makes you ostracized right there.

(Florence, interview #10)

It was my first relationship. First long-term relationship. But you
know I was—I was head over heels madly in love and I thought this
is the relationship for life. And it started out really good. This
woman was nine years older than myself. It was verbally abusive to
start off with and then physically, I was, quite often had black eyes
and she tried—she almost killed me once. Strangled me and then
this went on for three years. . . . I was too young and insecure
about the whole relationship—gay relationships, whatever. Anybody could have walked all over me.

(Ellen, interview #17)

I was just out for less than a year. This was my first experience with
a woman, I didn't care which woman it was.

(Sonia, interview #27)

Some women also mentioned that they now classify their abusive partners
as serial abusers, who were abusive in one relationship, and then the next,
and had a reputation for preying on women who were just coming out. In
fact, in one city where I conducted interviews four lesbians spoke to me
about the same abusive woman with whom they had each been involved
at different times, covering a span of fifteen years. They often learned of
the reputation of their partner only after the relationship ended.

This pattern of first relationships being abusive is not something that
has been reported in other research. The number I am reporting may in
fact be low because it was not something that I had asked about directly in
the first several interviews. In many ways, this pattern is not surprising,
given the additional social vulnerabilities lesbians (particularly young lesbians) face when just coming out. Lesbian women enter into a first relationship as outsiders to lesbian communities, and are often not plugged
into any support systems. It suggests that vulnerability to violence is part
of the cost of a heterosexist context in which lesbians are isolated, unable
to access meeting places, and often dependent on their first lover for information about living as a lesbian. Many young women also spoke about the
shame they felt in having to come out to friends or family by telling them
about their abusive lesbian relationship. For example, Wilma was twenty

when she was in an abusive first relationship. After the relationship ended her partner stalked her and made harassing phone calls for over three years, including calls to family members and her workplace. She described how her father could not understand what was going on:

> **W:** I think for my dad—like some 20 year old girl isn't very scary. . . . I think I couldn't really say how scared I was.
> **JR:** Were there some feelings of shame for you in having to tell other people what was going on?
> **W:** Yeah, there was for a long time and that kept me sort of more isolated with everything. . . . And that was kind of the circumstance of some of my coming out.
>
> (Wilma, interview #86)

It is also important to mention that in a few cases it was the abusive woman for whom it was a first lesbian relationship. Some women used their status as "new" lesbians who were perhaps unsure of their commitment to the relationship or to being lesbian as a way of making threats to get their partner to do what they wanted. Often connected to the context of first relationships is the context of some women being in the closet, another social factor that women themselves spoke about as mattering.

The Closet and Homophobia

Gays, lesbians, and transgendered people have all experienced the impact of living in a homophobic culture. Even though there have been many, many gains made in human rights and in visibility, some lesbians remain closeted, feeling that they must hide their sexuality from some people even when they are "out" to others. We also know that within abusive relationships, abusers can use the tactic of threatening to out their partner as a way of exerting power in a relationship.[20] In this study, fifty-two women mentioned homophobic threats as a specific part of the dynamic. Often these were threats of "outing" them, and sometimes this was part of the verbal abuse that women endured in which their partner would say vile things about lesbians, in a way that exhibited their own misogyny and homophobia. Internalized homophobia has been named as a factor in abusive relationships, where an abused lesbian is seen as internalizing society's negative attitudes, which leads to self-hatred and a feeling that you somehow deserve the abuse. Internalized homophobia, coupled with the fear of outing, is then said to keep a lesbian within an abusive situation.[21] Yet internalized homophobia is a term that can inaccurately describe what is going on. It suggests that the problem is individually based, residing within abused lesbians. The women that I spoke with did not demonstrate self-hatred but rather a well-founded fear of encountering homophobia/heterosexism. Fear of social forces, not self-loathing, contributed to their staying in an abusive relationship. For them, the power of homophobic threats was often connected to the context of the closet (itself a tactical response to homophobia) within which many lesbians still have to live. Forty-eight of the women that I interviewed said that being closeted was a factor within their abusive relationship. This was most evident for women who lived in small, rural, or northern locations in which there may be very real dangers to being out. This context added to their isolation and invisibility, leaving them unable to speak with anyone about what they were going through. For example, a college teacher in a rural town spoke of the fact that her partner used her past history of losing a job for being gay as a way to keep her in the relationship:

> I'm living in this small town, population five, six thousand. I was very concerned about people knowing that I'm gay because I just don't want the harassment. I meet this woman with two children . . . and within two weeks I realize that there is something seriously wrong with this woman. She's got a mean streak. And I was like, I'm outta there, this isn't good. She goes "if you even think about leaving or breaking up this relationship, I will ruin your life." Meanwhile I have the memory of this other harassment when I was an elementary school teacher and I don't want to have to leave this small town because it takes a particularly long time, in education, to get your career on track again.
>
> (Kelly, interview #41)

She remained in this relationship, which got progressively more abusive, for eighteen months. In another example, a woman and her abusive partner lived in a small, rural town and worked together in the same workplace where they were not out and were thought of as roommates:

> I would go to work, of course, with bizarre excuses for why I had a black eye or this that or the other thing. And we weren't out—we

worked together—we weren't out at work. So we were always just like buddies and "Ha, ha this happened." You know? Whatever . . . and she was a Baptist minister's daughter.

(Mary Ann, interview #95)

Another woman described the impact of homophobia and the closet in a different way. She was in her first relationship with another woman. It was physically and emotionally abusive and neither of them was out to anyone. She knew of no supports or services and turned to the church as the safest place that she could think of. She had to confess her sin of homosexuality and was then baptized again. She dated a man from the church and when she told him about her continued attractions to women he "outed" her in her job, to her family, her church, and her AA group (Rosie, interview #94). The social context of homophobia, heterosexism, and the closet continues to affect lesbians both within and outside abusive relationships.

Dislocation

Consistent with the context of first relationships being abusive and a context of the closet are similar contexts of social vulnerability to violence mentioned by some of the other participants in this research, such as moving to a new city, or moving from another country, or speaking English as a second language. One woman described the extra pressure that she and her partner felt as recent immigrants who were dislocated, which she feels contributed to the abuse:

I was around 24, I guess when I met her and we were both immigrants. She had just been in Canada for about 6 months. It was a really big thing for her and for me to find a lesbian who was Latina. That was a big thing for us. I could understand what she was going through in terms of learning the language and family. She has a sister who was married to a Canadian man and her mother was here. I was just getting divorced so it was a crucial time for us. . . . I think maybe that was what really put too much pressure on the relationship, because we were everything to each other. I was more out than she was and that put more pressure in the relationship too. . . . She considered herself lesbian, but she couldn't really handle the fact that her family was here. She didn't know how to come out to them. The family was starting to pressure her—why was she spending so much time with me? why was she sleeping over at my place? And I put pressure on her too, it's like we don't see each other as much and I would like to see you more. . . . The dynamics in our relationship were very weird. I think they were not healthy. At the time we were also best friends, we didn't have no supports whatsoever and we didn't know any other lesbian either.

(Rita, interview #32)

She is not excusing her abusive partner's behavior, but is describing the isolating context in which they found themselves. Similarly, another woman spoke of being a recent immigrant and being dependent on her French Canadian partner. She spoke of how her partner exploited the power dynamics of this context by threatening to disrupt her immigration process:

I didn't speak a word of French at the time; she was bilingual. I was totally dependent on her because I couldn't make myself understood. That is a really important context to understand that I was from another country in a French community.

(Heidi, interview #28)

Acknowledging these different contexts is in no way meant to minimize or explain away the abuse, but it does suggest that there can be multiple, overlapping, and compounding factors to consider when exploring when and how abusive dynamics emerge. The contexts that I have explored are also not exhaustive of the possibilities. For example, a few women mentioned more personal contexts like entering into a relationship soon after the unexpected death of their sister, mother, or friend; or getting involved too quickly after the break-up of a previous relationship. These considerations do not suggest that women who have been victimized are somehow weaker or more vulnerable than women who have not experienced relationship violence; rather they continue to point to the complexities of how violence in relationships might begin to take hold and be structured by certain social contexts.

Other factors that have been considered when trying to understand lesbian relationship violence include substance abuse and intergenerational violence.[22] Often, studies have suggested that lesbians, in general, may be at high risk for substance abuse because of the cumulative effects of living in a homophobic world that causes feelings of alienation and depression, and of the centrality of bars in many lesbians' communities.[23] In several studies on same-sex partner abuse, the use of drugs and alcohol has been found to be related to partner abuse in 33 percent to over 70 percent of the couples studied.[24] Most, however, report that although alcohol and drug use is often present in same-sex abusive relationships, it is not a sufficient cause for partner abuse.[25] In my view, we have to see drug and alcohol abuse not as causing violence in a simple sense, but yet as something more than a variable that may be correlated to violence. Heavy use of drugs and alcohol is a context into which abuse often fits and seems depressingly normal, and therefore may not be refrained from or fled.

Normalizing Violence: Drugs and Alcohol

In my study, forty-seven women mentioned drug and alcohol abuse as part of their relationship dynamic, while more than half (fifty-four) did not. However, what the forty-seven women reported reveals a variety of situations involving drugs and alcohol. For nineteen women, this meant that abusers would drink or use drugs and that this would lead to increased physical violence. For example, one woman spoke about this happening many times in their relationship and here speaks about one of the first incidents:

> So she's on disability [for a degenerative back problem] and stuff and on lots of pills. That's where a lot of this comes in—pills and drinking and stuff. That night she had a couple of drinks and probably a lot of pills. She was upstairs and she just started flipping out and crying and saying "I want my mother" and uhh, talking like a child. And I thought something is definitely wrong here. I thought it has something to do with her past and her parents and it was just coming out. Then she came down the stairs and that's where it started. Like she never really hit me but did everything else she could possibly do. She pushed me. And I said "What's wrong with you? Why are you acting this way? I didn't do anything." And it was just like push, shove, and then she threw me down and that was when I banged the coffee table right on the corner. And I just sat there and I looked at her and thought this is crazy. And then she started throwing things and a beer bottle landed up in the corner and it just smashed . . . and there was something with sour cream or I don't know what it was, that ended up on the couch. . . . She told me to clean that up, yelling that I did it. So it was really weird. I think a lot of it was pills.
>
> (Fran, interview #6)

Often, abusers use the excuse of medication or drinking too much to suggest that they were not in control of their actions, and in this way both partners can normalize and dismiss what happened. In a few cases, women reported that their partners were more abusive when not drinking. As Mary Ann said about her partner who became more abusive when she gave up drugs, "she could no longer numb her feelings with substances" (interview #95). A few others commented that their partners were less of a threat or "nicer" when they drank. For example, Wanda spoke of a relationship in which there had been several episodes of physical abuse (punching, pushing, shoving):

> **JR:** Were drugs or alcohol ever involved? Not that these cause abuse but . . .
> **W:** Not drugs but alcohol, I mean we were both going to AA, which we both had a hard time with. [laughs]
> **JR:** So did it change her behavior when she was drinking more?
> **W:** I actually hate to say it, but she was nicer when she was drinking. Oh, what an awful thing to say. [We both laugh.]
>
> (Wanda, interview #5)

In other cases, women who were abused reported that their drinking increased even if their partners never drank. They did this to numb themselves as a way of coping with the abuse that was being directed at them. Finally, in other situations, both women drank, which contributed to confusing interactions in which, again, violence could be made to seem normal. In one example, Yvonne was drinking heavily before her new relationship began. She and her new partner moved in together immediately. They both drank and her partner also smoked marijuana daily. Within six months, her lover physically assaulted her. She would spit on her, kick her, slap her, and call her a "fat, ugly, drunk." Yvonne felt like she deserved the abuse because she was drunk and felt worthless. The abuse got worse and continued for many years. She explains the normalizing effect alcohol had on her perception of abuse:

> Women are not going to leave that abusive relationship as long as they are using. They're not going to have the courage and strength because they are numb. I mean I drank for years so I wouldn't have to take a look at myself and my peers. I was sober for almost five years (in the abusive relationship) before I made that move [to leave].
>
> (Yvonne, interview #72)

Another woman described a first relationship that lasted for four years. Bev met her partner in a bar; neither had steady employment, and drugs, alcohol, and violence were a routine part of their lives:

> **B:** We started the day off smoking a joint and then all the way through the day . . . we didn't really have much in the way of verbal communication. It was basically having sex, going out to lunch, meeting our friends at the bar later . . . she was actually selling drugs at the time, that was her job.
>
> **JR:** Do you remember when she became physically abusive toward you?
>
> **B:** No. I'm sure that it was probably in a drunken flurry and that's why I don't remember. Plus you know, like everybody else we downplayed the violence so much that I don't even have a clue. There was everything from breaking my cheekbone, to hitting me, to pushing me into walls, to hitting me in the back. I got hit in the face quite a lot and I got bit once. . . . During the relationship we did a lot of acid, mushrooms, then coke, then I fell into the crack scene. It was on purpose almost because I wanted something to be so bad that I would have to be reached.
>
> (Bev, interview #31)

These accounts reveal the differing ways in which drugs and alcohol can be used by women within abusive relationships. It is an important context through which to understand some abusive relationships. In addition to substance abuse, many women also mentioned having experienced abuse in their lives before, and felt that this was significant in understanding the context of their abusive relationship.

Normalizing Violence: Histories of Previous Abuse

A few studies on lesbian abuse have asked whether women have had previous exposure to domestic violence in their families of origin. Like the research on drug and alcohol abuse, the findings are inconsistent. Some have found that those who witness abuse or experience abuse in childhood are more likely than those who have not to be victimized, and/or to be abusers in adult relationships.[26] Other studies have not found any correlation.[27] Again, the emphasis in asking a question such as this has been to isolate certain criteria that might establish who will be abused or will be abusive. However, treating previous experiences of abuse in this way ignores the complexities that women's stories reveal, which show how previous abuse can become part of a context that gives meaning and structure to violence that they experience within their relationship.

Of the women with whom I spoke, forty-nine mentioned that they had experienced abuse before, and fourteen women also specifically mentioned that their abusive partners had histories of abuse. (These figures may be inaccurate, as this was not a question that all women were asked, willing to discuss, or even able to answer. As well, I did not ask about forms of abuse such as gay bashing or other hate crimes, which also might have elicited different responses.) Their previous histories of abuse included a range from incest, to rape and sexual assault, to verbal, emotional, and/or physical abuse by parents or family members. Some women mentioned experiencing domestic violence in heterosexual relationships, and twelve women reported being in more than one abusive relationship with another woman. The context of previous abuse is important to explore because many women commented on how familiar the abusive dynamics sometimes felt to them. Looking back, they had become aware of a prewritten script and felt as if they had taken up their appropriate role within it. For example, a white woman, Michaela, who was forty-seven and spoke of being physically abused in three relationships with women, said the following about her previous history of abuse at the hands of her mother and father:

> I didn't know what to recognize and even when I did recognize and think, you know, oh someone's beating me up it wasn't of the same order of someone who's beating you up. Because of just the habit, of well that's what people do, they beat me up. You know childhood, people beating on you, I guess you walk through life thinking, well this is how it works. You know, if you love me then you'll beat me up. . . . There's a stun factor. In my experience we sort of go, oh my god this happened. And a terror factor and a feeling of being trapped. These things are true for me at least which correspond completely to the childhood and adolescent experience . . . you get afraid, you go brain dead.
>
> (Michaela, interview #47)

In other examples, some women who had histories of childhood abuse spoke of abusive partners using that information to add to their controlling behavior. For example, a woman who became intimately involved with her therapist spoke about this dynamic:

> She was my therapist and I was talking to you earlier about how my family situation set me up for this kind of situation [her mother was verbally abusive, controlling and her father was physically volatile]. I had never talked to anybody about anything in my life. . . . And what was profound about my connection with her, how she hooked me was by hearing me, paying attention to me . . . knowing all my vulnerabilities.
>
> (Jocelyn, interview #57)

Others spoke of different dynamics if they had both been abused, particularly in childhood. Sometimes they were each struggling with different triggers from their past. For example, one woman spoke to me about how her abusive partner would abandon her, going away for days at a time, often without a phone call, leaving her alone at Christmas or other holidays that she thought they would be celebrating. She explained what she went through in light of her own history of childhood sexual abuse, and how the familiar feelings of self-blame would arise:

> But mine [my abusive relationship] was in a context of changes I was already going through, Janice. In a way I've emerged from it grateful. I've been on a healing journey for the last five years. This was coincidental. It shocked me when I started getting panic attacks and stuff like that. I thought I had dealt with everything...did lay official charges against my father, told my mother, you know. I guess I'm thinking about the nights when you sit and you just try to pull through. It wasn't my fault. I didn't, I couldn't have done anything differently. All I could do was stay present in the moment. It's the realization sitting there alone, that I was alone. That I was absolutely isolated, which is a scary thing.
>
> (Cynthia, Interview #98)

She also explained that her abusive partner had been sexually abused as a child, sodomized almost daily for three years by an older cousin. She did not excuse her abusive partner's behavior because of her abuse history, but did suggest that her history had an impact on their relationship because she had never dealt with it:

> I had to realize that I was dealing with a six year old, a very defiant, very messed up, very angry six year old. . . . She would have rectal

pain after orgasms sometimes, there was some scarring that freaked her out. I started to see, to put it together. There's a kid in my bed. This is not a woman, this is a child in my bed. I don't want the child in my bed, I want the adult woman.

(Cynthia, interview #98)

In a few cases, abusive women told their partners about their own histories of abuse, which made them feel sorry for them and at times excuse their abusive behavior, as Mary Ann mentioned in the following excerpt:

She'd told me she had been in an abusive relationship where this guy beat her a lot and I quite believed it at the time. I've since had my doubts.

(Mary Ann, interview #95)

Previous histories of abuse are not uncommon in women's lives, when we consider the prevalence of male violence against women. It is perhaps more striking that fifty-two women did not mention histories of previous abuse. Their accounts remind us that some women who have never experienced abuse before experience lesbian partner violence. Yet histories of abuse are another example of a context in which violence seems ordinary, almost expected, and therefore not easily challenged or fled.

A Lifetime of Violence: Racism and Poverty

What also stood out for me, in listening to women's accounts such as Michaela's, was the context of a lifetime of violence that many women experienced, which occurred on so many levels. For example, Ruth spoke specifically about the context of colonization. She identified as Metis and her partner as Aboriginal. Each had backgrounds of experiencing sexual violence and racial violence, as did their families:

My mother is Cree and her parents were really devastated by residential schools and my mother grew up in an extremely violent, abusive, alcoholic home. And I remember thinking that I was living out that legacy. And I recall thinking . . . it was like two opposites. At one hand it was like this is the legacy that we carry. It is to be expected, I mean what do you expect from an Indian? Right? Just because we are so inundated with violence, we become normalized to it. And on the other hand, I also knew this is not normal, this is not acceptable.

(Ruth, interview #61)

She also spoke of understanding her abusive partner's feeling of power-lessness that she feels contributed to her abusiveness and that came from a context of racism in a way that did not affect her because she could often pass as white:

> 500 years of genocide. The legacy of residential schools. Because we are doing just what we were taught by Christians who represented God. You know and they raped and beat children. So we're doing just what we are taught. Not that that is acceptable, there's still something called personal responsibility. So I can understand my grandfather was a violent, drunken pedophile, it doesn't mean that it is acceptable or that it is okay.

(Ruth, interview #61)

Another Aboriginal woman spoke of her own experiences being sexually abused as a child, becoming a prostitute, being beaten by johns, using drugs and alcohol, getting involved with a woman who beat her up, and then she herself becoming abusive in another lesbian relationship. She explains:

> As I look back my mom's physically abusive, to me and my brother, I was sexually abused by my grandfather and that was huge for me . . . plus I'm from Alberta where there's a lot of racism towards Natives. People running people over and not caring . . . what I seen is what I thought was acceptable.

(Esme, interview #37)

She spoke without offering excuses. Her account reflects a context of vio-lence in which the neat categories of victim and abuser no longer seem to hold. The effects of racism and colonization show the ways in which per-sonal stories are linked to historical contexts that influence and shape peo-ple's lives. Their experiences are not shaped solely through racism, but reveal the way experiences of racism, sexism, and homophobia interact and affect each other in contexts of sexual abuse, child abuse, domestic vi-olence, and so forth.

Eight other women also spoke about a life of violence, often within a context of poverty. More and more, we have become aware of the ways in which poverty and violence are linked. For example, women are at risk of assault when waiting for buses on darkened streets, living in inadequate housing without locks or without telephones, or living on the street. We also know poverty contributes to ill health and lower self-esteem.[28] For the eight women with whom I spoke, the abuse they experienced within their relationship was just one small part of a larger story; it was being brought forward because of my focus on intimate relationships rather than on all the violence in their lives. Often, they remained in abusive relationships because it was their only option. They simply could not afford to move, and if they had come to see violence as normal there was even less reason to leave. A few other women spoke of how the relationship was still relatively safer than other areas of their lives. This is evident in one woman's account of how she and her partner moved in together in a rooming house:

> She actually ended up staying in my room because I had a bigger room with its own washroom. She just wouldn't go back down to her room. She didn't like being alone either.
>
> (Barb, interview #76)

They were together for seven and a half years. Sometimes they lived in hostels, sometimes on the street, sometimes in rooming houses. They were robbed and assaulted, and Barb was often physically assaulted by her partner, who had a crack addiction. Overall these accounts show how poverty, racism, and family violence have cumulative effects, deeply damaging people's lives. It makes sense that this legacy of violence is then carried into other relationships in a way that makes violence seem ordinary and inevitable.

I have brought forward many differing contexts in which women spoke about violence in their relationships including first relationships, a context of the closet and homophobia, being dislocated through immigration, using drugs and alcohol, poverty, racism, and experiences of previous abuse. Although not exhaustive, these contexts were prominent in creating isolation and invisibility for lesbians or in normalizing abusiveness. Each shows the specific ways in which violence takes hold and is reinforced within a larger context of social structures that creates and sustains inequalities and disadvantages. In focusing on social contexts, I am moving away from either/or categories or typologies that we have often relied on

to understand violence, but that only end up excluding some women's experiences or making them marginal. Examining contexts means recognizing the diversity of spaces in which lesbian partner violence occurs, so that
we can get inside and understand what they mean. For example, it is not
likely that violence is more prevalent among working-class lesbians; however, there might be specific ways in which violence is more likely to
emerge in a context of fewer economic resources, which would be different
from how violence might emerge within a context of greater economic resources—that is why contexts cannot be ignored. Rather than homogenizing lesbian partner violence I have tried to show the range and diversity of
violence about which women spoke. There is a similar diversity in the dynamics of abuse within the relationships.

Relationship Dynamics: Shifting Power

Many of the women interviewed described relationship dynamics that can
be explained as resembling the "cycle of violence" model often described
in abusive heterosexual relationships: this is where violence occurs in a
predictable cyclical fashion and intensifies over time. Part of the cycle includes a period of calm that follows an acute battering episode. More recently this has been described as a spiral, rather than a circular pattern, in
which each episode of violence moves higher up the spiral, building on
what has happened before in the relationship, until there is a resolution or
explosion. In this relationship dynamic, there is clearly a perpetrator and a
victim.[29] Perpetrators are seen as using abusive tactics as a way to gain
and maintain power and control over their partner throughout the relationship. Several women also mentioned the status of their partner, which
contributed to the power that they had over them. For example, some
women's abusive partners included their therapists, professors, and
bosses. In one case, the abuser was a police officer, which meant she could
not call the police for support, and in another case, the abuser worked at a
battered women's shelter, which limited her options for social services.
Other women spoke not of a cycle, but of a constant pattern of abuse; often this was emotional abuse that existed daily and throughout their relationship. Others mentioned that the physical violence increased whenever
they tried to leave the relationship or resist the abuser's control, and two
women spoke of the violence increasing when they were pregnant. These
are more familiar stories of what has come to be understood as abusive re-

lationship dynamics. Yet other women spoke of less predictable and even fluctuating power dynamics within their relationships. In their accounts, power is not something that resides fully in one person (the abuser) but is instead relational, as is evident in the following examples:

The imbalance of power between a man and a woman is constant just because a man has privilege in society. And so there's always going to be that, whether he's going to chose to work on it or not. Different factors may change some aspects of power but that power will remain constant. Whereas with two women, I think that the power fluctuates more . . . there's more variables involved that can change. I know with my relationship with S at certain times she was so weak I had the power. I remember at certain times I would say things and I would go, "oh my god, I can't believe I said that." And I think I was verbally abusive to her in several ways.

(Rhonda, interview #3)

It's a dance between two people of submission and dominance.

(Lindsay, interview #24)

B: The next thing you know we were in fisticuffs...
JR: and both of you were physically fighting?
B: Yeah, yeah well I wasn't going to stand there and let her beat on me you know, I mean I was a street kid myself, you know and you protect yourself.

(Becky, interview #20)

I don't like getting beat up and so you defend yourself physically. And your adrenaline runs. You get an energy no matter what size you are, you have more power and strength. I would say to her, you know, take your arm off me or whatever, the hair pulling or whatever was going on, or I will break your arm. And I knew I would; I was ready to break her arm. But what that does to you basically is it makes you taste—and it is a literal taste in the mouth—the adrenaline of your own violence. And it doesn't go away the next day. It's a really amazing, bitterish, after-taste thing. It's a horror and I resent the fact that another human being would bring me to a place where I would do that.

(Michaela, interview #47)

These excerpts suggest that we must explore the meanings of the concepts "power" and "control" that are most often used to describe relationship violence. Further, the focus on shifting power dynamics within abusive relationships has implications for how we understand the categories of victim and perpetrator. For example, the image of a victim as pure, innocent, and helpless looms large in dominant culture, and makes it difficult to speak about agency, strength, resiliency, and even a "taste" for revenge as other features of being a victim.[30] Yet many women with whom I spoke were not passive victims. Becky Marrujo and Mary Kreger suggest that rather than only two roles existing in violent relationships, victim and perpetrator, there may be a third—what they call a participant. A "participant" establishes a pattern of fighting back against her abusive partner with the intent not just to protect herself but to retaliate.[31] Yet, simply adding a third category to describe roles within abusive relationships continues to assume fixed positions within relationships rather than exploring the sometimes shifting nature of power relations and the differing contexts that can give rise to different reactions.

Fighting Back

In this sample thirty-eight women spoke to me about physically fighting back within their abusive relationships. There may be more opportunities for violence to go both ways in lesbian relationships because of the relatively similar physical size and strength of the two partners and because of the construction of femininity (unlike masculinity) as something not to be feared. Perhaps it is this particular gendered dynamic of two women that leads to different relations of power. For example, seven women described fighting back with the intent to hurt their partner and to retaliate, whereas twenty-three spoke of fighting back in self-defense throughout the relationship, and of those, six indicated that the self-defense then turned into a desire to hurt their partner. Nine women spoke of fighting back once or twice, often toward the end of the relationship (usually a single episode when they reached a point where they had had enough), whereas a few others said they tried fighting back to stop the violence but it did not work and so they stopped. Some women spoke to me of being abused in one relationship and then becoming controlling in the next. There is great diversity and complexity in what fighting back consists of and in women's reasons for fighting back, which, in this sample, included fighting back as a coping strategy, as a form of resistance, as an intentional act to cause harm, and/or as a self-defense reaction.

For example, a twenty-five-year-old woman, Kirstie, whose mother had just died when she got involved in a relationship, provides the following account: "I was very attracted to her and I was also trying to fill a void with my mom not being there. I just put all of my energy into this person." She described her partner as being very jealous and always calling to check up on her at work. The relationship began as emotionally and verbally abusive, and then became physically abusive:

> We would be okay as long as we didn't drink. We both started drinking heavily. She was dealing with stuff from her past and I was dealing with my grief and now my grief was shut off because I was just so involved with my relationship and just trying to appease her. I stopped grieving totally and the unfortunate thing is I stopped it in an angry period and I guess my anger took over. . . . We started out getting destructive. We just started cursing each other out throwing things around, destroying things. . . . The turning point for me was when I couldn't take it any more and I started becoming, I guess aggressive with her was when she had taken a picture of my mom and she tried to burn it. . . . I couldn't believe that she did that.
>
> (Kirstie, interview #78)

Their relationship got worse with more episodes of physical violence and with each partner upping the ante of intensity. Kirstie's partner then left her and got involved with another woman. Kirstie started stalking her, punctured her car tires, and also said she felt like killing her or herself. In her story, she explains a shift in her behavior as occurring because her partner attacked her core of vulnerability at that moment—a picture of her dead mother.

Another woman described fighting back that turned into retaliation because she knew what was going to happen next and thought she needed to defend herself so as not to be a victim. Barb had experienced so much violence in her life, she said she had "victim written all over my forehead." This is how she explained the start of fighting back:

> And the third time, I knew it was going to happen again, I beat her up. And I couldn't stop—I'm not that kind of person at all. I've never done anything like that before or since. I did it on the street

and I think that's why I did it, because I knew there was people around in case. And I was angry.

(Barb, interview #76)

In her story, Barb is both hurting her partner and protecting her by staging the violence where someone might intervene and stop her. Another woman spoke of a role reversal—she had been abused, never defending herself, and now had become the primary aggressor within the relationship. She suggests that she took on the role of abuser because she was tired of the control:

> **JR:** You say the dynamics have switched? How have they switched? What is happening for you?
>
> **Y:** I just got tired of her trying to control me all of the time so I guess I took over the role.
>
> **JR:** So you fought back? What happens now?
>
> **Y:** She just said she'd never hit me again and she never did. She's never hit me again but now I hit her.
>
> **JR:** And when do you hit her?
>
> **Y:** (laughs) Whenever she pisses me off.
>
> **JR:** Do you know why you hit her now?
>
> **Y:** Yeah because she really irritates me.
>
> **JR:** And why don't you end the relationship?
>
> **Y:** Because I couldn't care less now . . .
>
> (Later) **Y:** It's like she taught me to hit people because I never did before . . .
>
> **JR:** And she doesn't hit back? But do you feel she still has more power or control in the relationship?
>
> **Y:** She tries.

(Yvette, interview #11)

Each woman's story reflects different reasons for shifting power dynamics, and although they all suggest a resistance to being controlled, this is hardly what is normally imagined as "power and control" in abusive relationships. Too often, complex dynamics between women, where there is fighting back, have been labeled as mutual abuse. Like "innocent victim," "mutual abuse" is clearly a problematic term, in this case one that assumes equal power, motivation, and intention to harm when that is not what is being described. One woman spoke about this directly:

You know you have a very feminine woman who is beating her partner and a lot of people will find that hard to believe just because of
stereotypes and the mutual abuse thing. People will turn around
and go "well you're being just as abusive as she is." They don't see
it as a reaction to the initial abuse as in the heterosexual question
"Oh I lost it" you know," I went up and gave my husband some pills
and set his bed on fire and killed him." "Oh that's okay." I don't
know why they perceive it differently, it's like you aren't supposed
to react, the second you react you are also abusive . . . whether you
are doing it with intent or you are doing it in a reaction that's a really, really fine thing to pick out.

(Rhonda, interview #3)

Her comments are important to consider, as they also challenge some of
the distinctions that I have made between intention to hurt versus self-defense in listening to women's accounts of fighting back. Do motivation and
intention matter in all instances of partner violence? How do we decide?
How do we assess acts of resistance or differing levels of intention within
each partner when there is fighting back or when abuse continues? Grappling with these complexities in abusive relationship dynamics is necessary not only for theorizing and researching lesbian partner violence, but
also for developing effective responses.

In this chapter, I have presented women's accounts of their violent relationships, exploring a range of the types of abuse described, a variety of
contexts in which the abuse emerged, and finally some differences in
power dynamics. What stands out is the heterogeneity of women's experiences of partner abuse, the difference that social location makes to those
experiences, and the inadequacy of current concepts to capture the diversity of meanings. Terms such as victim/abuser, power/control, emotional
abuse, and sexual abuse each encompass such a wide range of behaviors;
it is important to unpack the terms to ensure that we know what women
are describing when speaking about violence in an intimate relationship.
In Chapters 5 and 6, I continue to explore the struggles with categories,
concepts, and the politics of responding to lesbian relationship violence,
where too often we find ourselves oversimplifying the stories we hear. But
first, because the material tale is not finished with an account of what
happened at the time, in the next chapter I continue to bring forward
women's accounts and look at the aftermath of relationship violence: their
feelings, responses, and experiences in trying to access support or help

that remain long after the abuse is over. Finally, I will turn to my conversations with feminist service providers and examine their responses to abuse in lesbian relationships.

FOUR
An Innocence Lost
Responses to Violence

What Did He Hit You With? The Doctor Said.

Shame Silence
Not he
She
I didn't correct him
Curled into myself like a bound foot
I looked at the floor ceiling evading
A fist
Hand that has spread me open Fingers I've taken inside me
Screaming I love you bitch You are the she who rocked
my head side to side
barrier reef for your rage boat
It's safe to beat me. . . .

You've hit me with that irresistible
deadly weapon
hatred dressed in the shoes & socks of the words
I love you

(Chrystos, Dream On)[1]

THIS EXCERPT FROM the powerful poem by Chrystos captures so much of
the trauma that is often a consequence of violence. Her words convey both
the pain inflicted by a lover's abuse, and the shame of having to disclose it

when seeking help in a heteronormative world. In this chapter, I focus on how women cope with, resist, and survive relationship violence. In subtitling this chapter "responses to violence" rather than "short- and long-term effects of violence," for example, I am following the work of Liz Kelly who suggests that the term "effects" ends up perpetuating an assumption of discrete physiological or psychological changes occurring as a result of violence that does not take account of "the range and complexity of the impact of abuse on women."[2] Within psychology, posttraumatic stress disorder is the clinical diagnosis most often given to label the after-effects of partner violence and other forms of violence. This diagnostic category covers symptoms that include fear, terror, flashbacks, denial and avoidance, psychic numbing, chronic anxiety, hypervigilance, difficulty sleeping, and nightmares.[3] Many women do indeed experience these symptoms, and naming them as an effect of violence can help lessen the self-blame and validate the severity of what an abused woman has gone through. However, it is a limited psychological framework that ignores women's subjective experiences of violence and therefore cannot account for the complexity of the effects of violence in women's lives.[4] This framework constructs the effects of trauma as external to a person, outside their control and involuntary; in that sense the effects are a betrayal of the body. As Sharon Lamb suggests, if we accept these assumptions, we are then very close to seeing women who have been victimized as "damaged goods," thereby reinforcing female passivity.[5] How do we understand women's responses, then, that fall outside this psychological construction?

As Kelly notes,[6] the responses of an individual woman depend on how she defines her experience, the context within which it occurs, and the resources that are available to her. Differences of age, race, class, disability, and degree of outness further affect a woman's access to support networks, and social, health, and legal services. Finally, when considering the consequences of lesbian partner abuse, it is important to bear in mind the larger surrounding context of the everyday indignities of lesbian life in a homophobic, sexist, racist culture to ensure that we see abuse as a social problem, not as an individual mental health issue: those subtle effects of living as a lesbian that are "not necessarily overtly violent or threatening to bodily well-being...but that do violence to the soul and spirit."[7] How do we understand the effects of what Maria Root calls "insidious trauma" on a woman's response to abuse, along with the further complicating effects of her own history of previous abuse, and experiences of power and privilege in the world?[8] These are the multiple spaces that need exploring in order to fully understand the impact of violence. In this chapter, I bring forward the varying contexts of women's experiences when exploring the impact of violence; in the latter part of the chapter I turn to my discussions with feminist service providers about their responses to this form of violence.

Responses to Violence

The responses of women that I interviewed show that they are often active agents during abusive relationships, doing many things to avoid, resist, control, and/or adapt to the distressing situation that they are in. At the same time, it is important to acknowledge that women also, in Sharon Lamb's words, "yield, look the other way, and 'take it.'" What is so complicated about the consequences of violence are these contradictions of agency and passivity, strength and vulnerability that women experience, making them both survivors and victims. Lamb has suggested that our culture inaccurately overemphasizes the helpless long-suffering victim, whereas victims tend to overemphasize the "survivor" victim to resist the feelings of helplessness, vulnerability, and weakness associated with being a victim. She concludes that we are caught between these two stereotypes, which then preclude a range of experiences.[9]

In this study, women who were victims of abuse did report a range of emotional responses that contest the either/or dichotomies of victim/survivor, active/passive. Many women spoke of being isolated, experiencing fear and terror, and not trusting other people. Yet within those reactions, women mentioned different ways of coping that included writing in journals so that they could reread them and know they were not crazy or making things up, or writing whole volumes of poetry, while others turned to drinking to numb the pain. One woman became agoraphobic and was unable to leave her home, and another said she suffered from amnesia that blocked out any memory of violence in her relationship for many, many years. A few women spoke of the impact on their physical bodies, which included losing weight or gaining weight. Others found comfort through physically exerting their bodies, with one woman increasing her involvement in competitive cycling, another playing hockey, and another kayaking. Some women who had disabilities felt that these grew worse with the stress of abuse. For example, two women reported experiencing increased back pain, and others spoke of worsening fibromyalgia and a progression in multiple sclerosis. Some women understood their reactions as occurring within a broader context, attributable not only to the violence within their relationship. As one woman said:

When you put everything together—my friend's death, the relationship, work just collapsing, my getting sick with MS and not knowing why I was so sick—so you put everything together and I
die. . . . I was so damaged by all that had happened.

(Lucy, interview #99)

Others feel forever marked by the abuse that they experienced. For example,
one woman spoke to me about a relationship that had occurred ten years
ago and that still deeply affected her: "That's what has been the big event in
my life" (Jocelyn, interview #57); whereas another woman who spoke of an
abusive relationship that occurred three years ago said, "I 've worked so
hard at putting it out of my mind, I've been very successful at that and I
don't think it will affect me negatively to talk about it now, you know?"
(Cybil, interview #71). A range of expressions of victimization is evident in
this overview of responses, suggesting that we cannot predict how someone
will be affected by that experience. Many women did, however, speak more
consistently of some emotional consequences of violence including feelings
of shame, of losing innocence, and of anger, depression, and suicide.

Shame

A common response reported by thirty-seven women in this study was
feeling a deep sense of shame, hardly a surprising response to violence
given its links to feelings of weakness and self-blame, with women believing that perhaps there was something that they could have done or should
have done to stop the violence. Butch women felt they should have been
able to stop a femme partner's physical violence; women who had never
experienced violence before felt they should have been able to identify
warning signs; women who had histories of previous abuse often felt they
should have known better. Some women that I interviewed as victims of
lesbian partner violence worked as counselors in the field. They expressed
a particular sense of shame, given their role in counseling other women
who were abused. As one interviewee said, "I was sort of seeing and not
seeing at the same time and the moment where I saw it was like, 'How
could I be in a situation like that?'" (Didi, interview #60). Her shame
came from having felt emotionally paralyzed and having stayed in the relationship after recognizing that it was abusive, despite the fact that she
was a counselor in this area.

These feelings of shame may be compounded for lesbians, because of the shaming enacted by the dominant culture toward people with marginalized sexual identities and toward women, as evident in the negative cultural constructions we have, lesbians and nonlesbians alike, of both lesbianism and femininity. I was struck, for example, by how many women spoke about a reaction to violence that included feeling shocked that another woman could do this to them: after all, men hurt women; women do not. They often excused the abuse and felt ashamed and weak because it was another woman who was inflicting violence. Others experience a shamed revulsion against their sexual identity, with some women questioning whether they were really lesbians after experiencing the abusive relationship. The following excerpts speak to the different ways in which we take on the views of the dominant culture, where we see women's violence as being more damaging than men's, or expect more intimacy from women than men, or see lesbian violence as a confirmation of the pathology of lesbian sexuality and then detach ourselves from lesbians either relationally or attitudinally:

I think for me the impact was much worse, I have that comparison because I've been in an abusive relationship with a man. I don't think I ever connected as deeply on an emotional level with a man and so correspondingly was never hurt to the same degree, if that makes sense?

(Carla, interview #100)

A lot of what happened between P and I, I do take further because I just felt really safe with the fact that she was another woman and I just couldn't imagine that that would happen.

(Ramona, interview #88)

After the relationship, interestingly enough I got involved with two men (laughs). Two different relationships for a couple of years, then the whole time thinking, "no this isn't it." But the thing is those relationships with those men were so much better than what I had experienced with K. In retrospect I think I did that as a way [to cope] it was part of the process for me.

(Samantha, interview #29)

The bigger thing—it's left me very misogynistic. I find it ironic for someone who prefers women.

(Tara, interview #96)

Shame, in other women's accounts, is both an internal feeling and an ago-
nizing awareness of how their abusive lesbian relationship will look to people who hold homophobic and misogynist views. Further, young lesbians,
often those who had been in their first relationship, described the impact of
violence as involving a loss of a piece of themselves—their innocence.

Innocence Lost

Angela, in her early twenties, was in her first relationship with another
woman. Her partner lied about having cancer, was emotionally controlling, and physically assaulted her on a few occasions:

> I am still healing. I am in this other relationship and I'm trying to
> get it to go and there's a lot of trust that I just don't have. My, kind
> of like, my spunk is gone. I don't want to sound too cheesy but the
> certain innocent part of me is gone.
>
> (Angela, interview #51)

Lorraine was twenty-four when her relationship began. It lasted six years
and included physical and emotional abuse:

> I think to survive—somehow we develop an incredible strength. You
> also develop a capacity for cruelty and this is something that I wish
> I didn't know. But I learned it because of that relationship. I saw
> how power in a love relationship could be manipulated, you know,
> could be wielded, could be used in so many really awful ways. It's
> almost as if I know all of the strategies. It's sick, it's a really sick
> kind of thing. . . . I mean in a way I lost a certain innocence.
>
> (Lorraine, interview #74)

The notion of innocence is connected both to an acceptance of romanti-
cized notions of lesbian relationships produced by lesbian feminists to
counter homophobia, and to happily-ever-after concepts of love produced
under patriarchy.[10] Part of the impact of abuse in lesbian partnerships,
then, is realizing that lesbians are not always gentle and caring, and that
relationships are not always within our control, in spite of our best efforts,
while also sometimes becoming aware of our own potential for violence.
These are harsh learnings in a homophobic world, compounding the many
other losses with which women who have been in abusive relationships

have to cope, including loss of self-esteem, loss of trust, loss of safety, loss of jobs, and loss of homes or property.

Acting Out of Anger

Fourteen women identified strong feelings of anger that emerged after the relationship had ended. Anger is not the first image that comes to mind when we think of someone who has been victimized, and many women were concerned about having these feelings and having acted on them. For example:

> There's been like a couple of things where I smashed through my ex-girlfriend's windshield and that was through drinking. You know I was upset. I guess I was just tired of being screwed around.
>
> (Fran, interview #6)

> I had this quiet little year and a half [after the abusive relationship] and then everything came to a fold. I had gotten into a relationship and it was fine but I started to be—well I was walking that fine line between having been abused and becoming abusive. In my anger, I was very in touch with my anger, and I couldn't understand why. And the relationship just fell apart because she was just, "get some help."
>
> (Connie, interview #77)

> I find it's affected my new relationship. She's a really wonderful woman and I'm fucking it up. Like because she's nice and stuff, I'm yelling at her. I haven't wanted to be around off and on because I've just thought I can't, I don't know how to function. Like when N makes me mad I want to beat the shit out of her. And I mean hard and like a lot. So . . . that's how it has affected me. . . . I went from being a really fun loving [crying] and I find that . . . friends and other women are really uncomfortable, they don't want to hear about it all.
>
> (Bonita, interview #80)

Anger seems like an understandable reaction to the experience of being abused. But as discussed in Chapter 3, when examining the context of shifting power relations and women fighting back, feelings of anger fall outside what is seen as acceptable for a "good" victimized woman to act on. Lamb describes the way that anger is written out of heterosexual women's stories because we see it as incompatible with being a female victim. For example, women who kill their abusive husbands are seen as acting in self-defense, possibly in robotic states, and are commonly labeled as having battered women's syndrome, but they are not seen as acting out of anger.[11] For lesbians, the necessity of being seen as a good female victim is even more complicated when we consider the images in popular culture of man-hating lesbians or killer dykes.[12] Becoming angry has women likely worrying that they are not only becoming like their abusive partner, but also like those negative images of lesbians with which we are all too familiar. In addition, some women described abusive partners who would tell them and others that they were the ones who were being abusive. This is a powerful tactic that made women doubt their own reactions within the relationship and afterward. For example,

> **T:** She threatened to go to the police to charge me with abuse. And then she threatened that if I ever went into the community she would tell everyone how awful I was.
> **JR:** That was her claim? That you were abusing her?
> **T:** Yes . . .
>
> (Trudy, interview #65)

Other women described engaging in controlling behaviors in their next relationships. They spoke of a new hypersensitivity to abuse, as they wanted to ensure that it would never happen again, so they scrutinized their new partners. For example:

> I'm so lucky—I thank my lucky stars that I have the person I have in my life—because the patience, the understanding—I put her through the mill—"Don't you dare open that door for me, don't you pull out a chair, don't you tell me how"—the second, the second and I would tell her, I would set the rules.
>
> (Gwen, interview #52)

Expressing anger and engaging in controlling behaviors are important to acknowledge as part of the range of responses that individuals might have to violence. They cannot simply be explained away as the effects of trauma, which would only reinforce a view that women are out of control

rather than having legitimate, rational reactions. These are also violent reactions for which women have to take responsibility, even though they
may not fit with the image of what it means to be a female victim. Of
course, many women also spoke of how they turned their feelings inward,
which is often seen as a more acceptable reaction for women to have.

Depression and Suicide

Now that we have a better understanding of the conditions of humiliation,
degradation, and terror in which abused women often live, it should not
surprise us that depression is a common response.[13] One recent study has
suggested that both lesbian and heterosexual women may have similar
emotional responses to abuse (despite the different gender of the batterer),
with greater frequency of physical abuse being linked to depression and
nonphysical abuse affecting feelings of self-worth.[14] In my study, twenty-
three women reported strong feelings of depression both during the relationship and afterward. Depression was often accompanied by isolation,
making women believe that they had no options within their abusive situation. Some lesbians discussed the pain of being estranged from their
communities. Lesbians of color noted the use of racist tactics that contributed to their isolation, for example, feeling that white lesbians would be
more likely to side with a white batterer or that women of color communities would minimize the behavior of an abusive woman of color to keep
their smaller community intact. Twenty women indicated that they had attempted suicide as the only way out of the pain and isolation. For example,
Beatrice was out of the relationship for two years when she overdosed. She
explained that she had lost her job due to the relationship, had credit card
debt created by her partner, was using drugs, and had recently beaten up
her ex because she was so angry at her. She explained her suicide attempt:

> I even tried to kill myself so I wouldn't have to deal with it anymore.
> I had had enough. I took a little bit of pills, a little bit of coke and a
> couple of shots of Kahlua that I had made. And everything worked
> fast . . . somebody found me and I was taken to the hospital.
>
> (Beatrice, interview #40)

Melissa was in her first relationship with another woman. She attempted
suicide three times as a way to try and get out of the situation:

> She had confined me once, she was looking around the house for rope, she was going to tie me up. And I just had my pills on me [medication for colitis] and had some water on the bedside table and I just took the pills—and I said I just overdosed. And she went crazy and then kicked me out of the house. I got to a phone booth and called a cab and went to the hospital I said "I've just taken 30 codeine." I mean I never lied to her that I had taken my pills, I really had.
>
> (Melissa, interview #8)

Describing these responses again reflects a range of meanings that shows how suicide can be both a desperate, self-destructive move and an active attempt to escape a situation. A few women spoke of cutting themselves, or slashing, not to commit suicide but to focus and control the pain in their bodies.

The many responses to violence that I have described are not final or static, often shifting throughout the relationship and afterward with some women feeling a combination of shame, and loss of self-confidence along with anger and depression. But against this backdrop of negative consequences, many lesbians felt they learned some things, showed strength, and made personal discoveries within their relationships.

Agency

Many lesbians are resilient within abusive relationships, coping and managing to continue working or functioning within extremely stressful and adverse situations without losing their will to live or self-respect. It is important to show the ways that women actively negotiated within their abusive situation, along with describing the negative effects that violence had on their lives. (In fact several women that I interviewed said to me that what they wanted to hear were stories of how other women survived.) Agency is more obvious, though, in the leaving than in the enduring. Many women described their efforts to leave abusive relationships more than once, or to show independence by going out to see family or friends only to be met by increased episodes of violence. Claire Renzetti's correlational analysis found that the greater an abused woman's desire for independence and the greater the abuser's dependency, the more likely the perpetrator was to inflict abuse.[15] Yet it was often within this more volatile context of a relationship nearing the end that women made active efforts to look out for themselves. They described three different contexts in which agency was apparent: where the victim is taking care of the abuser and making plans to leave; in the context of ending the relationship, and in the aftermath of the relationship.

Taking Care of the Abuser

In some cases women who were abusive would react to signs of independence in their partner by threatening or attempting suicide, or by hurting themselves as a way to bring their partner back and keep them in the relationship. In these cases, women often did respond by staying and taking care of their partner's pain. This is sometimes explained as an example of codependence, or fusion in the relationship, where the couple is merged and remains unable to act independently.[16] Fusion has been a term more widely applied to describe intimacy in lesbian relationships. Often it is interpreted as a sign of dysfunction because it implies that each partner has anxiety about any desire for separateness in the relationship. More recently, it has been seen as an adaptive response to a hostile, homophobic environment, suggesting that lesbian couples unite together against heteronormative forces that might tear them apart.[17] A few women described compassion for partners who hurt themselves, along with determination to get out of the relationship, rather than an obliterated sense of self. For example, Tracey described a relationship with a woman who would lash out at her unexpectedly, in dreadful scenes, often hitting, hissing, and spitting at her while she was in the bathtub. She would then turn around and run out of the bathroom and the house screaming and crying while Tracey would chase after her to comfort her. Tracey was concerned that her partner had a mental illness. She said the following about her reactions:

> I am really happy that I had the experience because I understand people in that position now. Okay, I mean not to say I'd love to have that experience again, but at least it has given me an understanding. So there's something positive that came out of it. So I decided well, I can't really leave, cause I would have felt more guilt. I didn't know if she would kill herself. She was a suicidal person, nowhere to go, and I had met her mother, there was no support from her, zero. So I stayed with her. I thought well, do I stay with her to try again or do I wait till September when she gets a student loan and has some money. So I just started looking for a place for her to

live. . . . She wanted the damage deposit money from me and I just said "no, I can't do this for you anymore." And she flipped out. I honestly thought she was going to kill me that night. I really did. So I left. I had to leave.

(Tracey, interview #102)

Tracey was able to leave while also ensuring that her partner had an apartment to live in that she could afford. In another example, Amy spoke of how she responded to her needy partner while also getting her five-year-old son and herself some space:

I would say, "Okay can we talk about this later, I need to get up in the morning." And if I wouldn't sit there and listen she would throw herself on the floor and start screaming and banging herself on the floor or just try to drink a lot more and run out to the car and drive off really drunk, fast. . . . And if I tried to walk towards the bedroom she would put herself in front of me and not let me get there, right? So there were several occasions where we were out on the street. . . . I would bundle up my child and take him out where we would look for a 24-hour donut place or something. Just to have some—just to get away from it until things calmed down. 'Cause we didn't know too many people in the city.

(Amy, interview #49)

Amy and her son eventually moved to another city after she successfully sought a new job, although her partner continued to harass her with late night phone calls. Amy's actions were also clearly about removing her son from an abusive environment. A recent article by Robin Nickel suggests that children who witness same-sex relationship violence are likely to experience the same fear and emotional pain as children who witness heterosexual abuse, with some additional burdens such as being afraid to disclose the abuse because it means revealing the sexual identity of their parents, and risks of misunderstanding or homophobic responses from those to whom they disclose.[18] My study did not directly explore the effects of witnessing abuse on children, yet this is something that needs to be addressed, as many more lesbians and gay men are adopting children, and having children through artificial insemination, in addition to raising children from previous heterosexual relationships. Overall, both examples point to the caring and resourceful actions of women, particularly given the difficulty of being with someone who is needy and self-abusive. Other women spoke of agency within the context of trying to end their relationship.

Ending the Relationship

Women were often very inventive in their efforts to try and bring the abusive relationship to an end. For example, one woman spoke of dressing to make herself less attractive in the hopes that her partner might end the relationship:

> I was doing everything in my will power to make her end the relationship. I wasn't cooperating anymore. I was trying to find ways for her to not want me anymore. . . . She was like "why do you always wear those overalls all the time?" I would deliberately wear them because I knew it ticked her off. . . . I am sort of guilty in the sense that I was trying to get her to get rid of me because I couldn't get rid of her.
>
> (Trudy, interview #65)

Another woman described getting involved with another woman as her attempt to save herself from a situation of escalating physical, emotional and financial abuse, and her partner forcing her to quit her job in the army:

> It had gone too far before I could even stop it. I realized that I had to leave. And then—I started up this other relationship—but it was doomed anyway because she was in a different city than me. So it was doomed to start with, but it gave me an out. She had friends that I went and lived with so I could stay there.
>
> (Ellen, interview #17)

In another example a woman spoke of planning a trip and how carrying through with that plan saved her:

> I started to talk about going on a trip and she's not coming. I decided that I was going to stop work, take six months and go to Australia and dive the Great Barrier Reef. So I had started to talk that I was going to go and she could stay in my house, she would finish her thesis and then when I got back we could sit down and decide whether we really wanted to be living together. . . . So I never had

the strength to say that we were going to break up. But I was like standing up and I was giving myself an out and I had created the out. I booked the tickets and I'm doing this for my soul.

(Sarah, interview #90)

These examples, and others like them (including leaving to care for a relative in another city, applying for work or school out of town, concealing plans to get a driver's license, and having affairs), are some of the actions that women took to try and bring the relationship to a final end. These acts, again, reveal women's agency in spite of being victimized. Not all relationships, however, ended through women's active planning efforts. In several interviews, women said it was their abusive partner who ended the relationship thereby maintaining their control through to the end. In a few cases, the relationships just seemed to run out of steam with both partners ending it, sometimes by starting new relationships or moving out. After abusive relationships end, the pain of having lived through it can remain very present. Yet many spoke of regaining strength and learning something from the experience.

The Aftermath

One woman described a seventeen-year relationship that was abusive, rendering her depressed and agoraphobic. She and her partner were closeted and isolated. She spoke about how she worked to get herself back after the relationship ended:

H: I just decided I've got to take the risks . . . if I'm not prepared to take risks, nothing is ever going to happen. I risked myself into doing things I was afraid of—I went on a heli-tour, white water rafting. I've done some things to challenge myself, things that I'm not totally comfortable doing. And I've had positive responses. . . .

JR: Do you know what brought you to the point of being able to make those decisions?

H: I think part of it that pushed me was when she started going out with that fellow. I thought "What am I doing, what am I doing with my life? I have to get out there." We were very isolated from the gay community; all of our friends were straight. So I got out there and met a few people and that sure helped. I think the biggest thing is being prepared to take risks, 'cause that is scary but once you do it once, it gets easier to do it again.

(Hannah, interview #82)

Another woman spoke of an abusive first lesbian relationship during which she lived in a small rural town where her ex-husband was trying to get custody of their four children because of her lesbianism. She spoke directly of being resilient:

I think there are some women who are very resilient and I think I might be one of those. My kids are an incredible amount of strength for me. . . . I definitely think it manifested itself in a physical ailment for sure [arthritis] and also um, it really—and this isn't corny, it's not the cliche but it made me stronger knowing what I want in a relationship and what my boundaries are as far as healthy and possessiveness and those sorts of things. You know my partner and I are now entering our fourth year. It is so much more healthier.

(Nadine, interview #62)

Overall, these examples of agency, along with the examples of the emotional impact of violence, illustrate the range of potential responses to lesbian relationship violence that individual women have. The interviews show the complexity of responses so that even while enduring violence, some women are also making choices, developing plans, and drawing on inner resources. There is not a survivor/victim dichotomy of emotions and actions in women's responses. However, some women have fewer options compared with other women, which further suggests the need to see agency within a social context. For example, being able to take a trip or go to school requires money that some women simply do not have, while other women may simply not have any positive inner resources left to draw on. It is important, then, to acknowledge women's strength as a part of what it means to be a victim, while not requiring victims to display positive coping strategies. Further, I have chosen the term agency to explain women's active actions and responses to violence, rather than using the term resiliency or survivor. Resiliency, in particular, has become a buzzword amongst policymakers filtering down into human service agencies. It is meant to describe an individual's competency in dealing with adverse situations. Therefore, it is conceptualized as a personality characteristic, a factor to be studied and then reproduced in others. This individualistic focus keeps victims responsible for their reactions to violence, rather than keeping a focus on violence as a social problem occurring within a context that must be addressed. Survivor, on the other hand, has been an important term for feminists to ensure that victimhood, as a result of sexual violence, is not understood as an individual, pathological state. Rather, being a survivor of violence means living through a violation that was enacted against you. Yet as Lamb states, "if we see the victim as 'survivor' then everything she does is given a 'spin' that makes it active and assertive," when that is not always the case.[19] From the interviews that I conducted, a consequence of violence for some women is indeed being unable to be active and assertive. Although agency implies active coping and making choices (some better than others), it is only one part of a continuum of both active and passive responses to violence that women may have. For many women, their degree of active responses depended on there being places that lesbians felt they could turn to for support.

Getting Support: Friends and Family

Most of the women that I interviewed reached outside their abusive relationships to other people to get some support. Consistent with other research, women in this study turned to friends and family members as a primary source of support.[20] Yet some women did not tell anyone what was happening because of a combination of shame, isolation, fear of homophobic responses, closetedness, and fear of retaliation from an abusive partner. Just as there is a range of consequences of violence, there is a range of experiences of support in terms of who women reach out to and what response they received. In this study, sixty-four women reported reaching out to friends, sometimes throughout the relationship and more frequently when it was ending or over. Friends played an important role by making comments to women about the inappropriateness of their abusive partner's behaviors, or even by naming a relationship as abusive. Women that I interviewed spoke of how they might not have been able to listen to the advice of friends at the time, but they remembered their words later, which helped them to see they were not imagining the abuse or exaggerating it. Some friends were helpful by directly intervening. For example, one woman described the way her friends protected her from her lover, whom she had just left but who was stalking her and following her to university classes:

> I stayed with two friends of mine (in a communal house). I stayed in their room for about a week. And I did go to class but the people in the class took turns going with me everywhere. She tried to find me and track me down. They spent time with her on the phone constantly—I wouldn't talk to her on the phone. They did crisis man-

agement on the phone with her. It was only recently when I saw someone from the house that they reminded me how awful it all was. Like I blocked a lot of that out over the years and the woman was just reminding me how scared they were of her, which I didn't know.

(Samantha, interview #29)

In some cases, friends were not helpful, and claimed they did not want to get involved or choose sides in the relationship, and would often minimize the abuse. This seemed more likely to occur when the abuse was primarily emotional and when friends did not see evidence of abusive behavior. Denial and minimizing by friends are also related to the on-going reluctance to acknowledge partner violence within lesbian communities because of concerns that this will contribute to our oppression. In a couple of instances, women that I interviewed described friends joining in on the verbal abuse being launched against them, often in a context in which drugs and alcohol were involved. Further, because some abusers told friends that it was their partner who was being abusive, the response of friends could be hostile and contribute to their isolation. As Ramona said about her friends' responses: "They said, 'We don't know who to believe, someone is lying' and then I was left to deal with it" (interview #88). Finally, many women commented on the charming public personality of their Jekyll-and-Hyde abuser, making it difficult for them to be believed by friends. Overall, their accounts suggest that although lesbians are most likely to turn to friends, they cannot be sure that they will receive positive responses because of lack of evidence of abuse, manipulative tactics used by perpetrators who claim to be victims, and assumptions about violent relationships that friends use to determine whether they are truly "victims" of relationship violence.

In addition to friends, some lesbians turned to family members for support. This was often a very difficult step, particularly when having to tell a parent that your first lesbian relationship is an abusive one. Many family members did come through in supportive ways, even though women may not have had any contact with them for a few months or years because of their isolation within the abusive relationship. Family members, like many friends, assisted women by offering places to stay, giving them money, or talking supportively on the phone. Yet, many women simply did not reach out to family members, because they expected a negative homophobic reaction. Sometimes, women also found support from unexpected places such as neighbors, co-workers, or strangers who intervened and helped them out in ways that they would not have anticipated. One woman explained that she and her partner were the only lesbians living in a housing cooperative, and that she was worried that people in the community would no longer want her once their already marginalized status was tainted by abuse. She explained,

> I really felt weirded out—I thought how are co-op members going to feel about me? I'm very committed to the garden committee and I really worried whether anyone would stay on the committee. But everybody came back onto the committee and I was really taken aback by how much support I had.
>
> (Trudy, interview #65)

Although several friends, family members, and acquaintances did respond in helpful ways many women still felt they needed to turn to formal support services to receive more consistent responses.

Getting Support: Formal Services

Recent studies on same-sex domestic violence have included discussions about a lack of social services available to lesbians and gay men. They report on the barriers gays and lesbians experience when accessing services, such as perceived or actual homophobia and racism;[21] and they comment on the inability of most services to respond fully to same-sex partner violence because of mainstream heterosexual approaches and assumptions.[22] Several survey studies report that lesbians who do access formal services are more likely to turn to counselors for therapy than to call the police, use the criminal justice system, access health care services, or turn to shelters for battered women.[23] My study found similar patterns; for example, only six women reported going to shelters for battered women, fourteen women told stories that involved the police, and more than half (fifty-seven) reported going to counselors. There are many regional disparities in the level of helpful resources available for lesbian partner abuse. Urban areas are more likely to have gay and lesbian resource centers, organizations for women who are victims of violence, and more and more agencies with programs or individuals who do specific work on same-sex domestic violence. This is not the case for smaller cities or rural areas. Further, a lack of knowledge about same-sex partner abuse is commonplace in formal service systems as a result of both lesbian invisibility and heterosexism. For example, several women reported going to the hospital because of their injuries, yet in none of these instances did healthcare providers ask them about how they got their injuries, even though most hospitals now have screening questions regarding domestic violence as part of their routine intakes. Another woman told me how she wrote to a counselor because there were none for her to see in the northern, rural area in which she lived, but got a response that ignored the issue of lesbian partner violence:

> I started writing to feminist therapists because there aren't any nearby. And so I wrote to this one woman who was advertising in [a feminist newspaper]. And I remember it must have been an awful letter (laughs). I poured everything out on just how awful I was feeling, and I was suicidal, and I was smoking too much, and drinking too much, and my mother had just died, and my best friend had just died and I was in this abusive relationship. That was the first time I named it, used that word. And this woman wrote back to me and addressed every single one of those things, with all she could offer, except the abuse. She went on for pages and pages about the alcohol abuse and about grief counseling and you know all the stuff she could help me with and didn't mention it. And I thought, you know, this was sort of the first time that I kinda twigged that there may be some resistance out there to believing this sort of thing.
>
> (Lindsay, interview #24)

Smaller cities, rural towns, and isolated areas present specific barriers for lesbians trying to reach out: few or no services, and great concerns about confidentiality and homophobia. A few women turned to books, printed resources, and the internet as ways of finding helpful information to validate their experiences. Others called crisis lines, sometimes paying long distance fees, to talk with someone who could understand their situation. These barriers are not limited to certain geographic regions because they are also related to a ubiquitous heteronormativity and the smallness of lesbian communities in general. Thus, many interrelated layers of complexity arise when lesbians seek formal services. For example, many women felt that the services set up to respond to domestic violence, such as shelters, were only for heterosexuals and therefore they do not think of or risk going there. In other research that I have done in which I surveyed shelter workers about their accessibility to lesbians, they had a different perception. They felt that shelters were open to serving all women. Yet their liberal and supposedly nondiscriminatory view most often did not extend to explicitly stating that lesbians were welcome in their service brochures and mandates,[24] which is why many lesbians get the message that they cannot qualify for services. Further, in small communities or within gay and lesbian or women's services, many women did not trust that there would be confidentiality, given another sometimes well-founded reason not to seek out support services. In fact, several women reported breaches in confidentiality within different services. For example, one woman with a physical disability that made it difficult for her to go to an organization in person explained her experience of the insularity of communities when calling a crisis line:

> I had a very negative experience when I called a crisis line for battered women. When I phoned there it turned out to be a former friend and colleague of my partner's and she didn't believe that I was involved in an abusive relationship with her. She started yelling at me on the phone.
>
> (Gio, interview #69)

This lack of confidentiality and anonymity is often compounded for lesbians of color seeking services in women-of-color organizations, and for lesbians who are themselves service providers and who may not be out. As one service provider who was very closeted and living in a community of just one hundred thousand people said,

> Because it is such a small area, I was trying to find someone for myself to go to. And it took me eight months. Eight months of me asking people that know me quite well, and that I am even willing to talk to about what happened. I finally found someone. . . . But it is a safety thing. I know at my agency [workplace], it doesn't feel safe for them to know [about her sexuality]. Yet, if I can't talk about domestic abuse, where the hell am I? (Ironic laughter) It's tough.
>
> (Donna, interview #101)

Another woman described the difficult interconnections within a smaller city, for example, when she attended a meeting for service providers:

> I was sitting beside the woman who counseled me and across from the woman was her [her abusive ex-partner's] therapist . . . and there was another individual in the room who was her girlfriend after me . . . and I just don't know, what did she tell them?
>
> (Heather, interview #79)

A further complication for responding to lesbian relationship violence is who gets to the service first. Because of an assumption that women are always victims, a few women described how their abusive partners were able to identify as victims and use victim services, which meant that they could not themselves access that service. Just as friends and family members may have trouble believing whether a woman has really been victimized, services that are set up to respond to the needs of women who are victims of violence often end up being unable to discern who is being abused and who is being abusive[25] and may rely on certain assumptions or stereotypes of "victims" and of lesbians. The responses of services, like those of friends, can end up reinforcing certain constructions of the "good, innocent" victim as they judge whether a woman has been victimized. Many lesbians who have been abused may not fit their assumptions, in particular if they are angry, have used substances, have used violence themselves, or are larger or less feminine than their partner. Several women gave examples of how they were judged negatively by the police.

Police and Criminal Justice System Responses

Responses from the police that women reported in this study reveal a continued belief in certain stereotypes. For example, they tended to assess lesbian partner abuse as a mutual fight rather than as domestic violence, and often dismissed the seriousness of the abuse because it was two women. Fourteen of the 102 women I interviewed reported that the police were called in to intervene at different times. It is not surprising that so few women called the police, given the history of police harassment of gay and lesbian communities, poor people, and people of color. In fact, research on hate crimes[26] has reported that police are often perpetrators of antilesbian and antigay violence. Yet the heterosexual battered women's movement has been successful in advocating for changes in law and policy so that domestic violence is seen as a crime not to be tolerated. In some American states, such as California, campaigns on the crime of domestic violence have included the example of same-sex partner abuse. What is difficult for lesbians, then, is not knowing how police and the criminal justice system will respond. In some cases, women called 911 directly for help (they were less interested in pressing charges), sometimes a neighbor called, and in a few cases, abusive partners tried to have the victim charged. The following extracts speak to the negative encounters that women had:

M: And of course who do the cops believe? They were making comments about having to use leather gloves with the situation, all that kind of thing. They did lay charges against her but they took it as kind of a joke. They called us the 'UDS.'

JR: What's that?

M: Ugly domestic situation . . . between two women, you know. They made jokes about it . . .

> (Meryl, interview #53, describing an incident in which the police were called by a friend because her ex-partner arrived threatening her and their daughter with a gun)

So my neighbor came over and I walked out the door with him and my kids and went to his house and called the cops. I put my kids in the car and drove to my girlfriend's and I phoned my place about an hour later and the cops are there and they said "you better get back here or else." So I go back and she had basically packed up 3/4 of my stuff and said it was her stuff and she told them that I had tried to kill her. They took her home and charged me! . . .

> (Sheila, interview #1; the charges were later dropped)

We were having an argument and she cracked a glass over my head. By the time the police got there, she was acting as if I was crazy— the one who did it. And they just totally ignored me, they were laughing it off and everything. I had glass in my hair and they didn't even want to look, they couldn't care less. They basically said "whose house is this?" At the time I was staying with her and they told me to leave.

> (Vanessa, interview #66)

Most often, women were hoping the police could defuse the situation and offer some protection. Those few who had more positive encounters with police, in which the police accurately assessed the situation, tended to be in larger cities with more sizable gay and lesbian communities where police might have had antihomophobia training.

A few women were successful in getting restraining orders, which offered them some temporary security. Very few women wanted to press charges against their abusive partner, and only three women spoke of these court cases. One case involved a woman trying to charge her partner with sexual assault, but the police refused to lay that charge because it was another woman, thereby denying the possibility of sex and sexual assault between women;[27] in another case a butch woman was countercharged by her abusive femme partner, which then resulted in each of them having to take a peace bond out on the other (implying they were equally at fault); the third case is still pending. Consistent with the conclusions of Pam Elliott, Claire Renzetti, and more recently, Evan Fray-Witzer, individuals at many levels of the criminal justice system (police, sergeants, lawyers, judges) fail lesbians who have been abused, which reinforces a reluctance to interact with these systems.[28] Further, we see that underlying third parties' responses to women who have been victimized are certain assumptions about what constitutes "domestic violence," "victims," and "perpetrators." These assumptions are most often based on heterosexual domestic violence and heterosexual women. As other research has suggested, people in general, and service providers are more likely to respond positively to battered women if they conform to stereotypes of "respectable femininity."[29] This, of course, is a double bind for lesbians who are always already seen as falling outside dominant constructions of femininity and battering. As Ruthann Robson suggests, based on her review of past and current legal treatments of lesbians, we are given the paradoxical message that our sexuality is invisible and not worthy of being included within legal texts and that our sexuality is deviant, worthy only of being criminalized.[30] A recent case that was covered by the media in Calgary, Alberta while I was conducting this research reveals this paradox. A white, forty-year-old, lesbian woman, Deborah Point, was charged with the grisly killing and dismemberment of another white woman, forty-four-year old Audrey Trudeau. The media normally reported that they had been roommates (Point shared Trudeau's condo), although a few stories also suggested that the two women had been lovers. Deborah was charged with second-degree murder and sentenced to life in prison with no chance of parole for twenty years, but there was much silence about the nature of her relationship with Audrey in media accounts of the courtroom proceedings. The media also reported that the murdered woman's family adamantly denied that Audrey was a lesbian, while they quoted friends who confirmed that Deborah was gay. In a further twist, several articles said that Deborah was known as "Chris in the local gay community," implying that she was perhaps transgendered, which was further supported by an accompanying picture in which "Chris" looks very much like a deranged man.[31] It seems the only way the court and media could understand this case was to ignore the context of the possibility of a lesbian relationship, and to see the perpetrator as a deviant male wannabe, exhibiting male-like behavior, while seeing the victim as heterosexual, "feminine" and "normal," and therefore able to occupy the victim category.

With these assumptions left in place, the heterosexual legal framework remained undisturbed. I was able to locate one story, written by the queer press, *PlanetOut*, that rightly summarized the case as one of domestic violence and that reminded gays and lesbians that we are not immune to experiencing abuse in our relationships.[32]

Counselors

It is perhaps not surprising that over half the women that I interviewed sought out the help of a counselor. Lesbians may well feel they have more of a chance of receiving positive support from a one-on-one setting, where you can pay for and choose the person to whom you will talk. In most urban areas, there are also lesbian and feminist counselors who may be more likely to be understanding and nonhomophobic. Women in this study went to counselors or therapists who worked in social service agencies or in private practice. The majority of counselors were women. Five women reported that they saw psychiatrists who were covered by work insurance plans, although for many women who were not out at work this was simply not an option, plan or no plan. As a woman in the armed forces said when I asked her if she thought of going to the army's psychiatrist when she was suicidal: "They'd kick me out—send me to a psychiatrist, then kick me out." (Ellen, interview #17).

It is also important to acknowledge women's reasons for not going to counseling, as a few women commented that counseling services tend to be set up based on North American, white, middle-class values. For example, women that I spoke to from Australia, South Africa, and Nicaragua felt that individual counseling was not a strong part of their culture, and they also felt that services would likely be unable to understand all the components of their identity (i.e., cultural, sexual). This feeling of not being understood was also expressed by some women who practiced s/m, by some young lesbians, and by some women who did not identify as lesbian. As one young woman said, "I feel like I can't talk about it, I mean how many therapists are going to understand queer, s/m, abuse, intersexed, interracial [all features of her abusive relationship]—it's too complicated, there is too much explaining that I'd have to do" (Natalie, interview #63). A few poor women, whose lives had been overly controlled by social services such as welfare, and child and family services, also did not see counseling services as a comfortable option. For women living on the streets, their most realistic options are often to try and minimize violence in their lives and get safety where they can, rather than go to counseling sessions. Finally, a few women saw counseling as something you turn to only if you are really "crazy."

Women who did seek counseling commented on the great expense. Free services often have long waiting lists, limits on the number of sessions you can have, and strict criteria for who qualifies. Therefore, some women were very creative when trying to get access to counseling services. For example, one woman spoke of being desperate and going to a drug crisis center where she knew they offered free services:

> I didn't have a drug problem but because it was a crisis center they let me in. And actually it was a guy and I wasn't sure I would be okay with a guy and I told him. But he said "why don't we just go with this and see if we can do it." And actually he was one of the best therapists I've ever had.
>
> (Judy, interview #87)

Most women went to individual counseling near the end of the relationship, or after it was over, although several had started out in couple counseling hoping that they could salvage their relationships. Several women described troubling, ineffective responses, seeing therapists who did not seem to understand or explore their lesbian relationships, and in one extreme case a psychiatrist who responded by asking if the woman wanted to change gender, a comment that she found to be both insensitive to her particular concerns and homophobic. Another woman described how her abusive partner killed herself and how full of guilt, anger, and self-blame she was. She went to a straight therapist who was insensitive to her loss and to the horrific abuse that she had endured:

> Like she'd say things to me, "I want you to think of five things you like about yourself." And I'm like, "you've got to be fucking kidding?" "Like I'm dying here, I'm bleeding on your nice leather chair and you want me to think of five things I like about myself?" So I think I had two or three more sessions with her and I just decided "O.K. . . . I can't do therapy now."
>
> (Sherri, interview #81)

Unfortunately, many counselors are simply not knowledgeable about lesbian relationships or partner violence. This is doubly unfortunate since often, women themselves struggle with whether to call a relationship abusive. As we have seen, responses from friends or the police can add confusion to their feelings by questioning their status as "victims." Understandably, then, many women sought out counseling for depression or anxiety attacks, or for help getting through the break-up rather than specifically identifying relationship violence as the issue they needed to address. For example, Anita went to a therapist because of anxiety attacks and after describing a recent episode her therapist named the relationship as abusive:

> **A:** She said that it was very abusive.
>
> **JR:** Did that change things, hearing your therapist say something like that, so strongly?
>
> **A:** Yeah, she named it and so did a friend of mine. And I didn't want to get caught up in that because my previous relationship had been abusive, like not as much, not to the same extent, but it was hurtful. And I knew it would be really hard and gut-wrenching to do this [counseling work] but it was something that I needed to do. And I was having anxiety attacks all the time...
>
> (Anita, interview #14)

Eight women spoke of being in support groups specifically for abused lesbians, although these groups were mainly available in larger cities and were not offered frequently. Women who went to them consistently commented on how helpful they were because of the validation of their experiences. For example, one woman said,

> I didn't want to get into the group. I'd have to sit and talk with other people and hash it all over again, um, it was just too much. But I decided it might be the only thing that would get me through. As it turned out it was excellent. . . . Sharing with other people, just hearing their stories and relating to it . . . not just that but dealing with anger and self-esteem and it just covers so much stuff. And we've all remained friends which is really nice.
>
> (Margo, interview #83)

After her negative experience with a therapist, Sherri joined a support group:

> I guess it was six months after she died that I started doing this group. And then I really started embracing and naming things and the denial was falling away. I heard other women's relationships and

heard how similar they were. And you know, I started to realize that
they use the same lines and they say the same things. I thought
there was "abuse college" because it's like they learned these same
tactics . . . it would blow me away—the exact same words.

(Sherri, interview #81)

Naming that they had been abused and seeing that they were not alone are
what women found most helpful about both individual and group counseling. Yet Susan Turell sees the popularity of counseling as the response to relationship violence a troubling one. In her view, this suggests that lesbians
think of relationship abuse as a personal, private issue needing an intrapsy-
chic response, rather than seeing violence as an outcome of a social context
that permits or encourages violence.[33] Her analysis is a challenging one for
service providers, who in her view, must educate glbt communities about
the public nature of domestic violence to lessen self-blame and encourage
connections to additional resources outside of counseling.

What has emerged in this chapter's exploration of the responses to violence so far is the complexity of emotional responses that women have to
partner violence, the difficulties they encounter in finding and receiving
help, and the way that responders emphasize certain features of being a
victim/survivor to keep dominant understandings in place within social
services, healthcare, and criminal justice systems. These dominant understandings are often reproduced through interactions with friends and acquaintances. What is lacking, then, is the ability of agencies and
individuals to respond to a range of women's experiences in a variety of
contexts. Lesbians are forced to figure out ways of coping on their own
while negotiating within a heteronormative culture that marginalizes and
misrecognizes them.

Responses of Feminist Service Providers: An Innocence Lost

Feminist counselors have always held the view that domestic violence is
not an individual or couple problem, but rather an outcome of a social
context that supports misogyny and patriarchy.[34] Yet a feminist, gender-
based explanation of domestic violence, as discussed in Chapter 1, is
clearly convoluted for explaining lesbian partner violence. Given the challenges of gender-based domestic violence theory, the question arises as to
how feminist service providers currently understand and respond to the issue of abuse in lesbian relationships.

Based on my discussions, many are providing services for lesbian partner abuse either within agencies or on their own. The majority provide
services for victims; very few specifically work with women who are abusive. Among the adjustments they are making to established models of
practice designed for heterosexual domestic violence are protocols for couple assessment (determining who is abusing whom in the absence of a
clear gender power differential), running support groups for lesbians who
have been abused, and creating more specific programs for lesbian
abuse.[35] Yet, feminist service providers often work in isolation (in private
practice or as lone voices within their agencies) when trying to respond to
same-sex domestic violence, and are most often lesbians themselves. Feminist service providers are aware of how this issue complicates feminist understandings of male violence against women because they have to
confront the fact that women can be both victims and abusers. Further,
they have to acknowledge that not all lesbian relationships are positive.
They can end up feeling like they are betraying both feminists and lesbians if they try to do work on this issue:

> **TO:** We have to look at are we supporting survivors or are we
> caught up in our own dilemmas about being part of this community
> [feminist and lesbian]? Perhaps it would be easier for a heterosex-
> ual to support a lesbian [who is dealing with relationship violence]
> [group laughter]. That has to do with where we are at historically
> and what we are talking about today—the conundrum of being part
> of what we are talking about. And it gives me some understanding
> of how men feel, in some ways, when they talk about male abusers
> and their discomfort sometimes when they have to expose other
> men. I mean it is a complicated thing. . . .
>
> **FL:** I just get what you are saying, that the struggle for us as
> workers is about who we betray and who we align ourselves with.
> It's also really important who supports us in the context of where we
> work and if there are program and policies on homophobia and
> other forms of oppression—how supportive our colleagues are or
> not and what kind of fights we're fighting internally.
>
> **Group:** Yes, yes.
>
> (Focus group #6)

Responding to lesbian relationship violence then often means acknowledging our own capacity for violence and reluctantly seeing an "innocence
lost" for feminism and "lesbian pride."

Naming Violence

The focus group discussions did confirm many of the patterns identified in the interview research. Service providers spoke of the barriers that women face in seeking services for abuse: concerns over confidentiality in small lesbian communities and feelings of shock and shame that another woman had done this to them. Service providers outside battered women's services, shelters, or programs for same-sex domestic violence confirmed the context in which women came to them, presenting issues such as self-esteem or depression or relationship problems, rather than presenting abuse as their primary issue. This means that service providers are often in the position of "naming the violence." Their perceptions become influential in how a woman will understand her own experience, in determining the kind of support she will receive, and how she will then respond. The following extracts from two focus group discussions speak to this:

> **TN:** In my experience when they come as a couple it is for communication issues or difficulties understanding each other, they don't recognize the dynamics. When an individual comes it is usually for depression, she's not sure what is wrong with her relationship . . . often they think being in a lesbian relationship means there isn't that [abuse] happening . . .
>
> **ZK:** And I find that they really don't want to, you know, when it is identified as abuse, it's really hard for them. They don't want it to be abuse, they don't want that to be the identification. They want anything else, anything else but that.
>
> (Focus group #1)

> **PD:** Naming abuse is really hard. Half of them would never come to a service with the word "battered." It's very sensitive, there is so much shame. [Group: mmm hmmm] The naming is sometimes a relief and sometimes causes a problem. My big problem is how to delineate power?—is it a power struggle or a power inequity? Because the person doing the abuse as M says often feels victimized.
>
> (Focus group #4)

It is clear that counselors often play a psychoeducational role helping women to define their experiences as abusive, and helping them to see patterns of power and control. Yet, many service providers spoke of seeing more muddled or confusing power dynamics than they had often seen in heterosexual relationships, because they cannot rely on a gender lens to help determine power dynamics. As one woman said, "The more I work with this issue [unlike working with heterosexual abuse] the less I know. I just know less and less and less all the time" (Focus group #2). They spoke of abusers often feeling victimized and not taking responsibility for their behaviors while many abused women felt responsible and identified as abusive.[36] Examining relationship patterns closely is necessary for accurate assessments. Service providers are often asking: what is abuse, what is an unhealthy relationship but not necessarily abusive, and how do we make such distinctions? Because naming violence is so important both to lesbians who have experienced abuse and to the work of counselors, it is necessary also to see the construction efforts that are a part of naming and categorizing. We need to examine, for example, the contradictions that might arise between our understandings of violence, our feminist beliefs, and the experiences we are confronted with when listening to the stories of women who have been abused. We need to ask how these pieces do or do not fit within the definitions and categories of abuse within which we operate. And feminist service providers are struggling with these distinctions, as the above excerpts show. This chapter has focused on the range of responses that women who have been victimized in their relationships experience. In revealing the diversity of women's responses as both active and passive, strong and weak, destructive and resilient, we see the need to deconstruct, revise, and expand our understandings of concepts such as "victim" if women are to truly get the support and services that they need.

The next chapter begins the discursive tale, in which I look more closely at the categories and language we have in place to help us talk about lesbian partner violence. In examining focus group discussions with feminist service providers, I explore the normative discourses that we have in place that at times hinder our efforts to address the complexities of lesbian partner violence. Examining the struggles with categories and concepts helps us see who and what are let inside, and who and what get left out of our constructions of power/control, victim/ perpetrator, emotional abuse, the rhetoric of fear . . . all important components of feminist discourses of violence.

A DISCURSIVE TALE
exposing language

FIVE
What's Written on the Body

IN PRESENTING the material tale of women's experiences of relationship violence, Chapters 3 and 4 revealed a number of differing contextual factors. The women that I interviewed spoke of experiencing many different forms of violence and of power dynamics that were entrenched and unchanging for some, and fluctuating and shifting for others. Their personal responses to abusive relationships were also varied and included contradictory feelings of shame and anger, strength and passivity. The material tale, then, gave voice to many different stories of violence in lesbian relationships. Yet, sometimes the language available to us to talk about violence assumes one story and requires the reproduction of one familiar plot line, no matter how the cast of characters and the setting change.

This chapter marks the beginning of the discursive tale in which I examine our struggles with categories and concepts to expose who and what are included and excluded by the assumptions embedded in our discourses. This chapter explores the efforts of feminist service providers to assess whether a relationship is abusive, the power dynamics within a relationship, and who the victim and the perpetrator are. It also raises some of the controversies with which they are grappling, such as the existence of the category "mutual abuse," whether consensual sadomasochistic (s/m) practices are inherently abusive, and whether they should provide services to batterers.

Feminist service providers are aware that the patterns, contexts, and experiences of women in abusive lesbian relationships are different and varied. Yet most often, they rely on certain assumptions about abusive power dynamics based on understandings from feminist theorizing of heterosexual relationships. Focus group discussions provided an opportunity to bring forward some of the dilemmas they encounter when trying to respond to women's differing experiences from a common, unifying under-standing of abusive intimate relationships.

As indicated in Chapter 4, many service providers are in the position of being the first to name a relationship as abusive. Making such an assess-ment involves relying on certain sources of information and assumptions. The most common understanding within feminist writings and recent gay and lesbian writings on domestic violence is that at the center of all violent relationships is a power imbalance, with one person using coercive con-trolling techniques such as intimidation, threats of outing, emotional abuse, isolation, and physical, and sexual violence. This imbalance is un-derstood to parallel that within heterosexual relationships, in which men are seen as having greater power because of male privilege and entitle-ment stemming from a larger historical context of patriarchy. For gay and lesbian relationships, determining who has the lion's share of power is of-ten difficult in practice, as discussed in Chapter 4. Yet the assumptions of a gender-based power and control model still frame the attempt. This is evident in the following excerpt from a focus group discussion:

> **TG:** I do feel violence is a manifestation of power. I am pretty stuck on that as a feminist. It is hard for me to believe that lesbians have invented a unique and devastating violence of their own. I don't think so. It's like, KR and AM [other focus group participants] and I were talking earlier and our whole society is built on these competitive methods of expressing power. I can see where it is mul-tilayered to understand lesbian violence, it is complex. I think there are some differences but I'm finding that it's almost like we don't have a language [to talk about the differences]. We have differences by culture or whatever but at the same time we all live with miso-gyny and male dominance, we all live in that context. [Much agree-ment from group]
>
> (Focus group #8)

As the quotation reveals, we are hanging on to certain understandings of violence while also recognizing that at times lesbian relationship violence seems not to fit them. How do we then struggle with the current under-standings we have in place? How does our language operate not just as neutral codings for our thoughts about violence, but rather to limit and shape what we are able to think, know, see, and talk about? By interrogat-ing the key concepts and constructs that are used in domestic violence work, we can begin to see their normative and regulating effects and expose our investments (conscious and unconscious) in maintaining current discourses.

In this chapter I pay attention to both dominant feminist discourses— those that feminists tend to give the status of truth—and marginal feminist discourses—those that challenge certain feminist thinking.[1] Focusing on the dominant and marginal discourses and the contradictory, intellectually fractious spaces between them reveals the difficulties we have in bringing forward complexities to our understandings about lesbian partner violence. I illustrate how we rely on white, feminist heteronormative categories and constructs to think about violence, and ultimately show how these can impede our efforts to respond effectively to same-sex partner abuse. There are many assumptions of normalcy at play that circulate in our discussions about violence: normative frameworks affect the way we think about victims and perpetrators, about lesbians, and about feminism. Even though feminist service providers in this study are struggling not to see lesbian abuse based on heterosexual understandings, and even though most of the women doing this work are lesbians, the tendency is to go back to certain standards of normalcy, certain dominant understandings based on feminist theories that were developed to explain heterosexual domestic violence. "Power and control" is the normative discourse that dominates much of our current thinking about domestic violence. I call it the "constellation of power and control," rather than the more familiar "power and control model" to signal the extent to which the discourse of power and control has been elaborated from its initial formulation into a discourse system that includes, for example, the rhetoric of fear, what Jeanne Maracek calls "trauma talk,"[2] and the binary categories victim/perpetrator. This highly elaborated discourse that works its way throughout our thinking about violence is maintained by "necessary speech," speech that reflects our struggles and even our inabilities to speak about those aspects of lesbian partner violence that do not fit dominant feminist understandings of relationship violence.

Power and Control

The constellation of power and control remains the foundational discourse for understanding all forms of abuse. We are thinking through it when we identify power and control (rightly or wrongly) as the core feature of an abusive relationship, and assume that we will find in that relationship a pattern of fear and intimidation that restricts the abused woman's move-

ments and thoughts and traumatizes her. It is not that power and control
are not features of abusive relationships, but we rely on a simplified version with a corresponding set of assumptions to distinguish a victim and a
perpetrator rather than exploring contextualized relations of power. All of
the service providers that I spoke with used the term "power and control"
to describe dynamics that they look for when assessing for abuse. For example, the following excerpts reflect the view that power and control are
central to all cases of relationship violence:

> Domestic violence is a power and control dynamic—I don't really
> care about what somebody's sexual orientation is, or what their gen-
> der identification is, um, I'm just looking at power and control dy-
> namics.
>
> (Interview with Kaitlin)

> The pattern I am interested in explicating is who is in control in the
> relationship, what abusive behaviors maintain this control, and
> what are the consequences of these behaviors—that is, fear and in-
> timidation.
>
> (Interview with Darcy)

As these quotations suggest, the focus when identifying relationship violence becomes the decontextualized couple and what one partner does to
another. Although the discourse of power and control is grounded in a
gender-based analysis of patriarchal culture, the original context of relationships between men and women in patriarchy is dropped when this
model becomes widely applied to all cases of domestic violence, so that it
no longer matters what "somebody's sexual orientation is, or what their
gender identification is." If the appropriateness of a gender-based model
is challenged, the answer usually given is that abusive lesbians have internalized patriarchy and misogyny.

Rhetoric of Fear

Because of the difficulties in assessing dynamics between two women, service providers working within a constellation of power and control would
often listen for patterns of controlling behaviors and the presence of fear
to help them determine whether the relationship was abusive and who the
victim was:

JR: How do you make the distinction that a relationship is abusive or violent?

WH: Well that's interesting—I consider emotional well-being, frequency, severity, long-standing patterns . . .

[other women in the group—"yeah, patterns, yeah"]

KL: I think the word fear comes to mind. Does the other partner feel really fearful that the person is going to retaliate or be physically abusive or so on?

(Focus group #3)

BW: For us [at her agency] it has been important to look at who is the primary aggressor—who is the one who is afraid? who is changing their behavior?—it is very similar to heterosexual abusive relationships.

(Focus group #5)

Nadya Burton notes that early feminist theorists articulated a relationship between fear and violence as a way of ensuring that rape, for example, was not understood as being about sex but rather about power and control.[3] Such a focus on fear is useful in maintaining the dominant status of the discourse of power and control: it displays the magnitude of the threat of violence under which women live in a patriarchal culture (whether they have been abused yet or not), and it unifies women in their experiences (heterosexual and lesbian alike). This universalizing construction of fear as an essential component of women's lives in patriarchy, in turn, helps keep a focus on the similarities of relationship violence: sexual, racial, and gender identity do not matter; what matters is whether fear is detectable in the relationship, and if it is, the power and control model is affirmed. This construction of fear as universal and as evidence of a violent relationship has its costs: we can end up seeing women who do not experience fear as having false consciousness or as perhaps not being true victims. We have to ask whose stories do we not hear when we listen only for fear?

Trauma Talk

The gender-based analysis of violence that is captured in the power and control constellation is intellectually compelling because it makes some sense out of the extent of violence against women in an opressive culture. But it is not fine-tuned to see the differing set of gendered relations between two women rather than a man and a woman. The insistence on fear as evidence of power and control quickly turns the focus of service providers from examining relations of power to attending to the trauma in individual women. Treating trauma once again permits a focus on the similarities of relationship violence. For example,

> Domestic violence assumes marriage, assumes spousal relationships, assumes a lot of things that do not apply to lesbians . . . so there is a problem with using that paradigm of domestic violence: the whole issue of heterosexism and homophobia in the relationship and sort of projecting maleness onto a partner or projecting issues around an abusive mother onto a partner with same-sex abuse. So I think those are issues—how those issues play out in the relationships—the issues of race and class—the power dynamics in the relationships—I think they are different than they are when I'm working with heterosexuals. But a fist is a fist. So the other part is entirely the same. Violence is violence and trauma is trauma. [murmurs of agreement from the group]
>
> (Focus group #5)

The statement "violence is violence and trauma is trauma" recuperates a homogenizing version of power and control to its dominant place, disavowing the significance of different contexts and making it difficult to explore any problems with current models that explain domestic violence. Moreover, trauma was often identified as being the result not only of the particular relationship violence at hand, but of a lifetime of sexual violence for many women:

> **AR:** Women who were abused as children I think are more likely to be abused as adults, so why should that change because of your orientation?—if you're prone to victimization and that is all you know then you might be more inclined to be drawn to a batterer, that goes for a woman as well.
> **PL:** That's been my experience as well, there are the occasional cases where that has not happened but the majority of women that I have seen in abusive female relationships either were in a prior abusive relationship with a male or female, or they were sexually abused at home, or they were neglected or physically abused at home. And it does set them up to choose people who are highly needy and abusers are highly needy.
> **All:** Yeah.

YK: I think it's partly learning. If you grow up in an abusive home, no matter what the abuse, you learn how not to recognize someone who is abusive. And so they would end up with a lesbian who is abusive because they do not know that these behaviors are abusive.

(Focus group #7)

As this excerpt suggests, service providers focus on the psychic trauma caused by violence that affects individual women and all of their relationships. Trauma is understood as a sustained injury "because it counters the cultural legacy of denying and minimizing the injustices that women, in particular, endure."[4] There is an implicit determinism in their comments where "if you grow up in an abusive home . . . they would end up with a lesbian who is abusive." The concepts constellated in the power and control discourse offer a compelling, common framework for the origin of violence in which power is understood as an entity held by one person and used against another, where fear is the acknowledged context of the relational dynamic and where trauma is the result often compounded by a lifelong experience of patriarchal violence against women. This constellation supports dominant feminist theorizing of all forms of male violence against women. So even though gendered dynamics and patriarchy are not spoken of, the familiar top-down understandings of the hierarchies of power are preserved, and the primary attention to victims, what Linda Gordon calls "the victimization paradigm" that dominates feminism,[5] is left in place. Yet the context of lesbian relationships and woman-to-woman abuse remains invisible and conveniently erased by this overarching assumption of sameness, as do the varied reactions and responses to violence that are inconsistent with the trauma paradigm.[6]

Despite their participation in this unifying discourse, it is clear that focus group participants are identifying differences between lesbian and heterosexual abuse; for example, the way homophobia is used as a threat within abusive relationships and the way a larger context of heterosexism can isolate a couple and make it difficult for them to access support. Equally clearly, participants are often uncomfortable with discussions that explore or speculate further on any differences that stray too far from the dominant feminist thinking in the area of domestic violence. A strong tension emerges when discussing similarities and differences, for example:

BP: I don't know if this is a good question or not, but I'm wondering if there is more insecurity in a lesbian relationship where one

partner may have been in a heterosexual relationship before and
their partner fears that they'll go back to a heterosexual relationship? I am just wondering whether insecurity could have something
to do with abuse, patterns of abuse.

WW: I myself, I have stayed away from analysis in terms of
"stress causes abuse."

MN: Though it does kind of add to that emotional pressure
cooker sort of sense in the relationship. So if there is a propensity to
handle problems in a physical way, [stress] may help to release, to
disinhibit that kind of response. (Pause) And I hate myself when I
talk like this because I feel really strongly when I talk about perpetrators being held responsible for their behaviors. I work with tons
of survivors who've been through hideously abusive experiences.
Uh, I have to do some deep breathing around it because [laughter] I
think it takes the onus of responsibility off the perpetrator and that
really bothers me. So having said what I said, I take it back.

(Focus group #8)

As this participant well knew, she took back what she said because it
threatened dominant feminist concepts in which we are deeply invested
for good reason: views that see perpetrators as making choices to be violent and never see stress as an exculpatory causal factor. The exploratory
conversation that was to examine different contexts and dynamics surrounding lesbian abuse was quickly recuperated into a known and accepted normative framework, in which perpetrators must be held
responsible and in which details such as lesbian partnerships perhaps being more vulnerable because they are not supported by heterosexist institutions and assumptions can remain underanalyzed.

In another example, a focus group discussion was exploring situations in
which a victim may also seek revenge and try to hurt her partner. This was
quickly reframed as self-protection and no room was made for the possibility of a victim having an additional motivation of retaliation and anger.

We would call that self-protection because we would talk about how
they'd been oppressed—that that oppression is always invisible and
they're saying "I don't deserve this, I'm a human being" and that
would be where the retaliation comes from—we would put that in
self-protection.

(Focus group #5)

Here, "victim" is constructed as always already in a state of oppression no matter what she does. These excerpts also reveal the ways in which the categories of victim and perpetrator become constructed as polar opposites: perpetrators choose to act violently and are never understood in a context; victims on the other hand are in a state of oppression and therefore cannot be held accountable for making choices. A homogenizing "trauma talk" discourse then often became the authoritative and overriding sentiment in focus group discussions about the similarities and differences that allowed us to focus on the similar effects of violence rather than work further to uncover and address the relational complexities and contextual differences.

The tendency in feminist services and counseling work is to focus our efforts on the results of domestic violence and to assume that we know all we need to know about the causes. Jeanne Marecek identified this focus on trauma in her interview research with feminist therapists. She defines "trauma talk" as a lexicon (a system of terms, metaphors, narrative frameworks) that circulates among feminists and others to talk about the physical and sexual abuse of women. Her interest in trauma talk is to show how therapists' language practices construct clinical realities. For some feminist therapists in her study, the trauma model has become the "sine qua non of feminism in therapy...retelling a woman's life as a trauma narrative was both the feminist way and the one true way to tell a life. Yet even though a woman has experienced abuse, narrating her life in terms of that experience produces only one of many possible stories."[7] Her comments are relevant for explaining the limiting effects of "trauma talk" in the discussion of lesbian abuse. In focusing only on the violence and in staying with universalist feminist assumptions of what motivates the perpetrator, we can erase and ignore any dissonance between heterosexual domestic violence theory and lesbians' experience of domestic violence, and continue with our current thinking and practices.

Necessary Speech

In another example of staying with known assumptions, participants in each focus group spoke about the concept of mutual abuse and the difficulties they have encountered in defining abuse when examining different dynamics. Again we see an acknowledgment of differences in lesbian relationship dynamics based on what they have actually heard from

women; yet the tendency is to hasten back to a known framework rather
than make room for new and different experiences. Consider the following
example:

> **HY:** I do think there is something called "mutual abuse," but I
> don't call it "mutual abuse"; I call it "bad fighting"—"bad dynam-
> ics," "power struggles"—I see it as fairly equal in terms of people
> being in trouble, feeling pretty powerless, pretty helpless, not know-
> ing how to get out of that kind of recursive cycle. Where I don't
> think it is mutual abuse is where the other person starts hitting
> back, even if it is not in self-protection, even if the hitting back is
> out of exhaustion, I don't see that as mutual. I see those actions as
> speaking more to the impact of abuse and the person [victim] has
> been so worn out that that's what they do. In the first example they
> don't talk about the impact in the same way; they were not afraid;
> they were not exhausted; they were not immobilized in their lives;
> they were not isolated from their friends; to me that's a difference
> [between bad fighting and abuse].
>
> **OM:** I'm still pondering the question, have I seen mutual abuse
> and whatever that means? I think about somebody who controls all
> the money and at the same time the other person is extremely con-
> trolling and jealous. And the one who controls the money is very ho-
> mophobic and doesn't want anyone to know they are lesbians so
> wants to keep them isolated—is that mutual abuse?
>
> **KR:** Where I find the language frightening is that working in a
> shelter with male violence, there are a lot of people in the popula-
> tion who would like to say "Hey this happens to everyone," so they
> can just defuse it. So I don't want to talk about this and that's why.
> I don't want to lose the funding, lose the momentum.
>
> (Focus group #4)

In this example we can see the force of very real contexts such as needing funds to keep shelters operating, and the fear that the scale of male
violence against women will be underestimated if we talk about woman-
to-woman abuse and try to explore differing power dynamics in which
both partners may be exerting power in different ways. This is the context
within which many feminist service providers work. Often we rely on
dominant discourses for solid strategic reasons, but this reliance shuts
down or limits the thinking and theorizing that we need in this area. I see

this tendency as an acquiescence to the demands of "necessary speech": speech necessitated by the realities of the conditions within which feminists work; in this case, the need for funding and the context of a backlash against feminism. Necessary speech is what is necessary to state so as to reassert the dominant understandings that provide strong explanatory power for the extent of male violence against women (understandings, as we shall see in Chapter 6, that are by now embedded in policies, mandates, and practices of social service organizations). However, speech made necessary by the power and control constellation has the unintended effect of constructing and affirming heteronormative frameworks to understand lesbian abuse. In this example, as in others discussed in this chapter, the reassertion of dominant feminist understandings limited the possibility of exploring certain distinctions in power dynamics that might well be important in same-sex relationships (such as possibly equal physical size, shared gender status) that make fighting back far more feasible than in heterosexual relationships.

Questions of Power

The normative discourse that I have brought forward suggests that women's use of violence is "anxiety-provoking for feminism" because it challenges theories that identify violence as male.[8] Yet at other times feminists clearly understand power as something more complex, requiring better-nuanced distinctions of power and powerlessness than the dominant discourse can afford to make. Many focus group discussions did explore questions of power. In the following conversation, power is understood more as contextual and relational rather than absolute or fixed in one person or one place.

> **DT:** I think women can exert their power and control in different areas sometimes. And not in an okay way, like each of them. It is like well, you've got the power there and I'm going to have the power here or I'm going to fight back in this way. And it doesn't necessarily have to be physical although it can be. Quite often there is the dynamic where each of them are trying to figure out ways of having power and control. And it is very difficult to sift. . . . I mean it is really a matter of working with them both to accept some responsibilities for those areas. And it isn't clear-cut in the traditional way of defining abuse.

JR: So then you tend not to use those categories (survivor, perpetrator)?

NZ: I agree with that.

MY: It's always interesting to me that we have to find a category to describe behavior. I find when I am working with people they say "you know I was really hurt by that." I mean they were victimized but I don't think their sole identity is as a victim, a perpetrator, a participant. I would rather describe it as they were victimized in this way, or this person perpetrated violence in that way.

JR: So neither has an identity?

MY: I think categories, we just use them for our own convenience. I don't know how helpful it is for the folks we work with, you know?

(Focus group #2)

Here, power is explored as relational and suggests that women can occupy more than one subject position. Rather than attaching a fixed identity of victim or perpetrator to individuals, this discussion explored how power operates in their actions. Questions of power were also raised when exploring abuse in different relationship contexts:

I think racism is another thing we don't talk about—the ways white women might use power over their partner who is a woman of color—there is power and control there. . . . How do we talk about that and then also talk about other power complexities in the relationship?

(Focus group #3)

I've noticed in my practice in lesbian relationships where one is the survivor [of childhood sexual abuse] and the other isn't. Then often in part of her healing, she doesn't want to be sexual any longer and we've got a partner who wants to be and a survivor who is saying "no"—would that qualify as sexual abuse? There is power and control . . . it could get that way.

(Focus group #3)

In these examples we see attempts to grapple with the complexities of power coming to a dead end because the power and control discourse is tied to a rigidly binary concept of victim/perpetrator. Such binaries cause dilemmas for feminist service providers who are used to working within clear dichotomies of women as victims and men as oppressors, where power and control are seen as being held by one person (the man) and used against the other (the woman). When practitioners are presented with complexities, such as both partners using power and control, or an interracial couple where one woman is physically abusive and the other is verbally and emotionally abusive through her use of racial attacks, the clear lines between perpetrator and victim break down and the need to understand power as something other than a fixed quotient becomes apparent.

Interracial Relationships

I turn now to some examples from my interviews with women who have experienced violence to show the effects of dominant discourses on their understandings of their experiences. I interviewed several women who identified as being part of an interracial couple. Most often I was interviewing a white woman who identified as a victim. However, in two interracial relationships in which I interviewed a woman of color, both identified as the abuser. When I asked each of them about the dynamics of their relationships they had not considered the racist comments made by their partner as also being a form of abuse. For example, Charlene, a South Asian woman, described her seventeen-year relationship with a white woman, which began when they were both fourteen years old. She herself had experienced sexual abuse by an uncle from the age of five to thirteen, and said she was often very angry because of that early abuse. She was very clear about incidents in which she was physically abusive, and described the worst incident in which she hit her girlfriend on the head with a metal bar:

> The blood brought me back to reality, a couple more inches on her temple and uh, I could have killed her. . . . And I could never understand it, like why am I taking out all of my anger, you know, all my past on her?
>
> (Charlene, interview #92)

But later on in their relationship, Charlene's partner physically attacked her. She said that her partner choked her and called her "every name in the book—'slut,' 'whore,' 'AIDS-infested' and even threw in 'you probably liked it when your uncle was on top of you.'" Charlene saw these hurtful actions as being justified because of her own previous abusive behaviors. I asked her if her partner was ever racist in her comments and she responded:

> **C:** Oh yeah.
>
> **JR:** Yeah?
>
> **C:** Oh yeah. Well even when I met her she was racist—"Chinks," "Pakis," "Niggers" you know all of that language. She did throw my heritage in my face.
>
> **JR:** But that must have been awful—how did you understand that? If she was racist in her attacks wasn't she being abusive toward you too?
>
> **C:** Um, I don't know, maybe you should be talking to her, the other side is worse. I know why she was doing that. She was racist because her daddy is and of course, I'm colored so she has to live with it even more.
>
> (Charlene, interview #92)

In her comments, it was as if the racism from her partner was a given, something that was to be expected and that could be explained away by her upbringing, whereas her own abusive actions, which could as easily have been attributed to her history of sexual abuse, were the ones defined as abusive. This example exposes the impact of a normative discourse of violence that uses victim and perpetrator as binary categories that in this case make even blatant racism seem beside the point: Charlene is the perpetrator. Any trauma that she experienced in the relationship cannot be accounted for because the power and control constellation assumes one person misusing power. Yet, we have to be able to see the complex workings of power that arise from women having multiple subject positions: the "perpetrator," too, experienced abuse. We then have to ask, whose experience is being privileged when we define, assess, and respond to relationship violence based on dominant understandings of power and violence? Dominant assumptions most often work to center and normalize white, middle-class women's experiences. When looking at the example of an interracial couple the unraveling of violence and power dynamics has to include an examination of the influences of power and privilege in the larger social culture.[9] I interviewed a white woman who was part of an interracial relationship with a black woman in which she was physically abused; however, she was also aware of her power and privilege in the relationship:

JR: You mentioned race or racism as part of the dynamic. Can you tell me more about that?

D: Yeah well for me I feel guilty about the fact that part of my lust/love kind of stuff for her was about exoticizing who she was. So I was aware of it and I felt guilty about that. It was about race in the sense that I stayed in there a lot longer because I felt guilty because she didn't have the advantages that I had. It wasn't because I thought I was gonna look racist, it was because she had had such a shitty awful life.

(Daphne, interview #43)

Daphne's comments show an awareness of her own abuses of power in the relationship, where she had acted from a white dominant position that sexualizes and "others" women of color; she expresses guilt and even stays longer than she should in the abusive relationship because of her guilt. Yet even with some insight into the negative effects of racism, her words reflect an embeddedness in binary understandings of power and control that ultimately make racism irrelevant to the understanding of abuse. Further they continue to center whiteness, making it difficult to speak about or "unravel the power dynamics" in her interracial relationship. In Charlene's case, the privileging of physical violence over racist comments is the necessary cost of preserving the victim/perpetrator binary. The gendered discourse of power and control demands that we maintain rigid opposition between victim and perpetrator so that we can see sexism as the root of violence. What remains concealed within this binary are all the hierarchies of power in which people can be situated. Women with less social power in the world can act abusively in some situations, whereas women with more social power can use their entitlement in oppressive ways *and* can also be in situations in which power is used against them. We need a language of power that allows us to map the multiple and interlocking nature of identity and systems of privilege and oppression that are part of the context of relationship violence.

Lesbian Perpetrators

At the end of the interview, Charlene was hoping that I could make a referral to a social service program for lesbian abusers. I could not. In that city there were, of course, several places to which I could refer her if she

had identified as a victim. Many questions about power are brought forward again when discussing responses to lesbian perpetrators. Service
providers are struggling with how best to offer services for lesbian victims,
yet are often unwilling to work with lesbian perpetrators. Some felt they
were incapable of working with women who were abusive because it requires a confrontational stance and others simply do not want to work
with women who are abusive, seeing them as undeserving of services. Others wonder if lesbian perpetrators, because they are women, may be able
to access their pain more easily than men, and may therefore be more
likely to change than male perpetrators. Still others want a political stance
to be taken, with names of lesbian perpetrators made public in lesbian
bars and community organizations, similar to the actions of radical feminists who exposed male rapists. Circulating within these discussions are
underlying questions of whether perpetrators are all the same in terms of
motivations, intentions, and psychological make-up. These distinctions remain blurred. For example:

> **MP:** Sometimes, there can be an attitude like: "Let's go get
> them! Let's go get the perpetrators and make them accountable!"—
> and that kind of stuff. I'm not saying people are saying that, but I
> feel that. And I guess I don't know what to do about that.
>
> **YA:** Yeah 'cuz we don't want to discourage women who are abu-
> sive from seeking help. I've seen a nice pattern in the last few years
> where women are saying, 'I have a problem with being controlling,
> I'm trying to control my partner.' You know that they are different
> from the more forensic type [of perpetrator] that are real serial and
> scary—all we can do there is advocate for victims to come forward
> and charge them.
>
> **HO:** I guess I'm being a devil's advocate here but if we leave it
> up to the woman to charge, the victim to be responsible for report-
> ing it—is that fair?
>
> **MP:** And how can we do outreach to perpetrators? Can we send
> a message? I don't think we as a community, that we have sent a
> consistent message. I think we have colluded in many ways over the
> years around the silencing of this issue and yet we can put the
> message out: This isn't okay. And also be clear that there is help
> available.
>
> **JR:** So are there any services specifically for lesbians who are
> perpetrators or is it mainly one-on-one counseling that is available
> at this point?

All: One-on-one.

UL: It's been so hard to even start up stuff for victims . . . we haven't even got to that point yet.

(Focus group #6)

The disparate ideas expressed about how to respond to perpetrators collide with one another because of the dominant power and control model that conflates all perpetrators as choosing to use power over someone to gain control over another. This assumes deliberate intention but cannot explain why some people make that choice and under what circumstances. Others have also considered psychological factors such as dependency, internal pain, or even personality disorders (as discussed in Chapter 1) as part of what makes someone abusive. What becomes clear is that the category "perpetrator" is too limited to contain these differences. Yet the discourse of power and control strictly prescribes the kind of identities that can be structured within it.

Mary Gilfus suggests that a dominant white, middle-class, never-victimized world view asserts that we live in a just world in which "bad things will not happen to good people and conversely where bad people will get their just desserts."[10] The feminist power and control discourse we are discussing here does not share this naive view of a just world, but in asserting a rigid victim–perpetrator dichotomy, it ironically helps maintain systems of oppression by ignoring the violence experienced by large groups of people on a daily basis. In assuming that these categories describe identities that are fixed, stable, and autonomous, we are not forced to critically examine the way someone can both be a victim and abuse systemic power. For example, a white woman may be a victim of relationship violence in her home while also employing an undocumented immigrant worker at extremely low wages. One of the effects, then, of maintaining categories that perpetuate domination is to continue to produce the white subject as innocent.[11] Another is to construct the lesbian perpetrator as an extension of maleness/badness. We need discursive possibilities that allow different narratives of subjectivities in which the whole person in all of her multiplicity can be considered within a larger context. As one service provider that I interviewed said,

As a family therapist I think that issues of power and control exist in ALL relationships, not necessarily emotional and physical abuse though. For example, many people have sex when they don't feel like it, and feel pressured without being coerced. I am "afraid" to

have a very messy house when my partner is in a bad mood cause I
know it will upset her and likely start a yucky fight . . . but I am
not overpowered by her or controlled by her or co-dependent. I
think that these are issues endemic to intimacy and living together.

(Interview with Leanne)

Here she is speaking of power and control not as an explanatory model in
which to understand violence; rather, she is asserting a view of power as
relational, negotiated, something that circulates within all interactions and
relationships, not related solely to position or status.

Many feminists, myself included, have found the work of Michel Foucault useful as a way of exploring power, which in his work is understood
as contextual and relational. He examines the "microphysics of power,"
constantly redirecting attention to the specifics of "how" power operates
in particular cases, rather than staying at the context-free level of the
"why" of power,[12] where a high-level concept of "patriarchy," for example, can account for the massive incidence of violence against women in
our society, but not for all individual incidents of it. Some feminists are
concerned that a more diffuse, relational view of power will depoliticize
the antiviolence movement, weakening our struggles in the larger sociopolitical context in which sexism and racism are huge problems, and resulting in batterers not being held accountable in specific situations. These are
valid concerns. However, the current view of power as a fixed entity held
by the perpetrator (the doer) and directed toward the innocent victim (the
done to) obscures the experiences of many lesbians in abusive relationships, ignores the multiple spaces that we occupy, and suggests strongly
that there is a need for more theorizing about power. A focus on the relations of power within a specific context could help us to move away from
abstract notions of victims and perpetrators toward an exploration of how
power operates in particular relationships, where we can examine the complexity of women's lives, and scrutinize the power dynamics in women's intimate relationships and in other areas of their lives.[13] This involves a
structural, personal, and relational focus; an analysis that involves both—
and constructions of social reality, in which we resist binary either/or positions.[14] The conversations that I have brought forward show that feminist
service providers are not simply accepting holus-bolus the dominant feminist understanding of violence through which they work on a daily basis,
but are in fact struggling between normative discourses and marginal ones
that offer more complexity but are often closed down within the terms of
the power and control constellation.

Marginal Feminist Discourses

I shift now to those topics in focus group discussions that revealed moments when people were working against normative frameworks rather than recuperating them. This was most evident in discussions about race and class differences, sadomasochism, and defining emotional abuse, where counterdiscussions about naming whiteness and other social differences, acknowledging the possibility of consensual domination, and seeing the constructedness of abuse were able to emerge. These marginal discourses are not as coherent and complete as the dominant power and control constellation; rather they are counterhegemonic challenges rooted in other discourses that are being brought into the discussion of lesbian relationship violence but have not yet been fully articulated within the feminist antiviolence movement.

Identity Politics: Naming Whiteness and Other Social Differences

Naming whiteness and acknowledging other social differences is rooted in a larger feminist discourse of identity politics, which has been central to contemporary feminist theorizing and political activism. Being organized around social identities, the discourse is characterized by struggles to recognize how women's experiences and perceptions are affected by socially significant differences such as race, class, and disability. Many writings on the battered women's movement critique the power and control paradigm as being derived from white, middle-class, able-bodied women's experiences and describe the ensuing difficulties that many women face when trying to access services. Even though participants were invested in the power and control discourse, all focus group discussions acknowledged social differences between lesbians and troubled the assumption that lesbians are a homogeneous group. For example,

> **JW:** Something I want to—it's going off topic a bit—but I want to get a sense of the women that other people work with because I know for me, my experience is primarily working with not a racially diverse group of women, primarily white women, maybe a small number of First Nations women. So I want to know who it is that we are talking about, who it is we are basing our experience on? It's a struggle and something that needs to be addressed that the women who come forward for services are usually not women of color and it's happening for particular reasons. I want that to be on the table when we are talking about whoever, our experiences are

coming from which groups of women? [Many voices commenting supportively, but with tension. People began reporting on how many women of color they have worked with and what they have done in their practices to address diversity.]

(Focus group #6)

In this discussion, a challenge was made to the group to resist centering lesbian relationships based on white, middle-class experiences, and although there was tension in the room when the issue was raised, no efforts were made to stop the conversation or change the direction to recuperate a white-normative approach. In this example, whiteness became named and marked as a category that demands scrutiny in order to disrupt its unspoken embodiment as truth, normality, and trustworthiness. But although focus group discussions raised the issue of whiteness, they were often difficult to sustain. Cindy Holmes also reports this difficulty in her focus group's discussions with antiviolence educators. She writes: "As white women we know we need to address racism and white privilege, and yet we frequently have difficulty sustaining a conversation about woman-to-woman abuse that includes a discussion about *our* privilege and complicity in the oppression of other women."[15] Similarly, in other focus groups, we had discussions about working with women from different social class backgrounds. For example,

> **WS:** I really want to talk about class issues because that is something that I really notice. Almost all of the women that I work with would not identify themselves as lesbian, they will say to me "WS I'm gay—I am not a lesbian—those are women who have nicer cars and an education." I find that they have a different sense of what gay is and also a different way of responding to violence, like knowing about the violence that is happening with each other and having an internal network to respond where so and so knows that so and so gets beat up and so goes to her house when it happens and that sort of thing—it is much more out there than for women, for example in my class [middle-class] where there is much more shame, humiliation, and unwillingness to talk about what is going on.
>
> (Focus group #5)

It is much more likely for working-class and poor women to be perceived as abusive than middle-class women, independent of what-

ever their behaviors are. And to some degree, the butch–femme
stuff maps differently depending on class too. The heterosexual domestic violence movement, the police, everybody else perceives
masculinity as violence. Class is about economics and a sense of entitlement and I think poor and working class women do not have
that sense of entitlement so they don't have that sense of advocating
for themselves within the systems that they have seen, for very good
reason, as oppressive. Plus service providers are very sympathetic to
women being able to talk about their pain, but in a certain language
and I think that particular language used in discussing the pain also
maps onto class.

(Individual interview with Amber)

These conversations show that there is an awareness of social differences
between lesbians based on race and class and acknowledgment that service provision is based on white, middle-class experiences making it difficult for some women "to talk about their pain" in the "right" recognizable
language. These conversations disrupt the homogenizing effect of the
dominant discourse. They show an opening for a feminist analysis of lesbian partner abuse that is able to address the interface of sexism, racism,
violence, and homophobia.[16] But although these conversations show evidence of a counterhegemonic discourse being able to be spoken, it remains
at the level of acknowledging women's differing attributes, rather than offering a full critique or challenge to the concepts and categories in the
power and control constellation that contain implicit assumptions based
on white, middle-class experiences of violence. The challenge remains
marginal because of an overriding acceptance of the power and control
constellation as the foundation of domestic violence work.

Consensual Sadomasochism

Similarly discussions on sadomasochistic sexual practices revealed attempts to disrupt certain dominant feminist homogenizing views. There
have been many debates within feminist, lesbian, and queer communities
about how to understand sadomasochism, with some arguing that it is
consensual, others arguing that it is impossible for women to truly consent
in a patriarchy, and still others stating that it is an empowering way to
take control and heal from experiences of sexual abuse. These issues all
resurfaced when discussing the therapeutic responses of feminist counselors to s/m. In each focus group, most of the participants were open to

seeing the complexities of women's sexual practices and experiences of abuse rather than forcing a dominant feminist ideological stance that s/m is abusive by definition. For example:

AM: I did see s/m practices as being abusive and then I changed my position as I learned more, found more out, gained more experience in the whole area . . . yet on a much broader level I still have a problem with it. Yet when I'm working with people I have to be very open so that we can work through different layers so that I don't totally lose them or alienate them.

GF: How do we learn about the complexities? I think for, myself, I think about my own ignorance about s/m, I'm not part of the s/m community and so I've needed to learn about different practices. I think when it gets difficult is when young women are learning about s/m and who they learn from and in what context and if there has been power imbalances in the relationship already and if you are just coming out and you are coming into s/m, who is teaching you about it? Is it in a context of an already abusive relationship or is it in a safe relationship?

AM: Those are really important questions. [Group voices—hmm hmm]

(Focus group #3)

The movement of this discussion shows efforts made by some of the participants to encourage reflexive stances (such as asking questions about the context of a relationship, being aware of your own limited knowledge) rather than asserting any either/or positions about the nature of s/m and its relation to abuse. In many of the focus groups, s/m was identified as an issue about which young queer women want to talk; for example, in four of the six cities in which focus groups were conducted, the participants mentioned that workshops have been held for glbt youth groups on this topic, at their request. Most feminist counselors saw their role as obtaining information and being able to create an environment in which women can talk about marginalized sexual practices without being judged. On this issue, there was more willingness to move beyond the usual polarization that exists between s/m feminists and anti-s/m domestic violence activists. Participants acknowledged s/m as a consensual sexual practice that many women did not experience as abusive, thereby resisting dominant feminist domestic violence theory that s/m equals abuse.[17] With this counterdiscourse, they could discuss the ways that some s/m relationships can be abusive and others can be consensual and nonabusive. Counterdiscourses in both of these examples (identity politics and s/m) create the possibility of moving away from discussing domestic violence in homogenizing abstract terms. Further, they point to the need for continued discussions on the meanings of power dynamics, and definitions of what constitutes abuse. One service provider that I interviewed generates discussions about s/m in workshops that she conducts on lesbian abuse:

> To have people think about where the limit of power is . . . and nobody knew, and I think that is the problem. The thing is, is it the restraint—your hand, a soft restraint, a handcuff—that gives the potential for power being misused, or is it the dynamic between two people? And I think some of the discussion about S and M, much like the discussion on abuse, has focused too narrowly on the object, you know it's not the thing it's the dynamic.
>
> (Interview with Amber)

I too have been part of these discussions in lesbian communities. One committee of service providers of which I was a part lost members during our heated discussion of whether to include s/m and mutual abuse in our definitions. Some committee members felt strongly that all s/m practices must be defined as abuse and wanted that stated in the brochure we were developing. Others also argued for a clear stance that said there was no such thing as mutual abuse because violence always includes a perpetrator and a victim. These strong assertions of the dominant view led us to become entangled in a binary debate, falsely positioning ourselves as either for or against s/m, and believing or not believing in the possibility of mutual abuse. Surrounding our discussions, of course, was the context of our position as lesbians working within feminist understandings of violence against women.

We came to an agreement that s/m would not be included as part of a working definition of lesbian abuse, that it should be considered abuse only if a woman experiences and defines these practices as abusive. Experience, in this case, was seen as (or at least treated as) unassailable knowledge. Yet quite contradictorily, mutual abuse was discussed by the same committee as an example of false consciousness, even when one woman on the committee spoke about experiencing an abusive relationship in which she felt the dynamics were different, more complex, and muddied than the descriptions of heterosexual battering with which she was familiar. Some committee members felt she was just unable to see the "real" pattern that was no doubt there, perhaps because she had left this abusive relationship so recently. Her experience was dismissed and we missed an opportunity to consider the complexities of some abusive relationships.

We seemed to be valuing experience on the one hand, while dismissing it on the other (when we could not make it fit the power and control paradigm). On reflection, as a committee we did not recognize the discursive dimensions of our own efforts at logic, and the politics of its construction. Although service providers in my focus group discussions resisted either/or positionings in our discussions of s/m, we shut down discussions that might have involved looking more closely at power relations and our assumptions of the meaning of categories such as "mutual abuse."

Constructionist Views of Abuse

Another area in which a counterhegemonic view emerged was in conversations about how the word "abuse" is being used, particularly when it is applied to situations of emotional abuse. As discussed in Chapter 3, all but one woman that I interviewed reported experiencing emotional abuse, with nineteen women stating that it was the only form of abuse that they had encountered. Emotional abuse includes a wide and divergent range of tactics and behaviors, some more subtle than others. This form of abuse, perhaps more than other forms, brings to the forefront questions about boundaries of the category abuse:

> **KK:** Abuse is a word that we use so easily and yet we don't know as women how to do conflict—ourselves or with other women. We don't know how to be angry in a way that is healthy, we don't know what that looks like. We know what violence is, but anger? How to be angry in a healthy way? how to work through difficulty? How to be in conflict in a respectful way? It's like you know people go you're not agreeing with me so you are abusing me—well I don't think so.
> (murmurs of agreement)
> **LN:** Yeah—you yelled at me so you are abusive!
> (Focus group #5)

> **RY:** I've struggled a lot with my own stance in doing violence work. I mean when I began I was very hard line—everything was abuse, just about. I saw everything from that lens.
> (Focus group #4)

Conversations such as these reflect a larger concern with definitions of violence being applied too broadly and uncritically. They also reveal a more
constructionist view of abuse; for example, the phrase "I saw everything
from that lens" acknowledges that there is a disciplinary structure of interpretation at work. Feminist writings, and in particular the trauma paradigm, have stressed an emphasis on understanding women's experiences
of violence. Yet the discussions that we had about the boundaries surrounding the category of abuse reveal a self-reflexive stance within feminism that challenges the once hegemonic view that asserts that women,
whose experience of violence has been ignored, silenced, trivialized, and in
general denied throughout history, must always be believed, *verbatim*, period. This literalist view has been strongest within the sexual abuse recovery movement in which adult women publicly and bravely defy their
fathers by speaking out about the unspeakable,[18] and is often in direct opposition to social constructionist discourses which acknowledge the level
of interpretation, reconstruction and perception that are also at work in
experience and certainly in emotionally traumatic ones in which the cause
of injury is not straightforwardly physical. Our focus group discussions
suggested that service providers are, at times, pushing against the extreme
literalist approach, in part because the cultural and historical terrain has
shifted where "believing women" becomes more complicated because of
woman-to-woman abuse. For example,

> In the 70's and 80's we had a strong clinical tool. Believe what the
> victim tells us, trust their experience, because perpetrators are in-
> credibly creative. So that is an important premise of the heterosex-
> ual domestic violence movement. But if you have two women
> reporting to you their experiences of victimization in the same rela-
> tionship who do you believe? We have to address that that is their
> internal experiences not their behavior.
>
> (Individual interview with Amber)

Feminist service providers struggle with this on-going tension between
honoring women's experiences and working therapeutically to figure out
what is really going on. Addressing "internal experiences" perhaps points
the way to more psychoanalytic discussions, where as Janice Haaken suggests, we can probe the deeper currents of conflict, internal desires, am-
bivalence, irrationality, identification, and hostility: although each of these
terms is loaded with a repressive history for women in general, and cer-

tainly for lesbians within the field of psychiatry, they grant women a fuller, more complex subjectivity.[19] A focus on the material conditions alone—who said what or did what to whom—cannot explain why a woman might lie (consciously or unconsciously) about having an illness—a form of emotional abuse that women in this study reported; or why a woman might make accusations that someone is abusive when they are not. These are delicate issues that need to be grappled with as they directly confront the voice of experience as authoritative "truth."[20] Feminist counselors have had to struggle with this issue of the "truth" of memories when working with adult survivors of childhood sexual abuse. Many understand memories as layered in meanings, constructed through meaning-making processes as the mind tries to come to grips with trauma, and therefore not simply about truthfulness or falseness.[21] Service providers in this study, at times, recognize the danger and the limitations of accepting all women's claims at face value. For example, one service provider gave an example of how she was falsely labeled as abusive:

> **HG:** I was in a situation about five years ago where a co-worker and close friend said all this shit about me [that I was abusive]. I was shocked, they were saying that I was a predator, luring all these young women in. And it was shit, so we've got to be very careful you know—that's from a very personal place—cuz you can destroy people.
> **LK:** That's where we put people in the good/bad category.
> **BG:** I think the challenge is not to oversimplify. Definitely keep your mind as open as it can be and still draw your line, I mean that is a real challenge, and allow your line to move because it will if you keep growing, right? It may move all over the place.
>
> (Focus group #4)

There is an awareness, then, that feminist understandings and concepts that we currently have at our disposal are limited constructions that serve to "oversimplify" when we need to "move all over the place" in order to develop an understanding of what is going on. Even though there was strong support for a power and control constellation, other comments suggest that this feminist understanding of violence "needs to be stretched" (Focus group #2) or even "doesn't fit, doesn't work" (Focus group #7). It can be difficult to make sense of these contradictions. The discussions reveal the normative discourse that feminist service providers both employ and at times struggle against. They show the investments we have in

maintaining dominant feminist understandings about relationship violence ("abuse is abuse") while also recognizing that dichotomous categories of good and bad do not capture the complexities of what an abusive
dynamic constitutes. In part, we want to preserve a dominant feminist
narrative because we want to keep the small space that has opened up in
the women's movement to address lesbian partner violence. We also feel
that we need to keep this discourse and speak its "necessary speech," because of the concerns about a backlash against feminism that denies male
violence against women. Service providers are perhaps most insistent on
keeping the power and control constellation because of its clarity and inclusion of "trauma talk," in which the real harms of violence against
women in the private realm can continue to be acknowledged and the
rigid categories of perpetrator and victim allow a strong stance to be
taken, with someone held accountable for the violence. The assumptions
of sameness that are inscribed in the dominant discourse, however, lead to
an erasure of lesbian existence, a denial of the complex ways women use
and experience power and control, and an insistence on centering the experiences of white, middle-class heterosexual women as universal. It is not
that power and control, fear, and trauma are all wrong; it is just that as a
discourse they assume too much about what is going on without telling us
anything.

Michel Foucault suggests, "a discourse can be an instrument and an effect of power, but also a hindrance, a stumbling block, a point of resistance and a starting point for an opposing strategy."[22] The chapter has
also shown that there were many moments in focus groups discussions
when marginal discourses emerged in places where the dominant discourse hindered understanding. Counterdiscussions more easily emerge
where there has been considerable antinormative discussion within academic and community feminisms. For example, the need to move beyond
white middle-class women's experiences has been stressed in all contexts
in which feminists work. There have also been many debates with feminist
and lesbian communities about sadomasochism (including debates about
pornography, censorship, and erotica), allowing for more openness to discussions of complexity with less need for recuperation. Finally, there has
been more awareness and understanding of how "abuse" is also a social
construct because of the very public and heated debates in the 1990s over
how to understand recovered memories of childhood sexual abuse.

Overall, this chapter suggests that we need more spaces and a better
language to talk about lesbian relationships and lesbian abuse. Calling attention to existing language practices shows how investments in a domi-

nant feminist discourse construct and shape reality in ways that are not always helpful to women's lives—in fact such investment often went against
the very experiences of lesbians that counselors had been witness to. Attention to discourse shows how lives are regulated by language and how
normative assumptions are asserted through categories that include the
experiences of some women and exclude the experiences of others; natu-
ralize certain forms of violence and repress knowledge of others. A fist is a
fist, yes, but there is more to abuse than that all-reductive claim tells us.
The impact of that fist involves not just a network of bones, blood, and
muscle, but also networks of two women's personal histories and social
identities. Service providers struggling against violence against women
and struggling to help lesbians in abusive relationships find again and
again that the constellation of power and control does not match up with
what women tell them. What the body remembers is very often not what is
written on the body by dominant discourse.

What I am suggesting is that we need to embrace a more complex understanding of power. This does not mean that I do not see power and control operating in violent relationships. Rather, I do not see power as fixed
and simply resting with one person. It is the "how" of that power and control that needs explicating. Just as my interviews with women who have
experienced abuse have suggested, we need analyses that account for the
complexities, the context, and the particulars of women's lives. The concepts we currently have in place, however, do not give us room for articulating these lives. Paying attention to the "microphysics of power" will
help to unlock our narrow focus on identifying the perpetrator as the one
with "power over" and the resulting paradigm of victimization.

Feminist service providers in these focus groups do wish to develop effective responses, understandings, and interventions in this area. They
recognize the lack of services for perpetrators; the barriers that exist for
lesbians of color, working-class, and poor women; and the fact that
woman-to-woman abuse challenges long-cherished ideals about women's
relationships with other women. Many identified the need to broaden our
focus in doing antiviolence work beyond relationships in a way that disrupts the dominant private/public binary. For example,

> **DM:** I think that doing work about violence between women can
> teach us about working with women in organizations—dealing with
> power issues there.
>
> (Focus group #4)

MF: There is so much we have to talk about dominance and nondominant groups, women in the sex trade who may have an abusive encounter with another woman, transgender issues—there is a whole group of women in terms of who women are in relationships with, in different places—it's a whole area we have not got to. [Lots of voices overlapping in agreement with different parts of this statement]

(Focus group #6)

But as I said earlier, conversations were just a beginning step in "collective consciousness work" with some windows opening up and others slammed shut. Challenges to the dominant power and control constellation are often quickly shut down because of institutional forces that further support and entrench the ideology while working against the emergence of counterdiscourses.

Chapter 6 explores the politics of responding to abuse in lesbian relationships by examining both the material and discursive regulation of lesbians' experiences of violence that is evident in social service practices and manuals. I turn to the process of institutionalization and explore the way certain understandings of lesbian partner violence become "regimes of truth" within social service organizations. I continue to critically reflect on what we are constructing in the field of lesbian relationship violence and look more specifically at the types of programs and services being offered within feminist, gay, lesbian, and queer communities, asking who is included and who is excluded? What "safety" is created, and for whom? In so doing, I recognize both the urgency of these efforts to respond, and, because of the critical persistence of focus group participants, the need to figure out the extent to which the language we use is interfering with that work.

SIX
The Politics of Responding to Violence in Lesbian Relationships

CHAPTER 5 EXPLORED the elaborate constellation of power and control on which feminist service providers rely, and also struggle against, when responding to violence in lesbian relationships. To better understand how and why this discourse remains so powerful, even when service providers are aware that it does not fit many women's experiences of abuse, it is necessary to look at the politics and practices of social service organizations. Organizations are often part of institutionalized approaches to battering that tend to conceptualize violence as homogeneous, and in effect, serve to mask more complicated dynamics. In Foucault's terms, discourses operate with institutional support as "regimes of truth."[1] We need to ask how "regimes of truth" on domestic violence operate in social services to obscure, delegitimize, or subjugate certain knowledges or subjects while legitimizing or normalizing others. This chapter examines both the material and discursive regulation of lesbians' experiences of violence by social service agencies. I examine the way that institutional mandates of social service agencies often reinforce the binary and gender-based understandings of violence embedded in the power and control discourse in spite of their considerable efforts to include a focus on marginalized sexual identities. I also look at how certain standard agency practices such as running survivor-only support groups, although often helpful to individuals, can inadvertently perpetuate heterosexist and gender-based assumptions of perpetrator and victim. I explore several organizational websites and manuals, including a booklet that I co-authored with Laurie Chesley and Donna MacAulay for Health Canada,[2] each of which reflects different strategic investments: some in mainstream intelligibility, some in feminism, and others in gay/lesbian and queer movements. Many terms such as lesbian relationship violence, woman-to-woman abuse, same-sex domestic violence, and queer domestic violence have been circulating within organizations and communities. Each term reflects some of the political struggles of naming violence in an accurate and inclusive way. All the texts I examine continue to make dominant the power and control paradigm that in some ways reproduces universalized categories of sexual identity and homogenizes experiences of relationship violence. Yet, I also bring forward some examples of innovative responses to lesbian abuse developed by social service agencies, reminding us that institutionalized discourses can be resisted despite their strong tendencies to achieve the status of common sense. In showing how exclusionary practices work even within marginalized communities, the chapter takes up ethical questions that point us toward more inclusive responses.

Organizational Mandates

Within the culture of social service provision in Canada and the United States there has been an increase in demands for efficiency and cost-cutting. For example, a number of service providers that I spoke with talked about the pressures to engage in short-term or brief therapy in which clients must resolve issues in a limited number of sessions and then move on, so that an agency can continue to work through their long waiting list. Further, there is often fierce competition for scarce funding, making it difficult for groups to collaborate or welcome innovations to service delivery. Instead, agencies must try to establish themselves as reputable experts, offering a definitive approach to addressing an issue. Focus group discussions with service providers acknowledged the ways in which organizations are limited by mandates that reinforce a tendency to conceptualize violence as homogeneous in terms of its relationships dynamics, its effects on the victim, and the motivations of the perpetrator. For example, most feminist-based organizations have a mandate to work only with victims of domestic violence, leaving women who are abusive without many, or in some cases any, options for services:

> NC: Can I ask if you were to see two of them coming where maybe one is the perpetrator—but you saw there was some willingness to change on her part—would you see them both or would you still say: "No we can't?"

BW: We can't because of our mandate. So that's a real gap for us.

(Focus group #5)

The focus on victims is historically rooted in the feminist sexual assault and domestic violence movements. Women's services developed to help support women while effectively demanding that the criminal justice system deal with abusers. Leaving this in place when responding to lesbian relationship violence allows organizations to preserve a gender-based analysis, and to maintain existing programs by simply fitting lesbian victims in and keeping lesbian perpetrators out along with their heterosexual counterparts. The gap created by this practice has certainly been recognized, as noted in the excerpt above and in Chapter 5. But as one service provider noted, "for some of us to start something where we work we're limited by the mandate" (Focus group #2). One of the regulating effects of this victim-only mandate is to enforce a specific victim script. For example, one service provider spoke of this effect in her work with some victims who were also abusive:

DP: You run the risk of losing clients when you start to push them to deal with their own anger and what they are doing because they are coming to you for some collusion that they are victims and they are feminists and so therefore they wouldn't, you know, they're not hurting anybody, when at times they're vile (laughs).

(Focus group #6)

In her comments, we see the way that both therapist and client get positioned within a normative discursive context that makes it very difficult to talk about other issues such as how some women may be victims in their relationship but abusive in other areas of their lives; it can be hard to discuss feelings of anger, or times when poor decisions were made within the abusive relationship. Although the common tendency of victims to blame themselves is certainly a concern, I was struck by the question posed by several women that I interviewed who wanted to figure out their "piece" in the relationship dynamic. Sharon Lamb states that we cannot simply oversympathize and tell women not to blame themselves: "it is crucial when working with victims to tease out the accurate level of responsibility, [and] to work away at the very odd self-destructive tendency of victims to assume more responsibility than they should."[3] This can be a very difficult task within institutionalized approaches that serve only victims, and often state in their service brochures "you are not to blame." As another service provider said,

RT: This is a big one for me and I'm afraid to mention it here in this room—that is the big R piece—the responsibility piece for victims—how do we talk about that without equalizing all of the abuse in the relationship?

(Focus group #4)

Such is the effect of institutionalized approaches that she was nervous about even raising the question. The interplay between service provider and victim within feminist services is scripted to be an empowering encounter in which we rebuild the self-esteem of victims, in part, to counter society's blaming of women and vilifying of lesbians. But who does this mandated script leave out, and what damage is done when a woman who comes to us for help is forced to rewrite the story of her experience in ways that deny any responsibility or complexity?

Other service providers commented on the very limited resources that are available to address the issue of lesbian abuse, both in terms of funding sources and personnel, and a larger process of professionalization. As one service provider commented, "I think there has been some mission shift. The original mission was to end violence. It's shifted now to serving women and children" (individual interview with Amber). Many feminists have been critical of this process of professionalization that has occurred within women's services, which includes an emphasis on standardizing and codifying practices as a way to "serve women and children" at the expense of the larger goal of ending violence. Service providers that I spoke with felt they were struggling not only against depoliticized and limiting mandates, but against a false compartmentalizing of issues that has occurred now that services for victims of violence have proliferated. For example,

MF: The shelter movement and the anti-rape movement still have two very distinct ways of looking at these issues. They don't bridge very well, partly because of fear of losing funding. It is sort of government initiated. It is being done so that all those women cannot bond together and be in one place, and all that violence and all those things we don't want to talk about can be dealt with in separate services. So that filters down into what we do; we tend to identify sexual assault here and partner assault here, as if the two rarely go together.

(Focus group #6)

Her comments show an awareness of how professionalization is part of an institutionalized process that further entrenches dominant discourses and binary understandings that keep domestic violence/sexual assault/sexual harassment/hate crimes, to name a few, as separate, discrete categories that are unrelated to larger systems of oppression such as sexism, racism, and heterosexism. It becomes very difficult to fight for changes within these large, interlocking systems that emphasize individual problems and solutions.

Responses to lesbian relationship violence have also been compartmentalized, primarily into two opposing streams: programs emerging within women's services, which are most often feminist based and have a history of responding to violence against women; and gay, lesbian, and queer services, which often see themselves as offering an alternative to outdated and inappropriate gender-based approaches developed by feminists. (It is important to point out that programs, whether in women's organizations or gay or lesbian services, are for the most part still a luxury of big cities.) Where feminist organizations emphasize the similarities experienced by lesbian and heterosexual women and keep a focus on female victimization, queer organizations emphasize the blending of men's and women's experiences by addressing same-sex or queer domestic violence and the experience of gays, lesbians, bisexuals, and transgendered people. Most often these services began by addressing bashing and homophobic hate crimes, but then received calls from gays and lesbians about abuse in their relationships and so developed new programs to respond to this largely unanticipated need. There are also a few examples of services that are lesbian/bisexual-only, such as the San Francisco Network for Battered Lesbians and Bisexual Women, which keep a feminist focus on women but have created separate services, often after experiencing little support from heterosexist women's organizations that remain reluctant to address lesbian issues.[4] Although the origins of each approach are different, the similarities of their programs and practices are striking. For example, queer organizations have tended to adopt the victim-only mandate of women's services, and have a clinical focus (reflecting the professionalization of most government-funded antiviolence services). One woman spoke of the complicated effects of dividing issues within their agency:

> If somebody were gay-bashed and they came here for services and that person was also battering their partner and their partner came here for services that would definitely affect our ability to provide services.

> (Individual interview with Cecily)

Here the limits of binary approaches that separate experiences of hate crimes and domestic violence, victimization, and abusiveness become apparent. Services end up focusing on individuals in a way that decontextualizes and rearticulates their experiences into a single problem that does not match the complexities that they are often describing. Further, many programs that address queer partner abuse are embedded in the same feminist power and control constellation found in women's services yet are often unaware of the similarities in their approaches and organizational responses. For example,

> I have never worked in a heterosexual agency, never dealt with heterosexual abuse. I think my philosophy is perhaps a little bit different because I was trained in queer domestic violence. In my work I'm just looking at power and control dynamics, I tend not to believe in the feminist model. I'm not saying that domestic violence is not a sexist-based dynamic, I believe that men do violate women. But if you just say that it is a gender-based dynamic then you totally cannot talk about queer domestic violence.
>
> (Individual interview with Shelagh)

Service providers are part of an elaborate social service system or culture that, in fact, constrains and shapes what can be said and what can be seen when responding to relationship violence. These institutionalized practices and discourses are based primarily on assumptions of liberal individualism in which the social, historical, and cultural contexts of issues and people's lives are ignored because of a focus on the individual. The discursive logic behind these practices sets certain roles for providers and for people seeking services. We have to become aware of how prescriptions for service provision have come into dominance and how they then shape our attitudes and the perceptions of those who seek services.

The Power and Control Wheel

The power and control constellation discourse that I discussed in Chapter 5 is institutionally supported by a visual diagram called the Power and Control Wheel, first developed by the Domestic Abuse Intervention project of Duluth, Minnesota.[5]

Joshua Price has found that the Wheel has become institutionalized in every shelter in Canada and the United States and is used in most antiviolence projects.[6] The Wheel was originally designed to be used as a pedagogical tool in workshops with battered women—a starting point to provoke discussion and encourage critical thinking about heterosexual relationship violence and other forms of violence that women encountered in their lives. Even though the Wheel provides a generalized abstraction of violence, it was designed to have women look at their situations, as well as other women's, and see the way abusers use various tactics to gain control in a relationship. It was never intended to be used as a template to define experiences or assess for violence. As a methodology, it was intended to capture the diversity of women's experiences and consider differing contexts of violence. Further, as Price explains, it was used in tandem with another chart, "Institutional and Cultural Supports for Battering," which asked women for examples of the ways institutions in society encourage and support male batterers to use controlling tactics. The exercise was

FIGURE 6.1: Produced by the Domestic Abuse International Project, 206 W. Fourth St., Duluth, MN 55806.

meant to develop a political analysis of woman abuse by considering the private, public, social, and cultural spheres of violence.[7] Overall, the diagram was a popular educational tool designed to generate critical, reflexive discussion rather than delineate the parameters of domestic violence. Yet Price has convincingly argued that through the process of institutionalization, the diagram is now used alone "to define, inform and provide a model of what domestic violence is."[8] He points out that the Wheel is also "employed unproblematically to define violence involving women of color and lesbians of any color."[9] Yet when taken as an explanatory model, the Wheel cannot easily map onto lesbians' experiences.

Several groups have revised the Wheel to address this problem; for example, the Southern Arizona Task Force on Domestic Violence has produced a diagram called "The Power and Control Wheel for Lesbians and Gays"[10] and The London Battered Women's Advocacy Centre of London, Ontario has produced a Wheel called "Lesbian Battering: Double Jeopardy."[11] These diagrams are almost identical to the original except for the section on the wheel describing social status and privilege which replaces the section on male privilege in the diagram describing heterosexual domestic violence, and the use of the female pronoun in the case of the wheel for lesbian abuse only. The homogenizing process is clear. The diagrams enforce the claim that lesbian abuse and heterosexual abuse are the same and further assert that all women's experiences of relationship violence are the same, thereby erasing and ignoring women's differing experiences of violence, power relations, and the social context in which it occurs. The diagrams further perpetuate gendered and binary assumptions that include seeing all perpetrators as acting rationally and intentionally using violence to control their partners. Further, replacing male privilege on the diagram with a section on using privilege merely reconstructs a familiar either/or binary: the lesbian abuser as male-like, someone who uses status and power-over, while the lesbian victim remains constructed as a universal female who lacks status and power and is subjected to control by her partner.

Another diagram is the one produced by the New York City Anti-Violence Project for lesbian, gay, transgender, and bisexual relationships.[12] (Figure 6.2)

This diagram departs more significantly from the original to include the tactics of abuse that are specific to a range of queer relationships, namely, transphobia, HIV-related abuse, heterosexism, and homo/biphobia. Further it expands the notion of male privilege to a broader category of entitlement. It also includes physical and sexual abuse as tactics rather than identifying them as the elements that keep all the tactics effective.

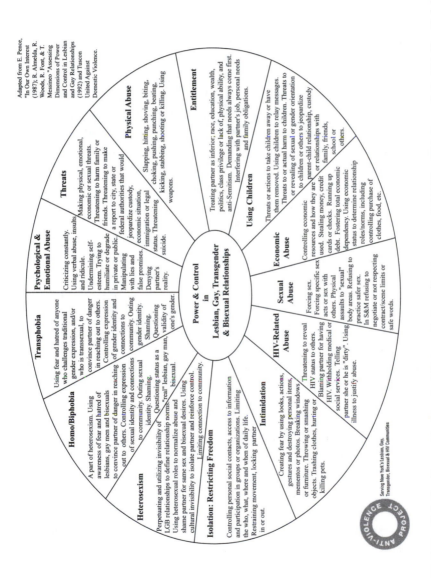

FIGURE 6.2: © New York City Gay and Lesbian Anti-Violence Project. All rights reserved. 240 West 35th Street, Suite 200, New York NY, 10001.

Yet even though this wheel is much more appropriate to queer contexts than it was in its original form, it still ends up oversimplifying particular experiences if it is used as a diagnostic tool rather than a starting point for discussion. For example, it reduces the context of homophobia and hetero-sexism to one of countless tactics exerted by abusers to control their vic-tims. Further HIV-related abuse is constructed as only involving an HIV-negative partner controlling an HIV-positive partner. Yet in my re-search several women reported partners who used illnesses as a way to manipulate them and gain control in the relationships.

A seamless grand narrative is reinforced by the power and control dia-grams in their transformation from critical thinking tools into a prescrip-tive diagnostic model. Although the underlying assertion of the power and control model (that violence is a learned behavior that one individual chooses to exercise against another) may often be applicable, the model is used too simplistically when placed like a template onto lesbian's lives rather than exploring the differing conditions that might give rise to vio-lence and the differing dynamics that might emerge in those contexts. In adhering to the power and control model, services do not have to pay at-tention to the social and cultural locations of victims or abusers because social contexts, like heterosexism, although noted on the diagram, are placed on the Wheel only to show that they do not matter. The diagrams are so readily interchangeable because there is one common mold of do-mestic violence. Lesbians who have experienced relationship violence have to make themselves fit the template by rereading their relationships in its terms or be denied services. The adaptations suggest that service providers are well aware of differing contexts that might give rise to violence. But the prevailing tendency is to reproduce a universalizing model that equates male violence against women based on a context of patriarchal entitlement with, for example, violence in HIV-related domestic situations based on a context of societal homophobia and the frustration, pain, and grief of caring for a dying partner. It is not that the violence in the latter situation should be excused, but the approach to understanding the dy-namics and intervening should surely be different.

I agree with Price, who concludes the following from tracing the use of the Wheel in several sites (battered Latinas in Los Angeles, men who bat-ter in rural New York, and lesbians who are battered in small towns in On-tario, Canada):

The institutions that I have looked at have turned this model into an instrument of normalization of violence through the homogeniz-

ing of the space of battering. . . . The tragedy of it is that method-
ologically, philosophically and politically the original diagram was
intended to instigate the contrary—to violate the public/private
split and to urge women to meditate on the connections or disjunc-
tion between various women's situations and in that context to assess the consequences of battering in cultural and socio-historical
terms.[13]

It is perhaps not surprising that the Wheel has been adopted within so
many services. I myself have used the diagram as a handout in courses
that I teach and in workshops that I have done on lesbian partner violence. Its heterosexist credentials lend it an authoritative familiarity that is
strategically useful when working with mainstream audiences: it is harder
to dismiss and minimize lesbian abuse when you are shown the parallels to
heterosexual partner abuse. As a handout in workshops or classes, it can
also be used to generate critical discussion. But I am suggesting that the
widespread adaptation and use of the diagram as a static, universal model
provide further evidence of how discourses become regimes of truth within
organizations, which then lead to certain standard practices and programs
being implemented that end up being exclusionary. When institutionalized, a focus on lesbian victims based on the power and control model
leads to programs being offered within services that are based on heterosexual relationship violence. Most often, these programs include binary
support services such as support groups for survivors, while excluding the
possibility of couple counseling, and forcing survivors to stick to a victim
script to obtain support even when, as seen in Chapter 3, they know very
well they have been abusive themselves or have experienced shifts in the
power dynamics that do not fit with the diagram's limited and mechanistic
view of power.

Support Groups: Safety for Survivors

Support groups for survivors of domestic violence have long been operating within women's services and are now offered for lesbians within many
feminist and gay and lesbian services. The rationale for groups is that they
provide a psychoeducational environment in which group members can
find support, validate their experiences and sense of isolation, and counteract the self-blame they often feel. Several women that I interviewed had
gone through support groups and spoke very positively about the transfor-

mative effect the experience had in making them feel that they were not the only lesbian on earth to have had this happen to them. Service providers who offer support groups, however, are struggling in their attempts to keep support groups safe for survivors by screening out perpetrators, a goal achieved in support groups for women abused in heterosexual relationships simply by screening out men. Service providers trying to construct an empowering support group for survivors struggle at the intake stage to do an accurate assessment of complicated relationship dynamics and often trace relationship histories to ensure no one in the group has been abused by anyone else in a past relationship. In small communities in which many lesbians know one another, ensuring safety and confidentiality can be a huge challenge. But do these practices always have the desired effect?

For example, two service providers who run support groups for survivors of same-sex abuse reported that when screening for group members, they accept only women who have never used violence (not even in self-defense), not because they categorically refuse to see women who have used violence as victims, but because they feel they cannot address the complexities such behaviors may raise in the group:

> **CD:** We have a very narrow paradigm that we're looking at for women in the group so the women in the group primarily experience violence. They haven't become violent themselves. And if they are violent themselves then they are not appropriate for this specific type of group. We've had a lot of difficulty with that because we have met women and spoken and spent a lot of time with women who have experienced some really hideous things but then at the same time they've acted out in violent ways themselves sometimes. And so it's a real dilemma because they can't come into the group with other women who have primarily experienced violence. But I think there is a tremendous need to and actually we've been talking about this more lately. There's a tremendous need for more of a mish-mash or something that's focused on that gray area of maybe primarily experiencing violence but they need some sort of anger management themselves—they act out themselves.

> **DY:** It is true that in our groups someone has come in and they have certainly defended themselves—there's been strong, pretty dramatic self-defense because you know a lesbian might have been fearing for her life and she took strong measures to defend her life.

So that would be where that line is drawn but it is very tough—it's become very, very complicated and I guess one of the principles that we're trying to stay with is a kind of safety for the lesbians in the group.

(Focus group #6)

An unintended consequence of this "nonviolent victim" approach is that the "real victim" is constructed as the one who never responds or defends herself. Here, the service providers are aware of the "narrow paradigm" of victim/perpetrator that they are working from, which excludes many lesbians, yet they feel they must continue to use it. Other service providers described a different approach to setting boundaries about who they will counsel: because of a mandate to work with victims, organizations that are confronted with both members of a lesbian couple may define the initiator of the violence as the abuser, or they may define a primary aggressor. Within these parameters, they can then work with a woman who has fought back or who now retaliates against her partner with physical violence. The strategy requires only a very minor discursive adjustment: "victim" gets reconstructed from "the one who is abused" to "the one who did not start it," or "the one whose actions are secondary," regardless of how abusive those subsequent actions or intentions are. This then reinforces the dichotomies of victim/perpetrator; passive/active; innocent/evil, female/male that underlie gender-based discourses of violence and mask complexities.

Further, other concepts such as "safety," which was raised as a central principle in providing services for victims, remain unproblematized and continue to homogenize women's experiences. Who are the groups made safe for? As one service provider said, "How safe are lesbians from heterosexual [homophobic] women in shelters?" (Focus group #8). Further, many focus group participants noted that it is primarily white women who have been seeking services for lesbian abuse. Whiteness, however, can remain unexamined as a barrier to safety for many women of color if the dichotomy of safe/unsafe remains rigidly linked only to gender-based constructions of victim/perpetrator. It is not that support groups for survivors or victim-only mandates are by definition wrong. I have cofacilitated support groups for survivors and have seen how important they can be in helping women to recover from the pain they have endured in their relationship. My concern is how these practices become disciplined into conventional, standardized practices that are universally applied and that have us ignore, minimize, and deny the specifics of some situations while making claims about safety to defend exclusionary actions that erase some women's experiences while normalizing others.

Another example is the practice of couple counseling, which has long been taboo in the field of relationship violence. There are many solid reasons as to why this practice has not been accepted, including the beliefs that the victim would never feel safe enough to share feelings; the abuser, who is often manipulative, could charm the therapist into being unable to see the dynamics of the relationship accurately; or the abuser could be absolved of responsibility when she arouses sympathy by offering excuses for her behavior (history of childhood abuse, alcoholism, etc.).[14] In focus group discussions, those service providers who worked in private practice seemed less constrained by rules of practice about couple counseling than those who worked in organizations that enforce policies; for example:

> **PW:** At the center, a couple, well two individuals will come for counseling almost at the same time. They are seeing different counselors and then certain stuff comes to light—It is a difficult thing we are trying to figure out. Many of these women are extremely isolated, they have no or very few connections with the lesbian community, and very awkward connections with the rest of their lives, and most of the people in their lives do not know they are a couple and there is this stuff going on and they have no place to talk about it or to even have someone else say "What is going on here?" because people do not even know they are together. So we are trying to figure out how to work with this?
>
> **JR:** Because does it feel inappropriate to have both partners there?
>
> **PW:** We're an agency.
>
> **JR:** Is that the issue?
>
> **PW:** As an agency we are trying to figure out if it is appropriate thing for us. We try and keep confidentiality but we are also trying to do safety planning—if we have a sense that something bad is going to happen. Do we talk to the other partner or not? I mean in regular counseling, of course, it is confidential.
>
> **CD:** I often suggest that couples both see the same counselor rather than encouraging secrecy and people going off in different directions rather than dealing with the issues. You can confront. Even with physical abuse too, depending on the level, how much it

has escalated, to what degree the person is in danger. But the whole secrecy thing is such a problem. And I find the more open it is between the two people the more likely it is they're going to work something out.

(Focus group #1)

This discussion reveals struggles concealed behind organizational policies such as not providing couple counseling, or not providing individual counseling to both members of a couple, even though in some circumstances couple counseling might help the counselor and the couple to determine the dynamics and find ways of stopping the violence. The process of institutionalization ("we're an agency") operates on assumptions of sameness in seeing abusive relationship dynamics and in determining responses that, for the most part, assume that victims must leave an abusive relationship because no resolution is possible. What we continue to see, then, is a pattern of structural/institutional forces interlocking with and supporting dominant discourses, making it difficult to address complexities.

Outreach: Creating Websites and Manuals

A newer institutionalized practice that has emerged is the development of informational websites. More and more domestic violence organizations are addressing the service needs of victims through web-based material.[15] Since many lesbians do not access services because of concerns about confidentiality, homophobia, or fear of reprisal from their abusive partner, web-based resources can be an important outreach tool. Women can access the information at anytime of the day, and can get information specific to lesbian partner abuse that may not be available within their local community. Of course, there are still limitations. Many working-class and poor women do not have access to computers, meaning that the sites are more likely to benefit middle-class women. As well, sites are limited by space and cannot be expected to provide all the information and resources that someone would need. Despite these limitations, the websites play an important role in raising awareness of lesbian partner abuse and in providing valuable resources and educational material. Yet the websites, like other institutionalized practices that I have reviewed, seem to actively work at foreclosing the complexities that arise in abusive relationships and end up asserting one coherent story of violence requiring the same solutions even though differing sexual identity categories are being used. Fol-

lowing the work of Cindy Holmes who examined three educational
brochures on lesbian abuse,[16] I ask what is being produced and what is being limited/erased/excluded in these websites.

As discussed in Chapter 2, I will look at five organizational websites
and two educational booklets. Although not unified in the information
they present, each makes public and mobilizes the category of abuse in
lesbian relationships and each reflects certain strategic investments in the
truth claims they are making and in those to whom they are speaking. I
provide a brief summary of each of the texts as a starting point for my examination of the institutionalized politics of deploying this category.

Advocates for Abused and Battered Lesbians (AABL), in Seattle,
Washington (www.aabl.org),[17] has the most comprehensive site, and perhaps the most influential, too, since other sites often provide a link to their
extensive resources. They provide a section on "tools to keep you safe and
help you know if you are being or have been abused," which begins with
statements related to power and control. They also provide "signs to look
for in a battering personality" including jealousy, controlling behavior,
isolation, and blaming others. They offer questions to consider about sex,
which include distinctions between consensual s/m sex and abuse. Post-
traumatic stress disorder is defined along with suggestions for healing.
They have also developed a section on "voices" in which survivors can
write personal narratives and poetry about what they have learned or
what has helped. An extensive global directory is included that lists the
contact information for services around the world including Africa, Asia,
Australia, Europe, and Central, North, and South America. Finally, they
include a description of their services that includes one-to-one counseling,
support, legal advocacy, and support groups "to lesbians/dykes who have
been emotionally, psychologically, physically and or/sexually abused by
their partners." They state, "we are also entrusted to provide a safe environment and assist in the empowerment process." They engage in community education and "encourage active community(ies) responses in the
recognition and elimination of the conditions and perceptions that perpetuate lesbian battering, homophobia and misogyny." Although they do not
claim that their services are feminist, they make a link between personal
experiences of battering and a context of homophobia and misogyny, as
well as emphasizing safety, empowerment, and women's voices, all of
which are consistent with dominant feminist values when addressing domestic violence.

Similarly, the Network for Battered Lesbians and Bisexual Women in
Boston (www.nblbw.org)[18] offers a focus on lesbians with the additional

inclusion of bisexual women. They provide a telephone hotline, run a free support group, provide legal and other referrals, produce a newsletter, and offer community education. Their site, like AABL's, is focused on victims, providing information on how to determine if you have been battered and how to do safety planning; they also list other resources and links. They, too, include a political analysis where "battering is but one aspect of a violent/abusive culture and cannot be addressed in isolation. To confront battering also means to confront all forms of oppression and other abuses of power." This site acknowledges that women might fight back, but always sees it as self-defense or an effort to stop the abuse.

Strategically, these sites center lesbian experiences of abuse and end up constructing an essentialized, universal lesbian/dyke/bisexual. Lesbian perpetrators are defined uniformly as intentional in their actions: "these are learned behaviors, she is choosing to use them, they are effective" (ABBL). Their investment is clearly in preserving a strict victim/perpetrator binary and in maintaining the power and control model. There is no suggestion that some victims might fight back, or that power is ever shifting, or that lesbians may be experiencing public and private violence. They stake out important but problematic political territory in which an abused lesbian is conceptualized as powerless and innocent. Lesbians who do not feel helpless, who have hit back or who are ambivalent about their relationship, will not see themselves in these sites. Women who do not identify as lesbian, or those who identify as queer or transgendered are also excluded.

The website by Women Organized To Make Abuse Nonexistent (W.O.M.A.N.) Inc., based in San Francisco (www.norcov.com/woman-inc),[19] describes their multiservice agency, which includes counseling, community education, a crisis line, Latina and bicultural services, and a lesbian domestic violence program. The services are once again for survivors, and they broaden a focus on lesbians to include bisexual, transgendered women, and all women intimate with women. A few facts about woman-to-woman abuse are provided, but the emphasis of the site is to conceptualize all domestic violence as the same. For example, they state, "Woman to woman domestic violence can be just as damaging as heterosexual domestic violence." The heterosexual framework then becomes normative with the pronoun "he" used in the website when describing abusers. The Power and Control Wheel is presented in diagram form and described as depicting the cycle of violence. Here, the claim of similarity and the construction of the site show the homogenizing and normalizing processes that are at work, in part to preserve their existing services (organized around the women-helping-women model) and knowledge base, and to assert that women share in their experiences of victimization. The effect is to view lesbian relationships through a heterosexist lens, see lesbian abusers as male-like, and ignore the social contexts surrounding and affecting our relationships. Their investment is in keeping the category woman at the center of any discussions of domestic violence. Yet, it is not only women's organizations that stress the claim of similarity. Both the L.A. Gay and Lesbian Center (LAGLC) (www.laglc.org)[20] and the New York City Gay and Lesbian Anti-Violence Project (www.avp.org)[21] make the claim that "domestic violence occurs in same gender relationships with as much frequency and severity as it does among heterosexuals" (LAGLC). As explored in Chapter 1, we do not have the research to back this claim, but it remains powerful as a way of legitimizing the issue. More than that, claiming similarity allows these gay-inclusive sites to dispense with any gender analysis or focus on women when discussing domestic violence.

   The New York City Gay and Lesbian Anti-Violence Project is part of The National Coalition of Anti-Violence Programs (NCAVP). The coalition includes programs throughout the United States that address violence against lesbian, gay, bisexual, and transgendered communities and who now also respond to domestic violence. The New York website offers resources on the many forms of violence, public and private, in glbt lives, including sexual assault and rape, hate crimes, HIV-related violence, and domestic violence. They address same-sex domestic violence in their site primarily by including a research report on domestic violence produced by the NCAVP. In their 1998 report,[22] twelve member organizations, including New York, provided information about cases of domestic violence addressed within their agency. The Coalition is invested in creating a national database for use in lobbying for policy changes, and funding for the creation of new programs and services. There is no question that this is important work, and given their aims it is understandable that the report brings forward an investment in criminal justice not found as strongly in the other sites. They suggest that they are following the steps taken by the battered women's movement in demanding protective orders for victims of same-sex domestic violence. But to do this, they pit themselves against women's groups, as is evident in the following example:

   Women's groups and others called for legislation designed to protect women victims of male abuse. This view of domestic violence framed the responses of lawmakers and was perpetuated through the resulting legislation. Even if the laws were later written (or revised) in a gender-neutral framework, the gendered conceptions of domestic violence became further entrenched in the application of the laws by police, court personnel, attorneys, and judges. Simply removing personal pronouns from a law does not ensure that it will be enforced beyond the gendered frame of reference within which the law was created.[23]

Here, truth claims are made about prevalence, and gendered analyses are dismissed in the desire to construct one grand narrative to account for all forms of domestic violence. They end up suggesting that women's groups deny equality under the law because of a focus on male violence "even if the laws were written in a gender-neutral framework." This is a strategically useful truth claim for gay men trying to get a place at the domestic-violence table, but it denies the realities of sexism, misogyny, racism, and the strong pan-societal patterns of male violence against women, all of which affect lesbians differently than gay men. In this site, sexual identities are lumped together and no differences are brought forward in the issues facing gay men, lesbians, or transgendered people.

This is also true of the website for the Los Angeles Gay and Lesbian Center, "the world's largest gay and lesbian organization and a leading provider of HIV/AIDS related care and other health and medical services." Their partner/domestic violence program includes survivors' groups, crisis and individual counseling, shelter information and referral, anger management groups, and a court-approved batterers' treatment program. The website does not provide information about the program for batterers but does have a section called "If you are abusing someone." They advise, "recognize that you are committing a crime. Assault is against the law and you can be charged. You do not have the right to abuse your partner." Although this is an important message for someone who is physically or sexually assaulting their partner, the statement can imply that all forms of abuse are crimes (when in fact emotional abuse is not), and fails to address anywhere in their site the problematic heterosexist context of the criminal justice system for the glbt community. For example, a California law exists requiring health practitioners to report to local law enforcement cases of domestic violence (including same-sex cases) in which some injury has occurred.[24] Legal, social service, and medical personnel who do not comply with this law can themselves be charged. Yet in maintaining this law, the justice system ignores the realities of a heterosexist, racist, and sexist society, to say nothing of its own prominent role in the history of discrimination against gays and lesbians, people of color, poor people, and other marginalized people. Many gays and lesbians who have been abused may not want their partners charged because they do not want to subject themselves to that system. Others will be concerned that being identified as gay or lesbian will put them at risk in their workplaces, families, and in housing. This law might prevent people from even seeking help or from talking about their experiences of partner violence, particularly if they are already at higher risk because they are HIV-positive, non-English speaking, or immigrants. The perpetrator/victim binary and the truth claim that we, and the abuse we suffer, are all the same becomes part of a criminological explanation that ends up privileging white, middle-class gay men. The discourse is directly linked to the organization's court-ordered batterers' program. The LAGLC site also claims in bold letters, "Couples counseling can make your situation more dangerous." Once again, there is no acknowledgment that violence might take different forms; that it is not always a criminal activity (even though their own definition includes emotional abuse) and need not be criminal to count as abuse; and that some couples might actually benefit from couple counseling. The claims that we make, the categories we mobilize, and the systems we enter are all political undertakings with consequences, not only for women experiencing abuse, but for advocates, activists, and people providing services.

I continue to interrogate such consequences of discursive choices in turning now to my own resource booklet, *Abuse in Lesbian Relationships: Information and Resources*, co-authored with Laurie Chesley and Donna MacAulay[25] and distributed by the National Clearinghouse on Family Violence, Health Canada (www.hc-sc.gc.ca/nc-cn). The booklet emerged from our work at the Toronto Counseling Center for Lesbian and Gays, where we had offered support groups for lesbian survivors, and where Laurie and Donna also provided individual counseling. The booklet includes information for lesbians who have been in abusive relationships, for friends and families, and for service providers. The primary focus in our writing is often, therefore, to make ourselves intelligible to mainstream audiences. We included a section on "what is lesbianism" and "the larger social context" as our way of educating readers and keeping a feminist political analysis. Yet here our efforts clashed with Health Canada, which wanted us to tone down our political language and use words such as "often," "sometimes," and "perhaps" when describing oppressive features in women's lives. We tried to make our language more palatable to Health Canada and perhaps mainstream service providers, while also trying to convey the heterogeneity of lesbians as a group so that women could see themselves included in the booklet yet we still exclude bisexual, queer, and transgendered women. Like many of the websites, the booklet defines violence, discusses myths of abuse, provides information on what to do if you are being abused, describes effects of abuse, suggests ways of getting help and how friends and relatives can help, offers advice to women who are abusive, and ends with a section on how professionals can respond. Yet we, too, rely on the simple conceptual framework of violence dominant in all of the materials that I have reviewed. In our case, this simplification helped to keep our allegiance to a dominant feminist model, and to make ourselves understandable to mainstream service providers. For example, in a section on myths (which most of the sites also include) we produced oversimplified corrections such as this one:

> Lesbian violence only occurs in butch and femme relationships. The butch is the batterer and the femme the victim. False.
> Beyond the fact that most lesbians do not assume explicitly butch–femme roles, the roles themselves do not automatically dictate who has more power or the desire to exercise more control in the relationship.[26]

On the one hand, we understandably try to dispel stereotypes about lesbian relationships, but in the process of doing so we imply that "normal" lesbian relationships are not butch–femme. Another example:

> Abuse between lesbians is mutual. Both partners contribute equally to the violence. False.

> This view stems from the belief that lesbian relationships are always equal partnerships. In violent relationships there is often a perpetrator and a victim. A perpetrator cannot be distinguished by any features such as size, height, or age. Defending oneself against an attacker must be examined closely as it may be mistakenly construed either as initiating or equally contributing to the abuse.[27]

In trying to dispel the myth of mutual abuse, we reinforce the victim–perpetrator binary, muting it only slightly by the qualifying word "often," missing an opportunity to turn from the myth of mutual abuse to the possibility of shifting power dynamics. Later, in the section on effects of abuse, we say that a victim "may have difficulty expressing her anger about the abuse. She may also turn the feelings of anger toward herself."[28]

We do not acknowledge that she may also act in anger toward her partner. Similarly, as Cindy Holmes accurately states, we end up depicting a white universal lesbian by "adding on" concepts of classism and racism without integrating them explicitly into our analysis of abuse. She writes, "it is at times hard to glimpse a woman whose life is structured fundamentally by racism and classism. When we do see her it is briefly at the margins—the violence she experiences and the realities of her life are added on as important issues for her but unconnected to everyone else."[29] The cost of mainstream intelligibility in this case is to oversimplify both lesbians and relationship violence.

Each of the sites and manuals, although varying in political perspective and content, ends up presenting one decontextualized, private form of relationship violence, and one explanatory model while asserting one primary identity cataegory—women or gay men. Victim and abuser are constructed as dichotomous identities that are conceptualized as autonomous and static, and further preserve a public/private binary. Further, lack of meaningful attention to class, race, and sexual/gender diversity leaves white, middle-class gay and lesbian sexual identities prominent despite add-on gestures to include transgender, bisexual, and queer communities and gays and lesbians of color. The truth claims that we reproduce are further entrenched in a structural context in which groups compete with one another in their efforts to keep themselves visible in the overarching dominant model. Gay/lesbian and queer communities are often pitted against mainstream services and women's services, and lesbians who want to keep lesbian/woman-only spaces are often pitted against glbt services.[30] Groups struggling for recognition and resources are strategically asking, do we show how lesbians are different or do we keep a homogenizing focus on women? Or do we dismiss gender altogether and strive for equal treatment of gays/lesbians/bisexual and transgendered people?

The booklet *'Out' of Sight*, produced by the Domestic Violence Action Resource Center (DVRC) in South Brisbane, Australia, begins by acknowledging the competitive context that has arisen because of a legislative reform to extend the provision of the Domestic Violence (Family Protection) Act 1989 to same-sex relationships. Although they see the extension as an important change, they argue that it is "inappropriate that there are no resources by the way of funding for additional services, training and policy and practice development to adequately and equitably assist victims of same sex domestic violence whether they choose to take up the legal protection option or not."[31] Their booklet, then, is targeted at mainstream service providers who are affected by this legislation. It includes a section on who is a lesbian, an analysis of domestic violence in lesbian communities, how to be supportive of lesbian/bisexual staff and clients, the legal system, police responses, and crisis accommodation issues for lesbians. In many ways, their booklet disrupts many of the truth claims in the texts that I have reviewed so far. For example, they suggest that more research is needed before they can provide a clear analysis of lesbian domestic violence, and want research to provide a basis for understanding effective service delivery. They conclude, "until this happens our response will be inefficient and ill informed."[32] Further, they acknowledge the oppressive history of the legal system in Australia, in which women remain unequal before the law, and where homosexuality in men was only recently decriminalized in 1990. They forcefully state that those in the legal system "must acknowledge the generally negative perceptions held about their care for women in same sex relationships in the past. It is the perception not the reality which is of crucial importance."[33] Overall, they resist providing simple answers, stress the diversity of lesbian communities, and urge service providers to do their own work in addressing heterosexism. Yet the booklet is still framed by a criminal justice perspective, as well as the feminist power and control model, that obscures the different faces of violence in different contexts. What would it mean if we acknowledged different contexts and spaces in which violence arises and the need for different understandings and responses? Can we push to make systems flexible rather than continuing to allow the inertia of institutional processes to keep us boxed in? Would a focus on ethics rather than political gains help us?

I have shown that our responses to lesbian relationship violence are based on one dominant discourse and a set of reinforcing institutional practices such as implementing victim-only mandates, using the Power and Control Wheel diagram as a definitive model, using problematic notions of safety in running survivor groups, opposing couple counseling, and producing oversimplified informational websites and manuals. Although our strategic investments in the story are often different, we end up telling one story of violence. Marginal discourses such as constructionist views of violence and naming whiteness and other social differences, as described in Chapter 5, for example, seem to have little impact on organizational practices. At the same time, many individual service providers do resist the cohesiveness of the dominant view. For example, service providers in one focus group discussion raised the concern that the language associated with domestic violence does not reflect the violence that surrounds every aspect of some women's lives and asserts a false assumption that safety will be achieved when they leave the abusive partner:

CJ: What do we do when two women do not use the language we are using here—where do they fit in what we are talking about here? (murmurs of agreement)

TU: I can speak from this position because I've been a street person—I've lived on the street and come out of the culture you are talking about. If violence has been the norm—which it has been for many people—where do they want to go with that? How much violence is too much violence? Is yelling okay and hitting not? Is hitting okay and punching not?

Someone: Harm reduction.

TU: Yeah it's a harm reduction model—let's speak to that place. It's more difficult in some ways but it's not impossible because if it wasn't a problem they wouldn't be talking to you about it. So what is your hope? What is the goal? What is the first step you would need to move toward that? Then to the other person—what do you think? Is this possible or not? How would you know if it was working or not? I've worked with a lot of people on the streets and I've been on the streets and that possibility exists absolutely.

(Focus Group #6)

A harm-reduction model offers a very different way of thinking about the public and private experiences of violence in people's lives. For example, service providers might negotiate with a couple to decrease their relationship violence rather than having a woman leave the relationship because together the couple might be better able to afford housing and avoid the additional dangers that come with homelessness. Another service provider questioned the effect of victim-only mandates:

SW: I thought I supported the survivor, but two years later she is actually more the batterer, she is the problematic one. And then I feel like the fool. You know, but then how do I know? And it's like what is our role as a service provider?

JR: So you are raising the question, does it matter if you did provide support to her?

SW: Right.

(Individual interview with Selena)

Her comments raise an ethical question: "What is our role as service providers?" She suggests it is more important to intervene than to accurately determine who the abuser is.

Finally, another service provider spoke of how they offer a mixed-gender support group even though the norm has been to offer separate groups for gay men and lesbians. She commented that they were concerned about the difference in culture but they found the group to have a positive impact:

> It was four women and six men—they were stunned at how well they related to one another and how much it meant to them. One woman, it was her first lesbian relationship, she had been married two times before and had children and she's an island woman. She thought that the abuse had to do with women, being with a woman. And after the group she saw it was the same across the board and she feels more comfortable about her identity and knows the violence is about that woman and that relationship. It was awesome.
>
> (Individual interview with Cecily)

Her experience is a reminder that we do not have to follow narrow prescriptive practices but can be open to seeing how different practices might be needed for different people, showing that disruptive efforts can be made within services despite the structural rigidity of institutions.

Community-Based Innovations

Some groups do try to engage in critical efforts that take us "outside the box." One strategy for escaping the constraints of a focus on responding to domestic violence is to have forums on building healthy relationships. For example, in Winnipeg, Manitoba, a group of service providers (Coalition of Lesbians on Support and Education, or CLOSE) had tried to offer a support group for lesbians, but found that very few women came forward to be in the group, likely over concerns about confidentiality given the relatively small size of the lesbian community in this city of 650,000. CLOSE then hosted an evening discussion on building healthy relationships, and the room was packed with a diverse group of women. The conversations covered a number of topics and abuse was one of them. Rather than dividing women into perpetrators and survivors, this discussion offered a more preventive intervention by discussing expectations in relationships, negotiating differences, and resolving conflict, while also addressing the lack of institution and social supports surrounding lesbian relationships. This is a community-based effort that certainly does not replace the need for domestic violence services, but offers an important shift in strategy from crisis intervention to support of relationships and prevention of abuse.

Similarly, another group of women were finding that queer Asian women were not utilizing the Asian women's shelter even though as an agency they had engaged in antihomophobia training. They decided to come up with a different kind of program. Selena described their challenge:

> How do we come up with a program that fits into what people like to do rather than make them talk to us when they really want to talk to their friends? So we are thinking of working with friends. My idea is to equip people, so if a friend came and said they are in a potentially violent relationship we could have a list of ideas of what they could do in that situation . . . so it's sort of an informal, not structured program. I've held one meeting with queer identified folks, a circle of friends. They wanted to talk about what a healthy relationship is. Rather than sharing with friends "hey that's abusive, that's not cool" we say, "actually a better way to do it is like this." So you know that's one approach.
>
> (Individual interview with Selena)

This approach reflects their attempts to respond to the local needs of queer Asian women. Rather than relying on a rigid domestic violence model of service delivery that immediately sorts out the abusers and the victims, this approach tried to acknowledge the complexities of being part of a small community of Asian queer women. As Selena said, if one woman in your friendship circle is a lawyer and is also abusive, you may need her expertise as a lawyer in the community so you cannot totally exclude her or toss her out because she is a batterer. In this approach, they are struggling to address the behaviors of the batterer while resisting the label batterer as a totalizing identity category. Similarly, another woman that I interviewed spoke of her work with recent immigrants from the Philippines. She, too, works through friendship circles to talk about all issues of violence—in relationships, workplaces, families, and so forth. She explained that Filipina women that she works with would not identify with the term lesbian, and would not participate in a domestic violence program. She was, therefore, responding to their context and their realities. Clearly, we need a variety of approaches that respond to local settings rather than standardizing programs if we are truly committed to eradicating violence.

Another example of a community-based response is the use of popular theater to provide education and information to lesbian communities. For example, a play called *Bruised* written by Lisa Allen-Agostini and Jhesekah presents four different scenes of relationship violence.[34] After the play, there is a discussion with the actors and writers; members of the community who have some knowledge of lesbian abuse are also in attendance as facilitators who can respond to questions. The play has traveled to different cities in Canada, and has been performed in lesbian bars. Because it is outside the realm of domestic services, it can reach different groups of women and provide a forum for information and discussion.

Finally, many cities are establishing coalitions of service providers who discuss and at times debate understandings and responses to same-sex partner violence. For example, Vancouver's Network Against Abuse in Same-Sex Relationships and Toronto's Coalition Against Domestic Partner Abuse are important efforts because they provide opportunities to disrupt dominant practices by encouraging discussion and critical thinking. Many feminist service providers who participated in my study wanted such opportunities for deliberation, noting that the everyday demands of working in services provides little time to reflect on practices, policies, and new information. Despite these innovative efforts, I remain concerned about our inability to sustain a focus on the complexities in our systems of caring and justice. Oversimplified concepts of domestic violence too often limit and shape our thinking about this issue in ways that can remain invisible to us because they are so thoroughly reinforced by the processes of bringing lesbian abuse into an institutional framework.

A Question of Ethics

Even though feminist service providers are aware of the limitations of the dominant power and control model, and are committed to responding to the needs of victims, we end up excluding and perhaps even harming some people with our normalizing practices. Claudia Card describes this as the gray zone—where we can have an illusion of innocence even though we are both victims and perpetrators of oppression.[35] The need to respond to complexities is ultimately an ethical issue. We need to make explicit the set of principles that guides and informs our actions rather than rigidly adhering to uninterrogated rules of conduct. Perhaps even more so, we need to be willing to see that principles can and should change, even ones that have served us well in some situations. I offer two examples that make ap-

parent the need to constantly question our practices. The first example is
the case of a twelve-year-old girl on trial for sexual assault, and the second
example involves a rape crisis center's rejection of a transgendered woman
as a counselor. Although neither is specifically about lesbian partner
abuse, both are cautionary tales of the ethical implications of universalizing and homogenizing discourses and practices within the area of anti-violence work.

Recently, a twelve-year-old girl in Toronto stood trial for sexual assault
against her two eleven-year-old girlfriends.[36] Apparently the three girls
had had a fight the day after engaging in sexual play. In the course of their
argument, the twelve-year-old girl accused the other girls of being lesbians. Presumably in retaliation, the two eleven-year-old girls went to
their parents and said that their twelve-year-old friend had "briefly forced
oral sex on them" (they also said she let the family dog rub against her
from behind). The parents called the police, who then charged the slightly
older girl with sexual assault because, according to the law, a person under
the age of twelve cannot consent to sex, making the issue of whether force
had been used irrelevant. The Crown Attorney (prosecutor) had the dis-
cretion to drop the charges and explore other options such as counseling,
but did not, because of the pressure to prosecute and the power of criminal
discourses such as "getting tough on crime" and zero tolerance policies for
violence. What is the effect of such well-intentioned discourses, however,
that are indiscriminate in their responses to different social contexts and
differing subjectivities? Brenda Cossman, a law professor wrote about this
case in the Toronto gay and lesbian newspaper, *XTRA!:*

> These are ideas run amok destroying the life of a little girl who was
> experimenting with sexuality. Gay men and lesbians should be very
> worried about this little girl and not only because it involves same-
> sex experimentation. We should be worried because it involves the
> criminalization of sexual experimentation, period (never mind the
> fact that it also criminalizes sexual experimentation between kids of
> the same age). The message sent to these kids is not only that there's
> something wrong with them, but that they might end up in jail.[37]

Here, we see that age-of-consent legislation designed to protect children
from sexual abuse by adults is too simply applied to a context involving
sexual experimentation and homophobia among children of roughly the
same age. My concern is that the law and order agenda evident in services
responding to lesbian abuse leads to similarly harmful outcomes that end

up regulating and further oppressing lesbians. For example, Canadian feminists pressed for a zero-tolerance policy on domestic abuse to counteract the widespread failure of police to make arrests in cases of domestic violence, leaving women at risk. The policy is not working as intended. Police responding to incidents of lesbian domestic violence often charge both members of a couple, either because they only see a fight between roommates when two women are involved (as described in Chapter 4), or because under a zero-tolerance policy anyone who uses violence (regardless of whether it is in self-defense) must be charged, with the Crown Attorney then determining how to proceed. Like the example of the prosecutor's response to the twelve-year-old girl, this one is not only about the limits of the criminal justice system; rather it shows the ethical dangers of letting policies guide our actions without stepping back to consider the assumptions on which they were based.

In another related example, a transgendered woman, Kimberly Nixon, recently filed a human rights complaint against Rape Relief, an organization in Vancouver, British Columbia, that is a woman-only space offering counseling and advocacy services to women who have been sexually assaulted.[38] Nixon had been taking the volunteer training program, and hoped to help other women because she herself had been in an abusive relationship and received assistance from a crisis center. Halfway through the volunteer training, a Rape Relief worker asked her if she was woman. Nixon explained that she was born male, had sex reassignment surgery, was now legally and medically a woman, and had lived as a woman for fourteen years. She was told that only women-born-women could work there and was asked to leave.[39] This case is not unique. Jacqueline Anderson has written about a similar discrimination complaint made against the women-born-women-only policy of Chicago's Mountain Moving Coffee House[40] and the Michigan Womyn's Music Festival has also been challenged for its women-born-women-only policy. The policy of having women-only spaces in services such as shelters and rape crisis centers is based on an important principle of safety implemented to ensure that women who had recently been victimized by men could feel comfortable. Yet, we have to ask safety for whom, given that women do sexually assault other women, if not in the same numbers as men. But even more disturbing is the assumption that Nixon would be unable to sympathize with victims of violence in counseling because she did not grow up female. They end up implying that all women-born-women are socialized in the same way and would make good, empathetic counselors; no transgendered women could. This logic reflects an investment in maintaining an essentialized, universal category of woman to preserve their unquestioned assumption of safety in women-only spaces. Most other rape crisis centers have taken a very different stance, arguing that the women's movement blatantly discriminates against transgendered women now the way it did against lesbians twenty-five years ago. I use this example to again reveal the potential limits of well-intentioned policies, such as women-only or victim-only mandates, that may be inappropriate and even discriminatory in different situations and contexts. Policy development is admittedly difficult; the challenge is to keep ethical dilemmas such as these at the forefront of our struggles.

In fact, in our political struggles to develop helpful responses to relationship violence I do think we have to bring forward what we might think of as an ethics of response, one that recognizes multiplicity and the limits of our insights into others lives'. This ethical stance would help us to move away from the moral and regulating stance that is embedded within systems such as social services and criminal justice where we, in effect, end up making judgments about who is deserving and undeserving of services. An ethics of response would be a self-reflexive one where we remain aware of who is let inside and left outside social services mandates, the naming of issues, and the setting of policies. That doesn't mean we should abandon women-only services or gay and lesbian organizations when addressing violence or other issues; nor does it mean that we should stop recognizing when someone has been victimized or stop calling abusive behaviors abusive. But we do need to consider more explicitly the effects of our exclusionary practices, showing how we are located and invested in them while letting others scrutinize, critique, and consider our efforts. For me this kind of querying (which I explore further in chapter 7) is a feminist ethical stance that can help us in our political struggles to name issues like lesbian partner abuse and develop helpful responses. It is a great but necessary challenge to imagine working from a place of multiplicity where we consider the particular people involved, the varied social spaces in which violence occurs and the need for diverse responses. Engaged and interlocked within systems that not only judge but assume homogeneous subjects with interests that can be met and justice served, we perhaps cannot even imagine or practice this ethic. But it is our ethical obligation to try—knowing what we do about the homogenizing, normalizing, and exclusionary effects of our current practices.

In this chapter I have explored the processes of institutionalization that make it difficult to struggle with the complexities and contextual differences so vital to the stories of women that I interviewed who had experienced relationship violence. In describing the politics and practices of organizations responding to lesbian abuse, we can begin to see why "regimes of truth" about domestic violence are so hard to disrupt even with many service providers and activists engaging in innovative responses. In the discursive tale, I have applied a critical, deconstructive lens to view our struggles with language and our efforts to build effective responses. I have tried to push the limits of understandings available to us, and have myself been pushed by the feminist service providers that I interviewed and with whom I share a concern with being responsive and responsible in our work. I turn now to the final chapter, part of a reflexive tale that summarizes the themes and issues I have stressed in this volume: I also suggest ways we might move forward and continue bearing witness to women's experiences of violence while keeping a critical reflexive examination of how we hear and respond to what we have witnessed.

A REFLEXIVE TALE

raising questions

SEVEN
Looking Forward

BECAUSE IN ANALYZING the interviews in an effort to understand women's stories, I have been continually struck by the diversity of women's experiences and by the difference that context makes to the dynamics of relationship violence, this has ended up being a book about problems with our categories. Our key categories—power and control, victim/perpetrator, domestic violence, trauma—just cannot capture either the range of contexts or their complexity. Although no concept can be expected to capture all of the details of a particular situation, these have been mobilized and institutionalized throughout lesbian, feminist, and social service communities in damaging ways. Sometimes the categories just do not fit the stories that women tell us when they first arrive at our offices and support groups, so we get women to retell their stories until they do fit, or we send them away; when the categories do fit, they often get mapped onto a situation in such a way that they obscure equally important factors.

One of the last interviews that I completed in this study involved both members of a couple, whom I interviewed separately. Blair and Jamie were two young, white, middle-class women, both graduate students, who had been in a relationship for three years. In that time, there were six or seven episodes in which Jamie would go into yelling rages, sometimes destroying objects, and on a couple of occasions biting, punching, and throwing water at Blair. One of the most hurtful things for Blair was finding out that Jamie had had a seven-month affair. Learning about the "lies and the elaborate structure of dishonesty" caused her the most pain, because the affair seemed more deliberate than Jamie's other actions. Blair described her reaction to Jamie's outbursts of anger in the following way:

B: My reaction was always to just leave, to get out of the house.

JR: Were you afraid of her?

B: It's funny, I'm not really afraid of her. It's not fear. It just feels like waiting for this moment to pass. Because I know it's not like that. Maybe it's the power dynamic between the two of us. It's never been about her trying to inspire fear in me. It's lashing out, it's a lashing out of sorts.

(Blair, interview #91)

Blair was clear that she did not like Jamie's actions, and does not think she in any way deserves the abuse. In fact, she sees many sides to Jamie, including being caring and fun, being depressed and in emotional pain, and being manipulative. All of these factors have made it difficult for Blair to leave Jamie because she sees the situation as complicated. For example:

B: I think it's complicated in that Jamie clearly has abusive behavior, but I don't see her as fitting the profile of "an abuser."

JR: Which is what for you? Just to make sure that I understand.

B: Well the wife beater who never lets his wife have any money or any access to the outside, sort of constantly isolating that person and just inspiring terror in somebody. Maybe that is a caricature but that is the image we have inherited.

JR: You're not isolated, you're not living in terror?

B: No, no. It gets complicated because when she is in these fits of anger or rage, there's no question she has the power. Just because I'm not trying to engage her, and there's nothing I can do when she throws a glass of water at me. I'm not going to go get one and throw it back. And yet in the relationship, in general, I probably still have a great deal of power.

JR: So you see the abuse as angry outbursts but not necessarily meant to hurt and control.

B: I don't think that is what drives it. I think the effects can be malicious but I do not think it is malicious in motivation.

(Blair, interview #91)

Her story is important because it reminds us that some abusive relationships do not have to include the victim feeling afraid and being controlled. Perhaps some readers will wonder if Blair is deceiving herself and protecting Jamie in this account of her story. But such a dismissal is a refusal to

hear the challenge that her story brings to the dominant feminist understanding of abuse. It may be that Blair is not afraid because she is larger
and stronger than Jamie, or perhaps she is influenced by dominant constructions of femininity that do not acknowledge women's capacity for violence, and thereby cause less fear. In my reflection notes, I am struck by
how their story challenged me:

> It's a very different dynamic that I don't know what to do with.
> Both of them said there were six or seven episodes where Jamie was
> acting angry and in out-of-control ways. Those behaviors were abu-
> sive yet the overall dynamic is not where there is fear or deliberate
> control and manipulation. I don't know why I feel like I'm strug-
> gling with this one and want to say that this is something else?
>
> (JR's notes on interview)

Further, unlike many abusers, Jamie did not try to put responsibility for
her actions onto Blair. She was seeing a therapist to address her anger, but
she felt therapists often minimized her behaviors and treated her as a victim because her father had verbally abused her when she was a child. She
spoke to me about how she understood her abusive behaviors:

> When I do those things it is protecting this whatever it is inside me
> that feels hurt. I feel hurt for some ridiculous reason, something in-
> significant that was said or that does not seem significant at the time
> and then I get angry and lash out. After I see Blair crying (and she
> doesn't cry very often) then at this point I think I do not feel the way
> normal people do. Because I don't think I have the same kind of grief
> or the same kind of sorrow or regret that a person should in those sit-
> uations. But I know enough to know that what I've done is really aw-
> ful and I know she is suffering and I do not want to see her suffer.
>
> (Jamie, interview #93)

As Blair said, Jamie's story does not convey the "profile of an abuser."
Therapists might argue that I spoke to Jamie for only a couple of hours,
whereas in a therapeutic context, in which you work with someone over
the course of weeks or months, you eventually are able to see not only who
is the abuser and who is the victim, but that the abuser is exercising power
and control and causing fear and isolation in the victim. In some initially
confusing situations, that might, indeed, turn out to be the real story, but

we have to acknowledge that in a context dominated by power and control discourse it is the only story allowed. It is a story that is scripted from the moment the counseling relationship begins. And it is a story that flies in the face of a great many women's experiences.

I think about Leita's story, for example, a white, forty-seven-year-old woman who was in the military, was closeted and isolated, lived in a small, rural town, and was in her first relationship with another woman who was a drug user and often physically violent. She described one of the last violent incidents before she fled the relationship:

> She slapped me and I said, "I wouldn't do that if I were you." And she says, "Fuck you" and she hit me again. And I said, "I'm telling you one more time do not hit me. I'm not going to take this, I've taken a lot of shit and abuse from you." You know, it was on and off for two and a half years. At that point she grabbed me around the neck and ripped my chains off and I just lost it. I literally picked her up with one hand and put my hand around her throat and put her up and against the wall and thought "I'm going to fucking kill you—you've caused me nothing but pain, grief and heartache, and financial, emotional and physical hardship." Somebody was looking after me, an angel was looking after me because I would have killed her. She went unconscious and that was like a dose of reality.
>
> (Leita, interview #84)

Her story reminds us that many women experience abuse in the context of a first lesbian relationship, in small rural areas, where they are extremely isolated. It also reminds us that women fight back, and then sometimes struggle with their anger and their own abusive behaviors in their next relationships. I think of other women who spoke of being raped by their partners and their strong feelings of shame and shock that came from being violated by another woman. I think of other women who described many different forms of emotional abuse revealing a wide range of experiences submerged within the category. Women described partners who threatened to commit suicide, or used homophobic threats to control them; a few spoke of women who lied about having an illness such as cancer; and others told of being stalked and terrorized by their partners or of having their sleep constantly interrupted. I think of women who have lived lives in which violence has been normalized, showing us the limits of a narrow focus on domestic, private violence: for example, Ruth, a two-spirited woman who understood her relationship violence as occurring within a larger social and historical context that included colonization, racism, and sexual abuse. As she said, "we are so inundated with violence we become normalized to it" (interview #61). Or Barb (interview #76), a homeless woman who spoke of the relative safety she and her physically abusive, cocaine-addicted partner found together, compared with the violence on the streets. And I am reminded of Charlene (interview #92), who dismissed the racist behavior of her white partner, reminding us of the dangers of defining violence based on white women's experiences that then limits our abilities to see certain forms of violence. These powerfully different stories of violence speak to the limits of relying on one all-explanatory power and control model, with its supporting binary constructions of victim/perpetrator, innocent/evil, private/public.

Some research on heterosexual relationship violence has suggested that there are different forms and patterns, a continuum of relationship violence depending on whether we look at samples from the general population ("common couple violence") or at clinical samples that are likely more extreme cases ("patriarchal terrorism").[1] This study has suggested that there are different contexts in which relationship violence emerges, such as within first relationships, where the larger conditions of heterosexism create social vulnerabilities for women who are negotiating marginalized sexual identities. Relationship violence also emerges in contexts in which violence has been normalized, including contexts of previous histories of abuse, something more likely to affect the relational dynamic between two women given the statistics that show women's greater rates of sexual victimization by men. I also brought forward examples of differing power dynamics in abusive relationships; some of them more clearly reflect the power and control model, whereas others show that power dynamics shift and fluctuate between two women and that fighting back can include self-defense as well as revenge. Finally, this study has shown the complexity of responses to violence that can include anger, shame, depression, and suicide, but also both active and passive coping behaviors.

In enumerating these trends that emerged from my interviews with women, I am not proposing a new typology for domestic abuse. As I argued in Chapter 3, I believe we need to move away from either/or categories or static models, stressing instead the need for more contextualized, multiple, and multifaceted understandings. This does not mean that I endorse a liberal humanistic framework, in which I see the diverse experiences of women as simply a reflection of individual differences without political significance. Feminist theorizing has important insights for understanding relationship violence in connection with oppressive social arrangements of gender, race, and class that illuminate specific contexts and power dynamics. As many feminist service providers that I spoke with agree, we can still work within a feminist analysis as long as we resist the ossifying tendencies of any discourse to become a regime of truth for those who participate in it. As one service provider said:

> We have to be very cautious and always remember that theory is just that, it's theory, it's not totally real. It's a way of trying to understand things and to be open to other ways of trying to understand things and gain new perspectives based on what we hear coming toward us. I would have had a different response five years ago, ten years ago, fifteen years ago and hopefully five years from now.
>
> (Focus group #6)

Yet this study has shown how difficult it can be to "gain new perspectives based on what we hear coming toward us," and how we become invested in our understandings, setting normative standards that make it difficult to bring forward counterdiscourses, and thereby erasing and excluding many women's experiences of abuse. Our investments also serve to support the institutionalized systems that have developed to respond to domestic violence, and that allow lesbian abuse to be slipped in, though in highly problematic ways.

Our biggest challenge is to see and respond to violence in lesbian relationships on its own terms—that is, as violence involving two women (with all the constructions of femininity and lesbianism at play) within a larger context that still renders sexual relationships between women invisible, and throughout which circulate the differing social and personal effects of heterosexism, racism, sexism, and classism on relationships and on women's subjectivities. We need to understand those spaces, how power circulates through them, between them, and around them, and not just focus on how the effects of abuse are all the same. Lesbian is itself a problematic, socially constructed category that excludes how many women self-identify; however, within dominant culture it is how women-loving-women are read: it is the space that we occupy. I believe we need to keep a specific focus (not a simple one) on the category of lesbian relationship violence, so that we continue to examine the surrounding relations of heteronormativity, and the different way lesbian subjects are gendered, racialized, and classed.

In examining lesbian partner abuse, a feminist postmodern analysis has guided my interweaving of the material, the discursive, and the reflexive components. I have provided a broad overview that includes listening to women's voices, exposing and deconstructing the assumptions in domestic violence language, and reflecting on the politics and processes of institutionalization that shape our responses and understandings. In many ways, this exploratory research raises more questions than it provides answers. For example, we need research that continues to explore the contexts of lesbian relationship violence and power dynamics as relational; we need research that includes the experiences of transgendered women; we need research that examines the contexts, motivations, and intentions of lesbians who are abusive; we need research that considers the public and private forms of violence that many lesbians experience; we need to consider the social consequences of lesbian relationship violence; and we need to evaluate the service delivery models that have become institutionalized within feminist services. I believe that to do any of these things well, we must take an ethical and political stance in our work that requires us to address the gaps and contradictions in our feminist theorizing of relationship violence, and to grapple with the complexities and multiplicity of women's lives.

Critically reflexive questions can help turn our efforts in research, in service provision, and in marginalized communities from striving toward ultimate explanatory models and making simple truth claims into a quest for deeper understandings and responses. We need to continually ask:

- Who benefits from the way we talk about lesbian relationship violence? What difference does this make?
- Who is telling the story and from what social location?
- Whose voices are and are not heard when we tell the story using the category lesbian violence?
- How else can this story be told? What difference would that make?

These questions can help make us more accountable, not only because they acknowledge our limited and partial perspectives, but because they provoke us to imagine what we do not understand. Although the focus of this volume has been on the particularities of abuse in lesbian relationships, critical questions such as these need to be raised about understandings of abuse in heterosexual and gay male relationships, and about our responses to domestic violence of all kinds.

Imagining Communities' Responses

Beyond these questions, I am aware of the need for a variety of responses and interventions that do not fit the current arrangements within services and their victim-only mandates. I think about the women that I spoke to who were far more likely to turn to friends than to formal services, often because of concerns about homophobia and racism, worries over confidentiality and trust, and heterosexist messages suggesting that they do not fit the existing services. We need, therefore, to develop many community-based innovations, similar to some of those described in Chapter 6, that consider relationship violence an issue facing communities, rather than an individual problem. One example we might be able to look to are those responses that have been developed within Indigenous communities. For example, the Community Holistic Healing Circle Program was developed in an Ojibway community to address childhood sexual abuse and the resulting problems of substance abuse, suicide, vandalism, and distress among youth that was devastating their small community of about 600 people.[2] This approach was developed as an alternative to a criminal justice system response where Aboriginal people most often encounter racism, and where offenders return to their communities in deeply damaged states. It involves a high level of commitment from volunteer community members and professionals (including representatives from schools and religious groups, a child protection worker, a community nurse, and representative of the Royal Canadian Mounted Police). The team works with victims and others affected by the actions of the offender, and together design a healing contract. An offender is required to make certain changes outlined in the contract and can be redirected to the criminal justice system for failure to do so. Personalized sharing sessions often confront and address an abuser's denial, manipulation, anger, and guilt, while also supporting them in upholding the contract. After successful completion of the healing process, a cleansing ceremony is held to honor the offender and mark a new beginning. As Anne McGillivray and Brenda Comaskey state, "the 'boundedness' of the community in terms of culture and geography, the intensive holistic approach, and the high degree of community commitment to the project" are what make it successful in combating the sexual abuse of children.[3] Lesbian communities, of course, are not bound in the same ways by culture, and are very diverse, yet this approach offers some insight into how we might work with lesbians who are abusive in a way that demands accountability, while also acknowledging that being abusive is not the sum of someone's identity, and that decent people can do awful things.

Similarly, we might follow the principles of Family Group Conferencing for Family Violence first developed in New Zealand within Maori communities and now being used in parts of Canada and the United States.[4] This approach is designed to work outside social service and legal responses, and to have friends and family members involved in resolving the abuse. A key assumption is that a family can develop a plan that fits its culture and situation. Abusers are held accountable, and the needs of the victim are at the forefront of this approach. Although operating on the victim/perpetrator binary, this model recognizes that many victims and perpetrators alike within Indigenous communities are recovering from the pain of past abuse and the whole "family should be invited to become partners in stopping the violence."[5] A project coordinator works to investigate and assess the situation to see if it is appropriate, and then meets with all the potential participants to determine who should be included or if anyone should be excluded from the conference. Like the Community Holistic Healing Circle Program, the family comes up with a plan that is presented to the project coordinator, who also works with community members and professionals to ensure that the plan can be monitored, and that it includes all of the necessary protective and caring measures. Perhaps an approach such as this could be adapted for those contexts in which both members of a lesbian couple have experienced a lifetime of abuse. These approaches cannot simply be appropriated for use within lesbian communities, but they can serve as examples of alternative routes we might explore. Community is very important to many lesbians, where we talk about our chosen family, and often have strong support networks that include ex-lovers as dear friends. This context might make this approach more feasible within lesbian communities. Further, the approach would break down the barriers of privacy that surround relationships and that keep individuals from intervening even when they know their friends are in trouble.

Mediation is another alternative, more appropriate for less extreme forms of relationship violence, or for those dynamics of emotional abuse in which a couple feels locked into a pattern that they want to get out of. Mediation may also help couples to end their relationships in more equitable ways. Feminists in the battered women's movement have long been critical of this approach as not clearly holding batterers accountable, and as implying that both parties are equally responsible. However, for some forms of relationship violence, it can offer lesbians a useful informal intervention that works within the community when formal legal avenues are unwanted or inappropriate. Volunteers or friends can be trained in mediation, guidelines can be established that outline clear parameters concerning when to use this approach, and each person can bring a friend to the mediation sessions, not as an advocate for innocence, but as a way to help build ongoing support networks for each person.

More initiatives can be undertaken that continue to educate communities about relationship violence. For example, there may be ways of reducing violence in first relationships by having educational campaigns and coming-out literature that specifically address this context. Materials could be developed for women who are just coming out that dispute harmful, limiting stereotypes of lesbian relationships, define healthy relationships, and identify some troubling warning signs of abusiveness of which they should be aware. Many young women (and women newly out of relationships that have ended, and women who have moved from other cities and countries) often still need supportive environments in which they can more easily meet and socialize with other lesbians. In focus group discussions, we also spoke of the need for developing a language to talk about our experiences as lesbians, and as lesbians in relationships—a challenge that might be undertaken at a grass-roots level. We also need to talk about resistance, survival, and triumphs, both within abusive relationships and within an oppressive society. These efforts can help us to mobilize grass-roots responses that consider abuse a community issue rather than an individual problem.

Finally, within communities, it remains important to keep our efforts to respond to relationship violence aligned with the broader struggles of combating racism, heterosexism, sexism, and classism—all systems of oppression that confine women to hellish situations and make abusive behavior more likely.

Imagining Social Services Responses

In addition to community responses, we need services that can offer a flexible range of programs that acknowledges different contexts and types of relationship violence, and therefore different responses to it. These could include couple counseling; programs for perpetrators, for victims, and for women who fit neither or both categories; support groups that address a range of violences in women's lives; outreach efforts that might reflect a harm-reduction approach, or other approaches more responsive to local communities; or preventive efforts, such as building healthy relationships. Organizations also need to make explicit the assumptions and analyses that inform their work, so that women seeking services can make more informed choices about where they might go. One service agency is, of course, unlikely to be able to offer all things to all lesbians, but we can develop more coordinated efforts between services, for example, that help reduce the false divisions between sexual assault and domestic violence. In smaller centers, we can also establish links between formal and informal groups to at least ensure referrals to nonhomophobic service providers. In addition to changing "victim-only" mandates, services need to acknowledge and respond to the layers of power that operate within agencies and between women to help us to get out of established dichotomies into greater conceptual complexity. Sherene Razack calls for a politics of accountability rather than a politics of inclusion in her writings about gender, race, and culture in education and law. Those services that include lesbians and respond to lesbian abuse would also benefit from a politics of accountability along with an ethics of response (as described in Chapter 6) that "begins with tracing relations of privilege and penalty. Only then can we ask questions about how we are understanding differences and for what purpose."[6] Programs, policies, and training on homophobia, racism, and others forms of oppression have to be firmly in place within any service that is addressing lesbian partner violence.

Adopting a stronger social constructionist and narrative approach in counseling is also something that can help us to get out of problematic binaries. Rather than using the terms victim/survivor and perpetrator/abuser, which reinforce the idea that these are stable identity categories, we could talk instead about women who use abusive behaviors and women who have experienced abuse. Feminist theories have long been critical of seeing mental health disorders and pathologies as ways of defining people. They have been clear in articulating the view that diagnostic categories, although sometimes convenient, are socially constructed and that categories can be harmful if they establish normative assumptions about human behavior.[7] Yet it seems we have lost this critical stance when responding to lesbian relationship violence. Therapists who are engaging in postmodern approaches, for example, are trying to acknowledge multiplicity and subjectivities, rather than stressing a core self. Often, counseling sessions bring in other voices as a way of helping to generate multiple realities for someone. In support groups when someone speaks, other people in the group may be asked to listen to their story from different perspectives, such as the ex-girlfriend, the best friend, the mother. They then are asked to voice their understanding of the individual's situation from the perspective from which they were listening. This helps to "open avenues for self-reflexivity and options for action."[8] Similarly, counselors can be thinking about how they are responding to women's stories, so that they can resist scripted, expected encounters, and move toward more transformative dialogue. These approaches do not minimize the realities of relationship violence, but include an awareness of the discursive level of counseling work in order to disrupt limiting prescriptive practices.

Clearly, there are many things that we can do within services and within communities to respond, intervene, and even prevent lesbian relationship violence in ways that do not enforce sameness, and that acknowledge the differing contexts of women's experiences of violence. At the same time, we are still confronted with barriers such as funding cuts, a backlash against feminist services, and societal homophobia. Geographic locations that are small or rural may be unable to start or even imagine any broader-scale initiatives. Often, the most we can hope for is committed individual efforts.

In 1998, Laurie, Donna, and I ended our resource booklet on lesbian relationship violence by saying, "We have only begun to scratch the surface of a complex and deep-seated issue" in our preliminary research.[9] I hope this study, involving 102 interviews with women who have experienced abuse, and eighty feminist service providers responding to this form of violence, has been able to offer a deeper understanding. I want to end by offering some information for lesbians who are experiencing abuse within their relationships, and some guidelines for service providers and friends who wish to respond to abuse. I am rewriting some of the information that was in our booklet and incorporating some of the understandings that my research has brought forward.[10] Although these guidelines are still limited and partial, I try to show how we might resist reproducing the homogenizing narratives that I described in Chapter 6, while also addressing, on a more individual level, a response to the question, "What can we do to respond to lesbian relationship violence?"

If You Are in an Abusive Intimate Relationship with another Woman . . .

You might identify as lesbian, queer, dyke, bisexual, gay, trans, two-spirited, or you might not use any of these terms to describe yourself.

There are many different forms that violence in relationships can take. Abusive experiences can include

- being hit, punched, slapped, shoved, restrained, choked; having weapons used against you;

- being raped, being forced to have sex against your will, being criticized and made to feel uncomfortable during sex;
- yelling rages, constant screaming, verbal put downs, humiliation, racist attacks;
- being stalked, terrorized, having your sleep constantly interrupted;
- hearing threats to harm you or your children or pets; threats to "out" you; threats to your immigration status; threats to use weapons; threats to commit suicide; threats to kill you—some women have been killed by their partners;
- destroying your property, throwing objects, controlling finances, creating debt, being lied to and manipulated.

You may have experienced some, many, or all of these different forms of violence. You may have experienced something not included in these lists.

Sometimes there is a pattern to abusive behaviors and you can almost predict when your partner will attack you, but this is not true of every situation. Sometimes the abuse gets worse over time or becomes more and more frequent. Sometimes the incidents are infrequent. Sometimes the dynamics remain constant. Things may feel confusing if your partner is always blaming you and telling you that you are abusive, when that does not seem to be the case. The dynamics in the relationship can also feel confusing if both of you are physically fighting, and if you are fairly evenly matched in terms of size and strength. Physical fighting can include defending yourself, or an intention to hurt your partner; sometimes it can include both. Often one person in the relationship will be directing more abusive behaviors toward her partner. Sometimes the dynamics can change where one person who was being abused gains the upper hand and is now abusing. Some women who have been abused in one relationship may go on to another relationship in which they become abusive. In some relationships, one person may be more physically abusive and another person more verbally and emotionally abusive. If you are both emotionally abusive, you may feel stuck in an ugly pattern in which you are constantly hurting and triggering each other. All of these situations are abusive.

Sometimes people think that certain groups or certain types of lesbians are more likely to abuse or be abused. These kinds of stereotypes (for example, about butch and femme women, or about women of color) can be inaccurate and very harmful.

Violence can also occur in different contexts. You may be in your first relationship with another woman and are isolated and worried that you will not meet anyone else. You may have moved from another city or country, and do not have any support networks. You and your partner may be using drugs and alcohol, which can sometimes increase physical violence and affect your perceptions of the abuse. If you have a history of violence (including childhood sexual abuse, rape, being the victim of a hate crime), violence in the relationship can feel familiar, almost normal, even though it is not.

You need to evaluate your relationship and ask yourself some questions, such as:

Am I being physically, sexually, or emotionally threatened or abused?

Are my thoughts, movements, and actions being negatively affected or controlled by my partner?

Am I disturbed, distressed, and anxious about how I am being treated in the relationship?

Am I isolated? Do I feel hopeless and helpless? Or am I afraid?

Answering "yes" to any of these questions means you need to gain some perspective on what is happening to you in your relationship. You need to think about your own internal signals that may also alert you to physical danger. If you fear for your safety, leave the situation. Go to the nearest safe place or call a friend. If you are in physical danger, you may want to keep a bag packed with money, identification cards, house keys, and clothing. Tell someone what is happening to you. It can be a friend, a family member, a neighbor, a service provider—someone you think will be supportive of you. If you are being abused you may feel a range of effects including shame, anger, self-blame, shock that another woman was abusive, depression, suicidal thoughts, low self-esteem, numbness, and confusion. It is important that you try to get some support.

You also need to ask yourself if you are physically, sexually, or emotionally threatening and/or abusive. You might consider the following questions:

Am I trying to control my partner, keep her to myself?

Am I constantly lashing out at her and hurting her?

Am I threatening my partner or trying to punish her?

Am I always finding fault with her, asking her to change her behaviors, to do things to please me?

Am I blaming my partner for my actions?

Do I feel out of control and in danger of hurting my partner or myself?

Answering "yes" to any of these questions is cause for concern. Take responsibility and accountability for your actions. Sometimes your actions may be intentional, and other times they may not, but they can still cause harm and there is no excuse for them, even if you too have been abused by her or someone else. Do not blame your partner but, instead, stop your behaviors. Leave the situation or the relationship, if necessary, to stop your abusive behaviors. You are likely experiencing a combination of feelings including anger, pain, anxiety, vulnerability, and fear. You will need the support of friends and possibly the help of a counselor to help you stop engaging in abusive behaviors.

If the dynamics feel more confusing, you may both need to go and get some support to help you figure out and stop the abusive dynamics. You may also each need some time alone or with friends to assess the situation. Your relationship might need to end. If you hope to preserve it, the abusive behaviors need to stop to enable you to rebuild a trusting, healthy relationship dynamic.

Sometimes your relationship, even though abusive, is better than other aspects of your life in which you also encounter violence. Think about things you might be able to do to reduce your chances of being seriously harmed. Think about places that you can go to for some peace, safety, and time alone. Try to find a supportive person that you can talk to.

Remember: We all want violence-free relationships. There are different forms of abuse, and different types of violent relationships, but they have this in common: the abusive dynamics need to stop. You cannot control or change your partner's behaviors; you can only be in control of your own actions. The person engaging in abusive behaviors is the only one who can stop these behaviors.

Getting Help

Getting help can be difficult depending on where you live, what resources are available, and your own financial resources. It likely requires you to come out as being in a lesbian relationship. Friends and family members can be supportive, or can react in ways that are homophobic, or that deny and minimize your experiences. For example, some friends may say that they do not want to choose sides in your relationship or get involved in your private issue. If you encounter negative reactions, keep trying until you find someone who will listen and support you. There are also some self-help books available on violence in relationships that include specific information for lesbians as well as some website resources. You are not alone in your experiences. Sometimes writing in a journal can help you to clarify your thoughts and feelings about what is happening.

You can find out about available resources in your community by contacting women's groups, gay and lesbian organizations, and domestic violence services. In some communities women of color have found help through Aboriginal organizations, AIDS organizations for people of color, and other multicultural organizations. Community resources such as these might include free services that you can access such as crisis counseling lines, support groups for lesbians and/or women who have been abused, shelters, as well as counseling, peer counseling and addiction programs. Fewer programs exist for women who are abusive in lesbian relationships, but there may be more general anger management programs that can be helpful. Ask services about their policies on confidentiality before you reveal your identity. Ask if they have had experience in working with lesbians and/or same-sex relationship violence. Unfortunately, social services can also be homophobic and racist in their responses. Many women have had more positive experiences in seeking the help of a counselor. There are often feminist and lesbian counselors who can offer support, and who will have a sliding-scale fee for women with fewer financial resources.

You may also need to call the police in some situations. They can and should be helpful in cases involving physical and sexual assaults and threats. However, sometimes the police can be unhelpful and wrongly assess the situation and/or be homophobic and/or racist in their responses, particularly in cities in which they have not received any antihomophobia, antiracism training. If you are concerned for your safety or your life, call the police.

Overall, seeking support from someone else helps reduce your isolation and provides other perspectives about your situation so that you can get some clarity and make some decisions about your relationship.

How Friends Can Help

If a friend who is being abused comes to you for help, you can listen to her and let her talk about what has happened. Do not offer excuses for the violence or minimize what has happened. If you suspect that a friend is being abused, express your concern and offer to help. Many women who have been abused may initially deny the abuse but will later re-member the supportive comment of their friend, which helps them immeasurably. If you think someone is being abusive, tell them that their behavior is unacceptable and work with them to get help and change their actions even though it may be hard and your friend may be angry with you for confronting her.

If you are worried about taking sides because you know both women who are in-volved, or because you are unsure of the dynamics in the relationship, think about ways that you can still offer each of them some assistance in finding resources and other peo-ple to talk to. Some abusive relationship dynamics really are muddled. Don't feel that you have to decide who is the victim or who is the abuser. Offering some support is better than offering no support at all. This can include helping a woman to find housing or a safe place to stay, referring her to a counselor, loaning her money, going with her to the police, or calling the police. Offer her opportunities to break her isolation and connect with oth-ers. Be clear about what you can and cannot offer.

Be respectful and supportive of women's decisions even when they might not be the ones that you would make, unless the decisions are harmful or dangerous. Examine your own responses, assumptions, and feelings. If you are a lesbian, this can be a difficult is-sue to face. You may want to explain it away rather than acknowledge that violence does happen in lesbian relationships. If you are not a lesbian, examine any stereotypes you may hold about lesbians and other marginalized sexual identities and try very hard not to let them affect your support.

Some people have become dismissive of abuse because words such as abuse, vio-lence, and battering have been used too loosely to describe every conceivable situation in which someone has been disappointed or hurt or has encountered meanness or rudeness.

Overusing these words trivializes the meaning of the terrible situation they describe, but if you think your friend is being abused or mistreated take it seriously.

How Service Providers Can Respond

Before doing this work, it is important to have done your own antioppression work so that you can scrutinize your own responses and change those that are based on stereotypes and ignorance. Be aware of the language that women use to describe themselves (lesbian, gay, two-spirited, bisexual, trans, queer, dyke). Some women may feel they are just in love with another woman, and will not identify with lesbian communities. Some women's primary identification may be racial or ethnic rather than focused on sexuality. Make sure that you have posters, brochures, and materials in your workplace that convey an open and accepting environment. Provide a woman with information about your confidentiality practices. If you are a lesbian, a woman may need even more reassurances about how you will maintain confidentiality. It is equally important for you to be open to hear the stories that women tell you that might challenge your feminist understandings of domestic violence. Think about your definitions of violence and make sure they do not privilege white, middle-class women's experiences. For example, challenge your perceptions of what a victim looks like. Also be aware that dichotomies of victim/perpetrator, with their underlying assumptions of innocence/evil and femaleness/maleness, can be very limiting and inaccurate when they mask or minimize harmful relational dynamics that need to be examined. For example, don't let the identification of abuse within an interracial relationship serve racist purposes by minimizing the racist comments that a white woman makes when describing the abusive behavior of her partner who is a woman of color. Similarly be aware that women may need to learn more about each other's cultural backgrounds and perhaps also about stereotypes. For example, a woman may feel threatened by a raised, excited voice that is part of a cultural norm for the other woman but not for her. You may find it helpful to read existing research, although most studies have focused on the experiences of white, middle-class lesbians. Overall, remember that we do not know all there is to know about lesbian relationship violence.

It is important that you begin where the woman is, or even where the couple is to begin to assess the relationship's dynamics. Be aware of the differing contexts that allow violence to take hold and give it structure in a relationship. Be aware of the differing dynamics that can exist between two women where, for example, fear may or may not be part of an abused woman's experience. Making a thorough and careful assessment may take a long time, but is crucial for determining the best course of action. It is important not to assume that power dynamics in a same-sex relationsip are mutual just because the dynamics are complex. For example, many women who have been victimized also fight back and have strong feelings of anger. This context has to be addressed along with their feelings of self-blame and guilt. Sometimes (though not if one woman is placed at greater risk or silenced), couple counseling might be appropriate, for example, for two women with histories of sexual abuse who are triggering each other in a mesh of emotional abuse. Be willing to work with both women's abusive behaviors as well as women's victimization. Women who are abusive often have the fewest resources and perhaps the most to gain from counseling. Some women have had the experience of being abused in one relationship and abusive in the next. Other women have had a lifetime of violence and may need to know that they are not to blame for it, that there is nothing wrong with them or with being a lesbian, but that they are responsible for stopping their own violent actions. Be willing to address the complex interplay between women's experiences of public and private forms of violence. Acknowledge the risks that women in lesbian relationships are taking in coming forward to receive help. For example, a lesbian of color who has experienced societal racism may feel very conflicted over betraying her partner of color to a white counselor and talking about the violence within her relationship.

Sexual assault and sexual coercion are not uncommon forms of abuse that lesbians experience, but they can be very hard for women to talk about. Make sure that you are comfortable in exploring this aspect of abuse. It is something you may have to ask about a few times in a number of different ways, because shame and self-blame often make women reluctant to discuss this. Make sure you are comfortable asking a variety of questions such as, has your partner ever forced you to have sex against your will? Have you ever felt sexually violated? Have you ever felt emotionally raped or sexually coerced? Acknowledge that this can be difficult to talk about. Be aware of the difference between consensual s/m sexual practices which are not abusive and non-consensual sex, which is. There is a diversity of language that women may use to describe their experiences of sexual assault or coercion and we need to be comfortable using that language and saying the words our clients use.

Establish supportive referral networks so that you can assist women in making connections with other services or with resources in lesbian or ethnic communities. For example, consulting with lesbian therapists or addiction counselors might be helpful in certain cases. It may be necessary to be more of an advocate for women and to have reliable contacts in shelters, with the police, and with lawyers. It is also important to understand the inherent racism and classism in these institutionalized systems and to forewarn and prepare women for this.

Talk with other service providers about this issue. Join or start a coalition or network of service providers. It can be very helpful to create spaces to talk about some of the issues and dilemmas in doing this work, as well as to share innovative approaches, insights, and new ideas as well as to develop plans for social action

Remember that violence in lesbian relationships is a political issue, in that it can be used against lesbians to support homophobic views that see our relationships as deviant and unhealthy. It is important, therefore, to be involved in and support all antioppressive efforts.

Looking Forward

I am grateful to the women who took the risk of breaking secrets by telling me their stories of lesbian relationship violence. I am grateful to the feminist service providers who struggled with me in conversations to break the analytical stranglehold of the dominant power and control discourse, and to painfully acknowledge the particulars of abuse in our own communities. Addressing violence in lesbian relationships is not easy, and much more work is necessary. We need to continue to think critically about how to engage in transformative work to disrupt the culture of violence; how to respond to and remember stories of relationship violence that are not our own. At the same time, we need to keep imagining a world without violence, in which secrets do not have to be kept, nor tragedies witnessed; a place in which lesbian relationships are affirmed, celebrated, and lived with dignity in all of their diversity. I look forward with hope.

NOTES

Preface: Bearing Witness

1. Dorothy Allison, foreword to *My Dangerous Desires*, by Amber H. Hollibaugh (Durham and London: Duke University Press, 2000), xv.

2. Roger I. Simon, "The Paradoxical Practice of Zakhor," in *Between Hope and Despair*, ed. Roger I. Simon, Sharon Rosenberg, and Claudia Eppert (Lanham, MD: Rowman and Littlefield Publishers, Inc., 2000), 18.

3. "No More Secrets," for example, was the title of several conferences held in Toronto, Ontario, organized by Natalie Zlodre, of Community Resources and Initiatives. See also Janice Haaken's book *Pillar of Salt: Gender, Memory, and the Perils of Looking Back* (London: Rutgers University Press, 1998), for her discussion of the incest survivors' movement in feminism.

4. Patti Lather and Chris Smithies, *Troubling the Angels* (Boulder, CO: Westview Press, 1997), footnote on xiv.

One: The Emergence of Lesbian Partner Abuse

1 Kerry Lobel, *Naming the Violence: Speaking Out About Lesbian Battering* (Seattle, WA: Seal Press, 1986), 7.

2 N. Boston, "Rise in Violence," *Gay Financial Network*, 2 November 1999; available from <http://gfn.com>; Internet, accessed 2 November 1999.

3 Lobel, *Naming the Violence*.

4 See Liz Kelly and Jill Radford, "Sexual Violence Against Women and Girls: An Approach to an International Overview," in *Rethinking Violence Against Women*, ed. Rebecca Emerson Dobash and Russell P. Dobash, vol. 9 of Sage Series on Violence Against Women (Thousand Oaks, CA: Sage Publications, 1998), 53–76; and Rebecca Emerson Dobash and Russell P. Dobash, "How Theoretical Definition and Perspectives Affect Research and Policy," in *Research and Public Policy Issues*, ed. Douglas J. Besharov (Washington, DC: AEI Press, 1990), 108–129.

5 Elizabeth L. Kennedy and Madeline D. Davis, *Boots of Leather, Slippers of Gold: The History of a Lesbian Community* (New York: Penguin Books, 1993).

6 Ellen Faulkner, "Woman-to-Woman Abuse: Analyzing Extant Accounts of Lesbian Battering," in *Unsettling Truths: Battered Women, Policy, Politics, and Con-*

temporary Research in Canada, ed. Kevin Bonnycastle and George S. Rigakos (Vancouver: Collective Press, 1998): 52–56.

7 See Barbara Hart, "Lesbian Battering: An Examination," in *Naming the Violence: Speaking Out Against Lesbian Battering*, ed. Kerry Lobel (Seattle, WA: Seal Press, 1986), 173–189; Lettie L. Lockhart and others, "Letting Out the Secret: Violence in Lesbian Relationships," *Journal of Interpersonal Violence* 9 (1994): 469–492; and Janice L. Ristock, "Beyond Ideologies: Understanding Violence in Lesbian Relationships," *Canadian Woman Studies* 12 (1991): 74–79

8 Janice L. Ristock, "'And Justice for All?'. . . The Social Context of Legal Responses to Abuse in Lesbian Relationships," *Canadian Journal of Women and the Law* 7 (1994): 415–430.

9 See Pam Elliott, ed., *Confronting Lesbian Battering: A Manual for the Battered Women's Movement* (St. Paul, MN: Minnesota Coalition for Battered Women, 1990); and Cindy Holmes, "The Politics of Naming the Violence: Examining Contradictions of 'Lesbian Abuse' in Community-Based Educational Discourses" (M.A. Thesis: Ontario Institute for Studies in Education, University of Toronto, 2000); Janice L. Ristock, "'And Justice.'"

10 Tonja Santos, "Woman-to-Woman Battering on College Campuses," *in Same-Sex Domestic Violence: Strategies for Change*, ed. Beth Leventhal and Sandra E. Lundy (Thousand Oaks, CA: Sage Publications, 1999), 147–156.

11 Liz Kelly, *Surviving Sexual Violence* (Minneapolis, MN: University of Minnesota Press, 1988); and Mary P. Koss and others, *No Safe Haven: Male Violence Against Women at Home, at Work, and in the Community* (Washington, DC: American Psychological Association, 1994).

12 See Patricia Hill Collins, *Black Feminist Thought: Knowledge, Consciousness, and the Politics of Empowerment* (Boston: Unwin Hyman, 1990); and Janice L. Ristock, "The Cultural Politics of Abuse in Lesbian Relationships: Challenges for Community Action," in *Subtle Sexism: Current Practice and Prospects for Change*, ed. Nijole Vaicraitis Benokraitis (Thousand Oaks, CA: Sage Publications, 1997), 279–296.

13 See Walter S. DeKeseredy, "Tactics of the Antifeminist Backlash Against Canadian National Woman Abuse Surveys," *Violence Against Women* 5 (1999): 1258–1276; Claire M. Renzetti, "On Dancing With a Bear: Reflections On Some of the Current Debates Among Domestic Violence Theorists," *Violence and Victims* 9 (1994): 195–200; and Chris Atmore, "Victims, Backlash, and Radical Feminist Theory (Or, the Morning After They Stole Feminism's Fire)," in *New Versions of Victims: Feminists Struggle With the Concept*, ed. Sharon Lamb (New York: New York University Press, 1999), 183–211.

14 DeKeseredy, "Tactics."

15 See Patricia Pearson, *When She Was Bad: Violent Women and the Myth of Innocence* (Toronto: Random House, 1997); and Naomi Wolf, *Fire With Fire: The New Female Power and How It Will Change the Twenty-First Century* (London: Chatto and Windus, 1993).

16 DeKeseredy, "Tactics."

17 Claire M. Renzetti, *Violent Betrayal: Partner Abuse in Lesbian Relationships* (Newbury Park, CA: Sage Publications, 1992).

18 Christina Hoff Sommers, *Who Stole Feminism: How Women Have Betrayed Women* (New York: Simon and Schuster, 1995), 200.

19 Donna Laframboise, *The Princess At the Window: A New Gender Morality* (Toronto: Penguin Books, 1996), 92.

20 Ibid., 94.

21 Ibid., 95; Laframboise is quoting directly from the Canadian Panel on Violence Against Women's *Changing the Landscape: Ending Violence-Achieving Equality. Final Report* (Ottawa: Minister of Supply and Services Canada, 1993), 14.

22 Pearson, *When She Was Bad*, 131.

23 See Janice L. Ristock, "Community-Based Research: Lesbian Abuse and Other Telling Tales," in *Inside the Academy and Out: Lesbian/Gay/Queer Studies and Social Action*, ed. Janice L. Ristock and Catherine G. Taylor (Toronto: University of Toronto Press, 1998), 137–154; and Janice L. Ristock, "Exploring Dynamics of Abusive Lesbian Relationships: Preliminary Analysis of a Multi-Site, Qualitative Study," *American Journal of Community Psychology*, in press.

24 Pearson, *When She Was Bad*, 117.

25 Renzetti, *Violent Betrayal*, 115.

26 See Renzetti, "On Dancing"; and Claire M. Renzetti, "Violence in Lesbian and Gay Relationships," in *Gender Violence: Interdisciplinary Perspectives*, ed. Laura L. O'Toole and Jessica R. Schiffmann (New York: New York University Press, 1997), 285–293.

27 Mary Louise Fellows and Sherene Razack, "The Race to Innocence: Confronting Hierarchical Relations Among Women," *Iowa Journal of Race, Gender and Justice*, 1, no. 2 (1998).

28 Melanie Kaye/Kantrowitz, *The Issue Is Power: Essays on Women, Jews, Violence and Resistance* (San Francisco: Aunt Lute Books, 1992).

29 Claire M. Renzetti, "Violence and Abuse in Lesbian Relationships: Theoretical and Empirical Issues," in *Issues in Intimate Violence*, ed. Raquel Kennedy Bergen (Thousand Oaks, CA: Sage Publications, 1998), 117–128.

30 Hart, "Lesbian Battering," 173.

31 See Nancy Hammond, "Lesbian Victims of Relationship Violence," *Women and Therapy* 8 (1989): 89–105; Elizabeth Leeder, "Enmeshed In Pain: Counselling the Lesbian Battering Couple," *Women and Therapy* 7 (1988): 81–99; and Lobel, *Naming*.

32 See Hammond, "Lesbian Victims"; Renzetti, *Violent Betrayal*; Ristock, "And Justice"; Teresa Scherzer, "Domestic Violence in Lesbian Relationships: Findings Of the Lesbian Relationships Research Project," *Journal of Lesbian Studies* 2 (1998): 29–47; and Susan C. Turell, "Seeking Help For Same-Sex Relationship Abuses," *Journal of Gay and Lesbian Social Services* 10, no. 2 (1999): 35–50.

33 Renzetti, *Violent Betrayal.*

34 Renzetti, "Violence in Lesbian and Gay Relationships."

35 I offer a similar but condensed discussion of prevalence studies in Ristock, "Exploring Dynamics."

36 Pamela A. Brand and Aline H. Kidd, "Frequency of Physical Aggression in Heterosexual and Female Homosexual Dyads," *Psychological Reports* 59 (1986): 1307–1313.

37 Joann Loulan, *Lesbian Passion* (San Francisco: Spinsters/Aunt Lute Books, 1987).

38 Valerie E. Coleman, *Violence Between Lesbian Couples: A Between-Groups Comparison*, (Ph.D. dissertation: University Microfilms International, 9109022, 1990).

39 Gwat-Yong Lie and Sabrina Gentlewarrier, "Intimate Violence in Lesbian Relationships: Discussion of Survey Findings and Practice Implications," *Journal of Social Service Research* 15, no. 1/2 (1991): 41–59.

40 Lockhart and others, "Letting."

41 Turell, "Seeking," 36.

42 Renzetti, "Violence."

43 Lisa K. Waldner-Hangrud, Linda Vaden Gratch, and Brian Magruder, "Victimization and Perpetration Rates of Violence in Gay and Lesbian Relationships: Gender Issues Explored," *Violence and Victims* 12 (1997): 173–184.

44 Murray A. Straus, Richard J. Gelles, and Suzanne K. Steinmetz, *Behind Closed Doors: Violence in the American Family* (New York: Doubleday Books, 1980).

45 Dawn H. Currie, "Violent Men or Violent Women? Whose Definition Counts," in *Issues in Intimate Violence*, ed. Raquel Kennedy Bergen (Thousand Oaks, CA: Sage Publications, 1998), 97–111.

46 Murray A. Straus, "The Conflict Tactics Scale and Its Critics: An Evaluation and New Data on Validity and Reliability," in *Physical Violence in American Families: Risk Factors and Adaptations to Violence in 8,145 Families*, ed. Murray A. Straus and Richard J. Gelles (New Brunswick, NJ: Transaction, 1990).

47 Geraldine Butts Stahly and Gwat-Yong Lie, "Women and Violence: A Comparison of Lesbian and Heterosexual Battering Relationships," in *Variations On a Theme: Diversity and the Psychology of Women*, ed. Joan C. Chrisler and Alyce Huston Hemstreet (Abany, NY: State University of New York Press, 1995), 51–68.

48 Waldner-Halgrud, Vaden Gratch, and Magruder, "Victimization," 182.

49 Currie, "Violent."

50 Stahly and Lie, "Women and Violence."

51 Renzetti, "Violence."

52 Currie, "Violent."

53 Scherzer, "Domestic Violence," 36.

54 Waldner-Halgrud, Vaden Gratch, and Magruder, "Victimization."

55 Scherzer, "Domestic Violence," 43.

56 DeKeseredy, "Tactics."

57 Ristock, "'And Justice.'"

58 See Anne Opie, "Qualitative Research, Appropriation of the 'Other' and Empowerment," *Feminist Review* 40 (Spring 1992): 52–69; and Janice L. Ristock and Joan Pennell, *Community Research as Empowerment: Feminist Links, Postmodern Interruptions* (Toronto: Oxford University Press, 1996).

59 Ristock, "Community-Based Research."

60 David Island and Patrick Letellier, *Men Who Beat the Men Who Love Them* (New York: Harrington Park Press, 1991).

61 Donald G. Dutton, "Patriarchy and Wife Assault: The Ecological Fallacy," *Violence and Victims* 9 (1994): 167–182.

62 Island and Letellier, *Men Who Beat.*

63 See Mary Eaton for her discussion of the misuses of limited definitions of gender as biology in "Abuse By Any Other Name: Feminism, Difference, and Intralesbian Violence," in *The Public Name of Private Violence: The Discovery of Domestic Abuse,* ed. Martha Albertson Fineman and Roxanne Mykitiuk (New York: Routledge, 1994), 195–224.

64 Island and Letellier, *Men Who Beat,* 3.

65 Valerie E. Coleman, "Lesbian Battering: The Relationship Between Personality and Perpetuation of Violence," *Violence and Victims* 9 (1994): 150.

66 See Gregory S. Merrill, "Ruling the Exceptions: Same-Sex Battering and Domestic Violence Theory," in *Violence in Gay and Lesbian Domestic Partnerships,* ed. Claire M. Renzetti and Charles Harvey Miley (New York: Harrington Park Press, 1996), 9–22; L. Gilbert, P. B. Poorman, and S. Simmons, "Guidelines for Mental Health Systems Response to Lesbian Battering," in *Confronting Lesbian Battering: A Manual for the Battered Women's Movement,* ed. Pam Elliott (St. Paul, MN: Minnesota Coalition for Battered Women, 1990), 105–117; and Beth Zemsky, "Lesbian Battering: Considerations for Intervention," in *Confronting Lesbian Battering: A Manual for the Battered Women's Movement,* ed. Pam Elliott (St. Paul, MN: Minnesota Coalition for Battered Women, 1990), 64–67.

67 Merrill, "Ruling the Exceptions," 13.

68 Ibid., 15.

69 Joan C. McClennen, "Partner Abuse Between Lesbian Couples: Toward a Better Understanding," in *A Professional Guide to Understanding Gay and Lesbian Domestic Violence: Understanding Practice Interventions,* ed. Joan C. McClennen and John Gunther (New York: Edwin Mellen Press, 1999), 77–94.

70 Eaton, "Abuse By Any Other Name," 201.

71 See Martha Lucia Garcia, "A 'New Kind' of Battered Woman: Challenges For the Movement," in *Same-Sex Domestic Violence: Strategies for Change,* ed. Beth Leventhal and Sandra E. Lundy (Thousand Oaks, CA: Sage Publications, 1999), 165–172; Arlene Istar, "Couple Assessment: Identifying and Intervening in Domestic Violence in Lesbian Relationships," in *Violence in Gay and Lesbian Domestic Part-*

nerships, ed. Claire M. Renzetti and Charles Harvey Miley (New York: Harrington Park Press, 1996), 93–106; and Lydia Walker, "Battered Women's Shelters and Work With Battered Lesbians," in *Naming the Violence*, ed. Lobel, 73–76.

72 See Eaton, "Abuse By Any Other Name"; and Suzanne Pharr, "Lesbian Battering: Social Change Urged," in *Confronting Lesbian Battering: A Manual For the Battered Women's Movement*, ed. Pam Elliott (St. Paul, MN: Minnesota Coalition for Battered Women, 1990), 142–157.

73 See Eaton, "Abuse By Any Other Name"; Kaye/Kantrowitz, *The Issue Is Power*; and Renzetti, "Violence and Abuse."

74 Kaye/Kantrowitz, *The Issue is Power*, 37.

75 Eaton, "Abuse By Any Other Name," 220.

76 See Eaton, "Abuse By Any Other Name"; Liz Kelly, "Unspeakable Acts: Abuse By and Between Women," *Trouble and Strife* 21, Summer (1991): 13–20; and Joelle Taylor and Tracey Chandler, *Lesbians Talk Violent Relationships* (London: Scarlet Press, 1995).

77 Renzetti, "Violence and Abuse."

78 See Kimberly W. Crenshaw for a discussion of this term in "Mapping the Margins: Intersectionality, Identity Politics, and Violence Against Women of Color," in *The Public Nature of Private Violence: The Discovery of Domestic Abuse*, ed. Martha Albertson Fineman and Roxanne Mykitiuk (New York: Routledge, 1994), 93–118.

79 Renzetti, "Violence and Abuse," 291.

80 See Valli Kanuha, "Compounding the Triple Jeopardy: Battering in Lesbian of Color Relationships," in *Women and Therapy* 9(1990): 169–184; and Charlene Waldron, "Lesbians of Color and the Domestic Violence Movement," in *Violence in Gay and Lesbian Domestic Partnerships*, ed. Claire M. Renzetti and Charles Harvey Miley (New York: Harrington Park Press, 1996), 43–51.

81 Rhea Almeida and others, "Violence in the Lives of the Racially and Sexually Different: A Public and Private Dilemma," *Journal of Feminist Family Therapy* 5, no. 3/4 (1994): 99–126.

82 See Claudia Card, *Lesbian Choices* (New York: Columbia University Press, 1995); and Carol Thorpe Tully, "Hate Crimes, Domestic Violence, and the Lesbian and Gay Community," in *A Professional Guide to Understanding Gay and Lesbian Domestic Violence: Understanding Practice Interventions*, ed. Joan C. McClennen and John Gunther (Lewiston, NY: Edwin Mellen Press, 1999), 13–28.

83 See Kathleen Ferraro, "The Dance of Dependency: A Genealogy of Domestic Violence," *Hypatia* 11, no. 4 (1996): 77–91; and Linda Gordon, *Heroes of Their Own Lives* (London: Virago, 1989).

84 Patrick Letellier, "Twin Epidemics: Domestic Violence and HIV Infection Among Gay and Bisexual Men," in *Violence in Gay and Lesbian Domestic Partnerships*, ed. Claire M. Renzetti and Charles Harvey Miley (New York: Harrington Park Press, 1996), 95–106.

85 Lola Butler, "African American Lesbians Experiencing Partner Abuse," in *A*

Professional Guide to Understanding Gay and Lesbian Domestic Violence: Under-standing Practice Interventions, ed. Joan C. McClennen and John Gunther (Lewiston, NY: Edwin Mellen Press, 1999), 175–199.

86 Michal De Vidas, "Childhood Sexual Abuse and Domestic Violence: A Support Group for Gays and Lesbians," *Journal of Gay and Lesbian Social Services* 10, no. 2 (1999): 51–68.

87 Faulkner, "Woman-to-Woman Abuse," 59.

88 Holmes, "The Politics of Naming," 21.

89 See Inderpal Grewal and Caren Kaplan, *Scattered Hegemonies: Postmodernity and Transnational Feminist Practices* (Minneapolis, MN: University of Minnesota Press, 1994); Donna J. Haraway, "Situated Knowledge: The Science Question in Feminism and the Privilege of Partial Perspective," *Feminist Studies* 14 (1988): 575–599; Ristock and Pennell, *Community Research*; and Gayatri Chakravorty Spivak, *In Other Worlds: Essays in Cultural Politics* (New York: Methuen, 1987).

90 Laura L. O'Toole and Jessica R. Schiffmann, eds., *Gender Violence: Interdisciplinary Perspectives* (New York: New York University Press, 1997).

91 Bat-Ami Bar On, "Introduction," *Hypatia*, special issue on *Women and Violence* 11, no. 4 (1996): 4.

92 Michel Foucault, *The Archeology of Knowledge and the Discourse on Language*, trans. A. M. Sheridan Smith (New York: Pantheon Books, 1972).

93 See Jane Flax, "The End of Innocence," in *Feminists Theorize the Political*, ed. Judith Butler and Joan Scott (New York: Routledge, 1992), 447; Patti Lather, *Getting Smart: Feminist Research and Pedagogy With/In the Postmodern* (New York: Routledge, 1991); and Ristock and Pennell, *Community Research*.

94 Ann Weick and Dennis Saleebey, "Postmodern Perspectives for Social Work," *Social Thought* 18, no. 3 (1998): 21–40.

95 Ristock and Pennell, *Community Research*, 114.

96 Linda Alcoff and Laura Gray, "Survivor Discourse: Transgression or Recuperation?" *Signs* 18 (1993): 260–290.

97 Sharon Lamb, ed., *New Versions of Victims: Feminists Struggle With the Concept* (New York: New York University Press, 1999).

98 Sharon Marcus, "Fighting Bodies, Fighting Words: A Theory and Politics of Rape Prevention," in *Feminists Theorize the Political*, ed. Judith Butler and Joan Scott (New York: Routledge, 1992), 385–403.

99 See Ruth Frankenburg, *White Women, Race Matters: The Social Construction of Whiteness* (Minneapolis, MN: University of Minneapolis, 1993); bell hooks, *Black Looks: Race and Representation* (Toronto: Between the Lines, 1992); and Sherene Razack, *Looking White People in the Eye: Gender, Race, and Culture in Courtrooms and Classrooms* (Toronto: University of Toronto Press, 1998).

100 Razack, *Looking*.

101 Anannya Bhattacharjee, "The Public/Private Mirage: Mapping Homes and Undomesticating Violence Work in the South Asian Immigrant Community," in *Fem-*

inist Genealogies, Colonial Legacies, Democratic Futures, ed. M. Jacqui Alexander and Chandra Talpade Mohanty (New York: Routledge, 1997), 308.

102 Crenshaw, "Mapping."

103 See Collins, "Learning"; and Razack, *Looking*.

104 See Nadya Burton, "Resistance to Prevention: Reconsidering Feminist Antiviolence Rhetoric," in *Violence Against Women: Philosophical Perspectives*, ed. Stanley G. French, Wanda Teays, and Laura M. Purdy (Ithaca, NY: Cornell University Press, 1998), 182–200; Ferraro, "The Dance"; Holmes, "The Politics of Naming"; and Damian O'Neill, "A Poststructuralist Review of the Theoretical Literature Surrounding Wife Abuse," *Violence Against Women* 4 (1998): 457–490.

105 Ristock and Pennell, *Community Research*.

106 Holmes, "The Politics of Naming."

107 Ristock and Pennell, *Community Research*.

108 Annamarie Jagose, *Queer Theory: An Introduction* (New York: New York University Press, 1996).

109 See for example the following edited collections: Beth Leventhal and Sandra E. Lundy, eds., *Same-Sex Domestic Violence: Strategies for Change* (Thousand Oaks, CA: Sage Publications, 1999); Joan C. McClennen and John Gunther, eds., *A Professional Guide to Understanding Gay and Lesbian Domestic Violence: Understanding Practice Interventions* (New York: Edwin Mellen Press, 1999); and Claire M. Renzetti and Charles Harvey Miley, eds., *Violence in Gay and Lesbian Domestic Partnerships* (New York: Harrington Park Press, 1996).

110 Nancy Ziegenmeyer, *Taking Back My Life* (New York: Summit Books, 1992), 218.

Two: Troubling Tales

1 This chapter expands and develops the methodological framework I described in Janice L. Ristock, "Community-Based Research: Lesbian Abuse and Other Telling Tales," in *Inside the Academy and Out: Lesbian/Gay/Queer Studies and Social Action*, ed. Janice L. Ristock and Catherine G. Taylor (Toronto: University of Toronto Press, 1998). See also Patti Lather, *Getting Smart: Feminist Research and Pedagogy With/In the Postmodern* (New York: Routledge, 1991); and Janice L. Ristock and Joan Pennell, *Community Research as Empowerment: Feminist Links, Postmodern Interruptions* (Toronto: Oxford University Press, 1996).

2 Patti Lather and Chris Smithies, *Troubling the Angels: Women Living With HIV/AIDS* (Boulder, CO: Westview Press, 1997).

3 See Claire M. Renzetti, "The Challenge to Feminism Posed by Women's Use of Violence in Intimate Relationships," in *New Versions of Victims: Feminists Struggle With the Concept*, ed. Sharon Lamb (New York: New York University Press, 1999), 42–56; Ristock and Pennell, *Community Research*; Jane M. Ussher, "Introduction:

Towards a Material-Discursive Analysis of Madness, Sexuality and Reproduction," in *Body Talk: The Material and Discursive Regulation of Sexuality, Madness and Reproduction* (London: Routledge, 1997), 1–9; and Marc A. Zimmerman and Douglas D. Perkins, eds., *Empowerment Theory, Research, and Application*, [Special Issue] *American Journal of Community Psychology* 23 (1995): 569–580.

4 See Ristock, "Community-Based Research"; Janice L. Ristock, "Exploring Dynamics of Abusive Lesbian Relationships: Preliminary Analysis of a Multi-Site, Qualitative Study," *American Journal of Community Psychology*, in press; and Ristock and Pennell, *Community Research*, where I have also described my methodological approach to this project.

5 This discussion expands on an earlier formulation of my methodology that appeared in my chapter, "Community Based Research." See Lather, *Getting Smart*, who has used a similar tactic to write up her research on students' resistance to liberatory curriculum.

6 Ken Plummer, *Telling Sexual Stories: Power, Change and Social Worlds* (London: Routledge, 1995).

7 See Angie Balan, Rhonda Chorney, and Janice L. Ristock, *Training and Education Project for Responding to Abuse in Lesbian Relationships: Final Report*, Ottawa: Department of Health, 1995, project no. 4887-07-93-011; Janice L. Ristock, "'And Justice for All?'. . . The Social Context of Legal Responses to Abuse in Lesbian Relationships," *Canadian Journal of Women and the Law* 7 (1994): 415–430; and Janice L. Ristock, "The Cultural Politics of Abuse in Lesbian Relationships: Challenges for Community Action," in *Subtle Sexism: Current Practice and Prospects for Change*, ed. Nijole Vaicraitis Benokraitis (Thousand Oaks, CA: Sage Publications, 1997), 279–296.

8 See, for example, Susan Hekman, "Truth and Method: Feminist Standpoint Theory Revisited," *Signs* 22, no. 2 (1997): 341–363.

9 Joan Scott, "Experience," in *Feminists Theorize the Political*, ed. Judith Butler and Joan Scott (New York: Routledge, 1992), 36.

10 Janet M. Stoppard, "Women's Bodies, Women's Lives and Depression: Towards a Reconciliation of Material and Discursive Accounts," in *Body Talk: The Material and Discursive Regulation of Sexuality, Madness and Reproduction*, ed. Jane M. Ussher (New York: Routledge, 1997), 10–32.

11 Ristock and Pennell, *Community Research*.

12 See Liz Kelly, *Surviving Sexual Violence* (Minneapolis, MN: University of Minnesota Press, 1988); and Shulamit Reinharz, *Feminist Methods in Social Research* (New York: Oxford University Press, 1992).

13 Patricia Maguire, *Doing Participatory Research: A Feminist Approach* (Amherst: Center for International Education, School of Education, University of Massachusetts, 1987).

14 See Claire M. Renzetti, *Violent Betrayal: Partner Abuse in Lesbian Relation-

ships (Newbury Park, CA: Sage Publications, 1992); Ristock, "'And Justice'"; Teresa Scherzer, "Domestic Violence in Lesbian Relationships: Findings of the Lesbian Relationships Research Project," *Journal of Lesbian Studies* 2 (1998): 29–47; and Susan C. Turell, "Seeking Help for Same-Sex Relationship Abuses," *Journal of Gay and Lesbian Social Services* 10, no. 2 (1999): 35–50.

15 Michelle Fine, *Disruptive Voices: The Possibilities of Feminist Research* (Ann Arbor, MI: University of Michigan Press, 1992).

16 See Anselm Strauss and Juliet Corbin, *Basics of Qualitative Research: Grounded Theory Procedures and Techniques* (Newbury Park, CA: Sage Publications, 1990); and Robert Stuart Weiss, *Learning From Strangers: The Art and Method of Qualitative Interview Studies* (New York: Free Press, 1994).

17 See Ristock, "Community-Based Research"; and Ristock, "Exploring Dynamics."

18 See Erica Burman, ed., *Deconstructing Feminist Psychology* (London: Sage Publications, 1998); Jeanne Marecek, "Trauma Talk in Feminist Clinical Practice," in *New Versions of Victims: Feminists Struggle With the Concept*, ed. Judith Butler and Joan Scott (New York: New York University Press, 1999), 158–182; and Sue Wilkinson and Celia Kitzinger, eds., *Feminism and Discourse: Psychological Perspectives* (London: Sage Publications, 1995).

19 Lather, *Getting Smart*.

20 See Michel Foucault, *The Archeology of Knowledge and the Discourse on Language*, trans. A. M. Sheridan Smith (New York: Pantheon Books, 1972); and Helen Malson, *The Thin Woman: Feminism, Post-Structuralism and the Social Psychology of Anorexia Nervosa* (London: Routledge, 1998).

21 See Ristock, "Exploring Dynamics"; and Marecek, "Trauma Talk."

22 See Ristock, "Exploring Dynamics"; and Janice L. Ristock, "Decentering Heterosexuality: Responses of Feminist Counselors to Abuse in Relationships," *Women in Therapy*, in press.

23 Laurie Chesley, Donna MacAulay, and Janice L. Ristock, *Abuse in Lesbian Relationships: Information and Resources*, rev. ed. [Booklet]. Ottawa: Minister of Public Works and Government Services Canada, 1992. Distributed by National Clearinghouse on Family Violence, Health Canada.

24 Cindy Holmes, "The Politics of Naming the Violence: Examining Constructions of 'Lesbian Abuse' in Community-Based Educational Discourses" (M.A. Thesis: Ontario Institute for Studies in Education, University of Toronto, 2000), 74.

25 Joshua M. Price, "Spaces of Violence, Shades of Meaning: The Heterogeneity of Violence Against Women in the United States" (Ph.D. dissertation: University of Chicago, 1998), 124.

26 See Janet M. Stoppard, *Understanding Depression: Feminist Social Constructionist Approaches* (New York: Routledge, 2000); and Ussher, "Introduction."

27 Melanie Kaye/Kantrowitz, *The Issue is Power: Essays on Women, Jews, Violence and Resistance* (San Francisco: Aunt Lute Books, 1992).

28 Donna J. Haraway, "Situated Knowledge: The Science Question in Feminism and the Privilege of Partial Perspective," *Feminist Studies* 14 (1988): 575–599.

29 Shoshana Felman, *Jacques Lacan and the Adventure of Insight: Psychoanalysis in Contemporary Culture* (Cambridge, MA: Harvard University Press, 1987).

30 See Debi Brock, "Talkin' Bout a Revelation: Feminist Popular Discourse on Sexual Abuse," *Canadian Woman Studies* 12, no. 1 (1991): 12–16; Holmes, "The Politics of Naming"; Joshua M. Price, "Spaces of Violence, Shades of Meaning: The Heterogeneity of Violence Against Women in the United States" (Ph.D. dissertation: University of Chicago, 1998); and Sherene H. Razack, *Looking White People in the Eye: Gender, Race, and Culture in Courtrooms and Classrooms* (Toronto: University of Toronto Press, 1998).

31 See Lather, *Getting Smart*; and Ristock and Pennell, *Community Research*.

32 Gloria Anzaldua, "La consciencia de la mestiza: Towards a New Consciousness," in *Making Face, Making Soul/Haciendo caras: Creative and Critical Perspectives by Women of Color*, ed. Gloria Anzaldua (San Francisco: Aunt Lute Books, 1990), 380.

33 James Baldwin, as quoted in Henry Louis Gates Jr., *Bearing Witness: Selections from African-American Autobiography in the Twentieth Century* (New York: Pantheon Books, 1991), 9.

Three: What the Body Remembers

1 See Liz Kelly's interview research with heterosexual women in *Surviving Sexual Violence* (Minneapolis, MN: University of Minnesota Press, 1988).

2 Ginny NiCarthy, *Getting Free: A Handbook for Women in Abusive Relationships* (Seattle, WA: Seal Press, 1986).

3 See Rebecca Emerson Dobash and Russell P. Dobash, "Violence Against Women," in *Gender Violence: Interdisciplinary Perspectives*, ed. Laura L. O'Toole and Jessica R. Schiffman (New York: New York University Press, 1997), 266–278; Liz Kelly, "The Continuum of Sexual Violence," in *Women, Violence and Social Control*, ed. Jalna Hanmer and Mary Maynard (Atlantic Highlands, NJ: Humanities Press International, 1987) and Claire M. Renzetti, "Violence and Abuse in Lesbian Relationships: Theoretical and Empirical Issues," in *Issues in Intimate Violence*, ed. Raquel Kennedy Bergen (Thousand Oaks, CA: Sage Publications, 1998), 117–128.

4 See Gregory S. Merrill, "Reports of Gay Domestic Violence Up Sharply," *San Francisco Examiner*, 8 May 1998, p. A3; and Renzetti, "Violence and Abuse."

5 Claire M. Renzetti, *Violent Betrayal: Partner Abuse in Lesbian Relationships* (Newbury Park, CA: Sage Publications, 1992).

6 Pam Elliott, "Shattering Illusions: Same-Sex Domestic Violence," in *Violence in Gay and Lesbian Domestic Partnerships*, ed. Claire M. Renzetti and Charles Harvey Miley (New York: Harrington Park Press, 1996), 4.

7 Arlene Istar Lev and S. Sundance Lev, "Sexual Assault in the Lesbian, Gay, Bisexual and Transgendered Communities," in *A Professional Guide to Understanding Gay and Lesbian Domestic Violence: Understanding Practice Interventions*, ed. Joan C. McClennen and John Gunther (New York: Edwin Mellen Press, 1999), 35–62.

8 Caroline K. Waterman, Lori J. Dawson, and Michael J. Bologna, "Sexual Coercion in Gay Male and Lesbian Relationships: Predictors and Implications for Support Services," *Journal of Sex Research* 26 (1989): 118–124.

9 See Istar Lev and Lev, "Sexual Assault"; Janice L. Ristock, "The Cultural Politics of Abuse in Lesbian Relationships: Challenges for Community Action," in *Subtle Sexism: Current Practice and Prospects for Change*, ed. Nijole Vaicraitis Benokraitis (Thousand Oaks, CA: Sage Publications, 1997), 279–296; Janice L. Ristock, "Decentering Heterosexuality: Responses of Feminist Counselors to Abuse in Lesbian Relationships," *Women in Therapy*, in press.

10 Michael P. Johnson, "Patriarchal Terrorism and Common Couple Violence: Two Forms of Violence Against Women," *Journal of Marriage and the Family* 57 (1995): 283–294.

11 As quoted in Renzetti, "Violence and Abuse," 123.

12 Anne McGillivray and Brenda Comaskey, *Black Eyes All of the Time: Intimate Violence, Aboriginal Women, and the Justice System* (Toronto: University of Toronto Press, 1999).

13 See Patricia Hill Collins, "Learning From the Outsider Within: The Sociological Significance of Black Feminist Thought," *Social Problems* 33, no. 6 (1986): S14–S32; and Kimberly W. Crenshaw, "Mapping the Margins: Intersectionality, Identity Politics, and Violence Against Women of Color," in *The Public Nature of Private Violence: The Discovery of Domestic Abuse*, ed. Martha Albertson Fineman and Roxanne Mykitiuk (New York: Routledge, 1994), 93–118.

14 Elaine Leeder, "Enmeshed in Pain: Counselling the Lesbian Battering Couple," *Women and Therapy* 7 (1988): 81–99.

15 Johnson, "Patriarchal Terrorism."

16 See Renzetti, *Violent Betrayal*; and Claire M. Renzetti, "Violence in Lesbian and Gay Relationships," in *Gender Violence: InterdisciplinaryPerspectives*, ed. Laura L. O'Toole and Jessica R. Schiffmann (New York: New York University Press, 1997), 285–293.

17 Renzetti, "Violence."

18. Ann Duffy and Julianne Momirov, *Family Violence: A Canadian Introduction* (Toronto: James Lorimer and Company, 1997), 34–37.

19 I have written about this pattern elsewhere. See Janice L. Ristock, "Community-Based Research: Lesbian Abuse and Other Telling Tales," in *Inside the Academy and Out: Lesbian/Gay/Queer Studies and Social Action*, ed. Janice L. Ristock and Catherine G. Taylor (Toronto: University of Toronto Press, 1998), 137–154; and Janice L. Ristock, "Exploring Dynamics of Abusive Lesbian Relationships: Prelimi-

nary Analysis of a Multi-Site, Qualitative Study," *American Journal of Community Psychology*, in press.

20 See Renzetti, *Violent Betrayal*; and Teresa Scherzer, "Domestic Violence in Lesbian Relationships: Findings of the Lesbian Relationships Research Project," *Journal of Lesbian Studies* 2 (1998): 29–47.

21 See Renzetti, *Violent Betrayal*.

22 See Joan C. McClennen, "Partner Abuse Between Lesbian Couples: Toward a Better Understanding," in *A Professional Guide to Understanding Gay and Lesbian Domestic Violence: Understanding Practice Interventions*, ed. Joan C. McClennen and John Gunther (New York: Edwin Mellen Press, 1999), 77–94; Renzetti, *Violent Betrayal*; Rebecca Schilit, Gwat-Yong Lie, and Marilyn Montagne, "Substance Use as a Correlate of Violence in Intimate Lesbian Relationships," *Journal of Homosexuality* 19, no. 3 (1990): 51–65; and Rebecca Schilit, Gwat-Yong Lie, Judy Bush, Marilyn Montagne, and Lynn Reyes, "Intergenerational Transmission of Violence in Lesbian Relationships." *Affilia* 6 (1991): 72–87.

23 See McClennen, "Partner Abuse"; and Renzetti, *Violent Betrayal*.

24 See Valerie E. Coleman, "Violence Between Lesbian Couples: A Between-Groups Comparison" (Ph.D. dissertation: University Microfilms International, 9109022, 1990); Carl E. Kelly and Lynn Warshafsky, "Partner Abuse in Gay Male and Lesbian Couples" (paper presented at the Third National Conference for Family Violence Researchers, Durham, NH, July, 1987); and Rebecca Schilit, Gwat-Yong Lie, and Marilyn Montagne, "Substance Use as a Correlate of Violence in Intimate Lesbian Relationships," *Journal of Homosexuality* 19, no. 3 (1990): 51–65.

25 See David Island and Patrick Letellier, *Men Who Beat the Men Who Love Them* (New York: Harrington Park Press, 1991); and Renzetti, *Violent Betrayal*.

26 Gwat-Yong Lie and others, "Lesbians in Currently Aggressive Relationships: How Frequently Do They Report Aggressive Past Relationships?," *Violence and Victims* 6, no. 1/2 (1991): 41–59.

27 See Coleman, *Violence Between*; and Renzetti, *Violent Betrayal*.

28 Lee Lakeman, "Why Law and Order Cannot End Violence Against Women and Why the Development of Women's (Social, Economic, and Civil) Rights Might," *Canadian Woman Studies* 20, no. 3 (2000): 24–33.

29 Carol Thorpe Tully, *Lesbians, Gays and the Empowerment Perspective* (New York: Columbia University Press, 2000); and Lenore E. Walker, *The Battered Woman* (New York: Harper & Row, 1979).

30 Sharon Lamb, "Constructing the Victim: Popular Images and Lasting Labels," in *New Versions of Victims: Feminists Struggle With the Concept*, ed. Sharon Lamb (New York: New York University Press, 1999), 108–138.

31 Becky Marrujo and Mary Kreger, "Definition of Roles in Abusive Lesbian Relationships," in *Violence in Gay and Lesbian Domestic Partnerships* (New York: Harrington Park Press, 1996).

Four: An Innocence Lost

1 Chrystos, *Dream On* (Vancouver: Press Gang Publishers, 1991).

2 Liz Kelly, *Surviving Sexual Violence* (Minneapolis, MN: University of Minnesota Press, 1988), 159.

3 Mary P. Koss and others, *No Safe Haven: Male Violence Against Women at Home, Work, and in the Community* (Washington, DC: American Psychological Association, 1994).

4 Judith Herman, *Trauma and Recovery: The Aftermath of Violence from Domestic Abuse and Political Terror* (New York: Basic Books, 1992); and Lenore E. Walker, "Post-Traumatic Stress Disorder in Women: Diagnosis and Treatment of Battered Woman Syndrome," *Psychotherapy* 28 (1991): 21–29.

5 Sharon Lamb, "Constructing the Victim: Popular Images and Lasting Labels," in *New Versions of Victims: Feminists Struggle With the Concept*, ed. Sharon Lamb (New York: New York University Press, 1999), 108–138.

6 Kelly, *Surviving*.

7 Laura M. Brown, "Not Outside the Range: One Feminist Perspective on Psychic Trauma," in *Trauma: Explorations in Memory*, ed. Cathy Caruth (Baltimore, MD: Johns Hopkins University Press, 1995), 107.

8 Cited in Brown, "Not Outside the Range," 107.

9 Lamb, "Constructing the Victim," 120.

10 bell hooks, "Violence in Intimate Relationships: Interdisciplinary Perspectives," in *Gender Violence: Interdisciplinary Perspectives*, ed. Laura L. O'Toole and Jessica R. Schiffmann (New York: New York University Press, 1997), 279–284; and Janice L. Ristock, "Beyond Ideologies: Understanding Violence in Lesbian Relationships," *Canadian Woman Studies* 12 (1991): 74–79.

11 Lamb, "Constructing the Victim."

12 Janice L. Ristock, "The Cultural Politics of Abuse in Lesbian Relationships: Challenges for Community Action," in *Subtle Sexism: Current Practice and Prospects for Change*, ed. Nijole Vaicraitis Benokraitis (Thousand Oaks, CA: Sage Publications, 1997), 279–296.

13 Rebecca Emerson Dobash and Russell P. Dobash, "Violence Against Women," in *Gender Violence: Interdisciplinary Perspectives*, ed. Laura L. O'Toole and Jessica R. Schiffmann (New York: New York University Press, 1997), 266–278.

14 Beverly D. Tuel and Richard K. Russell, "Self-Esteem and Depression in Battered Women: A Comparison of Lesbian and Heterosexual Survivors," *Violence Against Women* 4 (1998): 344–362.

15 Claire M. Renzetti, *Violent Betrayal: Partner Abuse in Lesbian Relationships* (Newbury Park, CA: Sage Publications, 1992).

16 Jo-Ann Krestan and Claudia S. Bepko, "The Problem of Fusion in the Lesbian Relationship," *Family Process* 19 (1980): 277–289.

17 Kathryn Greene, Vickie Causby, and Diane Helene Greene, "The Nature and

Function of Fusion in the Dynamics of Lesbian Relationships," *Affilia* 14, no. 1 (Spring 1999): 78–97.

18 Robin S. Nickel, "Children Witnessing Abuse Between Their Same-Gender Caregivers: Impact and Prevention," in *A Professional Guide to Understanding Gay and Lesbian Domestic Violence: Understanding Practice Interventions*, ed. Joan C. McClennen and John Gunther (New York: Edwin Mellen Press, 1999), 145–164.

19 Lamb, "Constructing the Victim," 127.

20 See Renzetti, *Violent Betrayal*; Teresa Scherzer, "Domestic Violence in Lesbian Relationships: Findings of the Lesbian Relationships Research Project," *Journal of Lesbian Studies* 2 (1998): 29–47; and Susan C. Turell, "Seeking Help for Same-Sex Relationship Abuses," *Journal of Gay and Lesbian Social Services* 10, no. 2 (1999): 35–50.

21 See, respectively, Turell, "Seeking Help"; and Valli Kanuha, "Compounding the Triple Jeopardy: Battering in Lesbian of Color Relationships," in *Confronting Lesbian Battering: A Manual for the Battered Women's Movement*, ed. Pam Elliott (St. Paul, MN: Minnesota Coalition for Battered Women, 1990), 142–157.

22 See Janice L. Ristock, "'And Justice for All?'. . . The Social Context of Legal Responses to Abuse in Lesbian Relationships," *Canadian Journal of Women and the Law* 7 (1994): 415–430; Ristock, "The Cultural Politics"; and Ann Russo, "Lesbians Organizing Lesbians Against Battering," in *Same-Sex Domestic Violence: Strategies for Change*, ed. Beth Leventhal and Sandra E. Lundy (Thousand Oaks, CA: Sage Publications, 1999), 83–96.

23 See Renzetti, *Violent Betrayal*; Janice L. Ristock, "Community-Based Research: Lesbian Abuse and Other Telling Tales," in *Inside the Academy and Out: Lesbian/Gay/Queer Studies and Social Action*, ed. Janice L. Ristock and Catherine G. Taylor (Toronto: University of Toronto Press, 1998), 137–154; Scherzer, "Domestic Violence"; and Turell, "Seeking Help."

24 Ristock, "The Cultural Politics."

25 See Nancy Hammond, "Lesbian Victims of Relationship Violence," *Women and Therapy* 8 (1989): 89–105; and Renzetti, *Violent Betrayal*.

26 See Kevin T. Berrill, "Antigay Violence and Victimization in the United States: An Overview," in *Hate Crimes: Confronting Violence Against Lesbians and Gay Men*, ed. Gregory M. Herek and Kevin T. Berrill (Newbury Park, CA: Sage Publications, 1992), 19–45; and Gary David Comstock, *Violence Against Lesbians and Gay Men* (New York: Columbia University Press, 1991).

27 Ristock, "'And Justice for All?'"

28 See Pam Elliott, "How Should Battered Lesbians Seek Help and Justice?," *Lesbian Battering Intervention Project Report* (St. Paul, MN, Spring 1991), 3; Renzetti, *Violent Betrayal*; and Evan Fray-Witzer, "Twice-Abused: Same-Sex Domestic Violence and the Law," in *Same-Sex Domestic Violence: Strategies for Change*, ed. Beth Leventhal and Sandra E. Lundy (Thousand Oaks, CA: Sage Publications, 1999), 19–42.

29 Demie Kurz, "Emergency Department Responses to Battered Women: Resistance to Medicalization," *Social Problems* 19 (1987): 277–289; Renzetti, *Violent Betrayal*; Ruthann Robson, *Lesbian Outlaw: Survival Under the Rule of Law* (Ithaca, NY: Firebrand Books, 1992); and Edwin M. Schur, *Labeling Women Deviant* (New York: Random House Publishers, 1984).

30 Robson, *Lesbian Outlaw*.

31 From the *Calgary Herald*, 6 August 1999.

32 "Lesbian Guilty of Partner's Murder," *PlanetOut*, 2000; [online], available from <http:// www.planetout.com/news>, Internet, accessed 21 November 2000.

33 Turell, "Seeking Help."

34 See Ginny NiCarthy, *Getting Free: A Handbook for Women in Abusive Relationships*. Seattle: Seal Press, 1986; Lenore E. Walker, *The Battered Woman* (New York: Harper & Row, 1979); and Kersti A.Yllo, "Through a Feminist Lens: Gender, Power and Violence," in *Current Controversies in Family Violence*, ed. Richard J. Gelles and Donileen R. Loseke (Newbury Park, CA: Sage Publications, 1993), 47–62.

35 Susan Cayouette, "Running Batterer Groups for Lesbians," in *Same-Sex Domestic Violence: Strategies for Change*, ed. Beth Leventhal and Sandra E. Lundy (Thousand Oaks, CA: Sage Publications, 1999), 233–242; Alma Banda Goddard and Tara Hardy, "Assessing the Lesbian Victim," in *Same-Sex Domestic Violence: Strategies for Change*, ed. Beth Leventhal and Sandra E. Lundy (Thousand Oaks, CA: Sage Publications, 1999), 193–200; and Arlene Istar, "Couple Assessment: Identifying and Intervening in Domestic Violence in Lesbian Relationships," in *Violence in Gay and Lesbian Domestic Partnerships*, ed. Claire M. Renzetti and Charles Harvey Miley (New York: Harrington Park Press, 1996), 93–106.

36 Also reported in Hammond, "Lesbian Victims"; and Barbara Hart, "Lesbian Battering: An Examination," in *Naming the Violence: Speaking Out About Lesbian Battering*, ed. Kerry Lobel (Seattle, WA: Seal Publications, 1986), 173–189.

Five: What's Written on the Body

1 Two earlier publications of mine examine the discourses operating in the focus groups: see "Exploring Dynamics of Abusive Lesbian Relationships: Preliminary Analysis of a Multi-Site, Qualitative Study," *American Journal of Community Psychology*; and "Decentering Heterosexuality: Responses of Feminist Counselors to Abuse in Lesbian Relationships," *Women in Therapy* (both in press). Jeanne Marecek brings forward dominant and marginal feminist discourses in her study of "Trauma Talk in Feminist Clinical Practice," in *New Versions of Victims: Feminists Struggle With the Concept*, ed. Sharon Lamb (New York: New York University Press, 1999), 158–182.

2 Ibid.

3 Nadya Burton, "Resistance to Prevention: Reconsidering Feminist Antiviolence Rhetoric," in *Violence Against Women: Philosophical Perspectives*, ed. Stanley G. French, Wanda Teays, and Laura M. Purdy (Ithaca, NY: Cornell University Press, 1998), 182–200.

4 Janice Haaken, *Pillar of Salt: Gender, Memory, and the Perils of Looking Back* (London: Rutgers University Press, 1998), 75.

5 Linda Gordon, *Heroes of Their Own Lives* (London: Virago, 1989).

6 Haaken, *Pillar of Salt*.

7 Marecek, "Trauma Talk," 170–171.

8 Brid Featherstone, "Victims or Villains? Women Who Physically Abuse Their Children," in *Violence and Gender Relations: Theories and Interventions*, ed. Barbara Fawcett, Brid Featherstone, Jeff Hearn, and Christine Toft (London: Sage Publications, 1996), 178–189.

9 Rhea Almeida and others, "Violence in the Lives of the Racially and Sexually Different: A Public and Private Dilemma," *Journal of Feminist Family Therapy* 5, no. 3/4 (1994): 99–126.

10 Mary E. Gilfus, "The Price of the Ticket: A Survivor-Centered Appraisal of Trauma Theory," *Violence Against Women* 5, no 11 (1999): 1251.

11 See Cindy Holmes, "The Politics of Naming the Violence: Examining Constructions of 'Lesbian Abuse' in Community-Based Educational Discourses," (M.A. Thesis: Ontario Institute for Studies in Education, University of Toronto, 2000); Mary Louise Pratt, *Imperial Eyes: Travel Writing and Transculturation* (New York: Routledge, 1992); and Sherene Razack, *Looking White People in the Eye: Gender, Race, and Culture in Courtrooms and Classrooms* (Toronto: University of Toronto Press, 1998).

12 Michel Foucault, *Discipline and Punish: The Birth of the Prison*, trans. A. Sheridan Smith (London: Allen Lane, 1997).

13 Featherstone, "Victims or Villains?"

14 Janice L. Ristock and Joan Pennell, *Community Research as Empowerment: Feminist Links, Postmodern Interruptions* (Toronto: Oxford University Press, 1996).

15 Holmes, "The Politics of Naming," 132.

16 See Valli Kanuha, "Compounding the Triple Jeopardy: Battering in Lesbian of Color Relationships," in *Confronting Lesbian Battering: A Manual for the Battered Women's Movement*, ed. Pam Elliott (St. Paul, MN: Minnesota Coalition for Battered Women, 1990), 142–157; and Claire M. Renzetti, "Violence and Abuse in Lesbian Relationships: Theoretical and Empirical Issues," in *Issues in Intimate Violence*, ed. Raquel Kennedy Bergen (Thousand Oaks, CA: Sage Publications, 1998), 117–128.

17 Jennifer Margulies, "Coalition Building 'Til it Hurts: Creating Safety Around S/M and Battering," in *Same-Sex Domestic Violence: Strategies for Change*, ed. Beth Leventhal and Sandra E. Lundy (Thousand Oaks, CA: Sage Publications, 1999), 135–146.

18 Haaken, *Pillar of Salt*

19 Ibid; see also Janice Haaken, "Heretical Texts: 'The Courage to Heal' and the Incest Survivor Movement," in *New Versions of Victims: Feminists Struggle with the Concept*, ed. Sharon Lamb (New York: New York University Press, 1999), 13–41. Haaken's work looks at women's memories of childhood sexual abuse to show the layers of complicated meaning-making involved and shift the discussion from the quest to distinguish true from false memories.

20 Joan Scott, "Experience," in *Feminists Theorize the Political*, ed. Judith Butler and Joan Scott (New York: Routledge, 1992), 22–40.

21 Haaken, *Pillar of Salt*.

22 Michel Foucault, *The History of Sexuality* (New York: Random House, 1978/1990), 100.

Six: The Politics of Responding to Violence in Lesbian Relationships

1 Paul Rabinow, ed. *The Foucault Reader* (New York: Pantheon Books, 1984).

2 Laurie Chesley, Donna MacAulay, and Janice L. Ristock, *Abuse in Lesbian Relationships: Information and Resources*, rev. ed. [Booklet] (Ottawa: Minister of Public Works and Government Services Canada, 1992). Distributed by National Clearinghouse on Family Violence, Health Canada.

3 Sharon Lamb, *The Trouble With Blame: Victims, Perpetrators, and Responsibility* (Cambridge, MA: Harvard University Press, 1996), 180.

4 Jennifer Grant, writing for the San Francisco Network for Battered Lesbians and Bisexual Women, "An Argument for Separate Services," in *Same-Sex Domestic Violence: Strategies for Change*, ed. Beth Leventhal and Sandra E. Lundy (Thousand Oaks, CA: Sage Publications, 1999), 183–192.

5 Ellen Pence, *In Our Best Interest: A Process for Personal and Social Change* (Duluth, Minnesota: Minnesota Program Development Fund, 1987).

6 Joshua M. Price, "Spaces of Violence, Shades of Meaning: The Heterogeneity of Violence Against Women in the United States" (Ph.D. dissertation: University of Chicago, 1998).

7 Pence, "The Duluth Domestic;" and Price, "Spaces of Violence."

8 Price, "Spaces of Violence," 97.

9 Ibid., 110.

10 The Southern Arizona Task Force on Domestic Violence produced a Wheel for gay and lesbian partner violence in 1995, as cited in Joan C. McClennen, "Partner Abuse Between Lesbian Couples: Toward a Better Understanding," in *A Professional Guide to Understanding Gay and Lesbian Domestic Violence: Understanding Practice Interventions*, ed. Joan C. McClennen and John Gunther (New York: Edwin Mellen Press, 1999), 81.

11 This Wheel is published in the booklet by Cheryl Champagne, Ruth Lapp, and Julia Lee, "Assisting Abused Lesbians: A Guide for Health Professionals and Service Providers" (London, ON: London Battered Women's Advocacy Centre, 1994), and is discussed in Price, "Spaces of Violence," 134–135.

12 Adapted by the New York Gay and Lesbian Anti-violence project

13 Price, "Spaces of Violence," 145.

14 Lisa J. Fox, "Couples Therapy for Gay and Lesbian Couples With a History of Domestic Violence," in *A Professional Guide to Understanding Gay and Lesbian Domestic Violence: Understanding Practice Interventions*, ed. Joan C. McClennen and John Gunther (New York: Edwin Mellen Press, 1999), 107–126.

15 Jerry Finn, "Domestic Violence Organizations on the Web: A New Arena for Domestic Violence Services," *Violence Against Women* 6 (2000): 80–102.

16 Cindy Holmes, "The Politics of Naming the Violence: Examining Contradictions of 'Lesbian Abuse' in Community-Based Educational Discourses" (M.A. The-

sis: Ontario Institute for Studies in Education, University of Toronto, 2000).

17 Advocates for Abused and Battered Lesbians [homepage]; available from <http://www.aabl.org>; Internet, accessed 10 November, 2000. I am aware that they have recently changed their name to Northwest Network of Bisexual, Trans, and Lesbian Survivors of Abuse. When writing this volume their new website was under construction.

18 Network for Battered Lesbians and Bisexual Women [homepage]; available from <http://www.nblbw.org>; Internet, accessed 11 November 2000.

19 Women Organized to Make Abuse Nonexistent (W.O.M.A.N.) Inc. [homepage] available from <http://www.norcov.com/womaninc>; Internet, accessed 10 November, 2000].

20 Los Angeles Gay and Lesbian Center (LAGLC) [homepage]; available from <http://www.laglc.org>; Internet, accessed 11 November 2000

21 New York City Gay and Lesbian Anti-Violence Project [homepage]; available from <http://www.avp.org>; Internet, accessed 11 November, 2000.

22 New York City Gay and Lesbian Anti-Violence Project (AVP) and the National Coalition of Anti-Violence Programs (NCAVP), "1998 Report on Lesbian, Gay, Bisexual and Transgender Domestic Violence" [online, 52 pages]; available from http://www.avp.org; Internet, accessed 12 November, 2000.

23 Ibid., 19.

24 This mandatory reporting law in the state of California falls under the *Domestic Violence Prevention Act, Family Code*, division 10, sec. 6200§ (1994).

25 Chesley, MacAulay, and Ristock, *Abuse.*

26 Ibid., 10.

27 Ibid.

28 Ibid.

29 Holmes, "The Politics of Naming," 74.

30 Domestic Violence Resource Centre (DVRC), *"Out" of Sight* 7 (March 2000): 1.

31 Ibid., 7.

32 Ibid., 6.

33 Ibid., 15.

34 Lisa Allen-Agostini and Jhesekah, "Bruised," performed 12–13 June, 1996, Winnipeg, MB.

35 Claudia Card, "Groping Through Gray Zones," in *On Feminist Ethics and Politics*, ed. Claudia Card (Lawrence, KS: University Press of Kansas, 1999), 3–26.

36 Brenda Cossman, "The Crime of Playing Doctor," *XTRA!*, 8 March, 2001, p. 16.

37 Ibid.

38 As reported by Stephanie Nolen, "Fighting to Do a Woman's Work," *The Globe and Mail*, 9 December, 2000, sec. A, p. 2.

39 Ibid.

40 Jacqueline Anderson, "Revolutionary Community," in *On Feminist Ethics and Politics*, ed. Claudia Card (Lawrence, KS: University of Kansas Press, 1999), 140–149.

Seven: Looking Forward

1 See Jana L. Jasinski and Linda M. Williams, eds., *Partner Violence: A Comprehensive Review of 20 Years of Research* (Thousand Oaks, CA: Sage Publications, 1998); and Michael P. Johnson, "Patriarchal Terrorism and Common Couple Violence: Two Forms of Violence Against Women," *Journal of Marriage and the Family* 57 (1995): 283–294.

2 Canada, Solicitor-General, *The Four Circles of Hollow Water* (Ottawa, 1997).

3 McGillivray, Anne, and Brenda Comaskey, *Black Eyes All of the Time: Intimate Violence, Aboriginal Women, and the Justice System* (Toronto: University of Toronto Press, 1999), 168.

4 Gale Burford, Joan Pennell, and Susan MacLeod, "Manual for Coordinators and Communities: The Organization and Practice of Family Group Decision Making," rev. ed., 1995 [online]; available from <http://social.chass.ncsu.edu/jpennell/fgdm/Manual>; Internet, accessed January 2001.

5 Ibid., appendix A.

6 Sherene H. Razack, *Looking White People in the Eye: Gender, Race, and Culture in Courtrooms and Classrooms* (Toronto: University of Toronto Press, 1998), 170.

7 Laura S. Brown, "Discomforts of the Powerless: Feminist Constructions of Distress," in *Constructions of Disorder: Meaning-Making Frameworks for Psychotherapy*, ed. Robert A. Neimeyer and Jonathan D. Raskin (Washington, DC: American Psychological Association, 2000), 287–308.

8 Kenneth J. Gergen and Sheila McNamee, "From Disordering Discourse to Transformative Dialogue," in *Constructions of Disorder: Meaning-Making Frameworks for Psychotherapy*, ed. Robert A. Neimeyer and Jonathan D. Raskin (Washington, DC: American Psychological Association, 2000), 347.

9 Laurie Chesley, Donna MacAulay, and Janice L. Ristock, *Abuse in Lesbian Relationships: Information and Resources*, rev. ed. [booklet] (Ottawa: Minister of Public Works and Government Services Canada, 1992), 20. Distributed by The National Clearinghouse on Family Violence, Health Canada.

10 Our booklet has different sections that include: If you are being abused; The effects of abuse; Getting help; If you are abusive; Friends and relatives can help; and How professionals can respond. I alter that framework, but still rely on some of the sound information that we originally wrote. My new writings have greatly benefited from the contributions and insights of Laurie and Donna in our original collaboration. I also wish to thank Cindy Holmes and Sherri McConnell who each offered a critical reading and provided me with alternate wordings.

BIBLIOGRAPHY

Advocates for Abused and Battered Lesbians. [homepage] Available from http://www.aabl.org; Internet, accessed 10 November 2000.

Alcoff, Linda, and Laura Gray. "Survivor Discourse: Transgression or Recuperation?" *Signs* 18 (1993): 260-290.

Alexander, M. Jacqui, and Chandra Talpade Mohanty, eds. *Feminist Genealogies, Colonial Legacies, Democratic Futures*. New York: Routledge, 1997.

Allen-Agostini, Lisa, and Jhesekah. "Bruised." Performed 12–13 June 1996, Winnipeg, MB.

Allison, Dorothy. Foreword to *My Dangerous Desires*, by Amber L. Hollibaugh, xv. Durham and London: Duke University Press, 2000.

Almeida, Rhea, Rosemary Woods, Theresa Messineo, Roberto J. Font, and Chris Heer. "Violence in the Lives of the Racially and Sexually Different: A Public and Private Dilemma." *Journal of Feminist Family Therapy* 5, no. 3/4 (1994): 99–126.

Anderson, Jacqueline. "Revolutionary Community." In *On Feminist Ethics and Politics*, edited by Claudia Card, 140–149. Lawrence, KS: University of Kansas Press, 1999.

Anzaldua, Gloria. "La conciencia de la mestiza: Towards a New Consciousness." In *Making Face, Making Soul/Haciendo caras: Creative and Critical Perspectives by Women of Color*, edited by Gloria Anzaldua, 377–390. San Francisco: Aunt Lute Books, 1990.

———, ed. *Making Face, Making Soul/Haciendo caras: Creative and Critical Perspectives by Women of Color*. San Francisco: Aunt Lute Books, 1990.

Atmore, Chris. "Victims, Backlash, and Radical Feminist Theory (Or, the Morning After They Stole Feminism's Fire)." In *New Versions of Victims: Feminists Struggle With the Concept*, edited by Sharon Lamb, 183–211. New York: New York University Press, 1999.

Balan, Angie, Rhonda Chorney, and Janice L. Ristock. *Training and Education Project for Responding to Abuse in Lesbian Relationships: Final Report*. Ottawa: Department of Health, 1995. Project no. 4887-07-93-011.

Bar On, Bat-Ami. "Introduction," *Hypatia*, special issue on *Women and Violence* 11, no. 4 (1996): 4.

Benokraitis, Nijole Vaicaitis, ed. *Subtle Sexism: Current Practice and Prospects for Change*. Thousand Oaks, CA: Sage Publications, 1997.

Bergen, Raquel Kennedy, ed. *Issues in Intimate Violence*. Thousand Oaks, CA: Sage Publications, 1998.

Berrill, Kevin T. "Antigay Violence and Victimization in the United States: An Overview." In *Hate Crimes: Confronting Violence Against Lesbians and Gay Men*, edited by Gregory M. Herek and Kevin T. Berrill, 19–45. Newbury Park, CA: Sage Publications, 1992.

Besharov, Douglas J., ed. *Research and Public Policy Issues*. Washington, DC: AEI Press, 1990.

Bhattacharjee, Anannya. "The Public/Private Mirage: Mapping Homes and Undomesticating Violence Work in the South Asian Immigrant Community." In *Feminist Genealogies, Colonial Legacies, Democratic Futures*, edited by M. Jacqui Alexander and Chandra Talpade Mohanty, 308–329. New York: Routledge, 1997.

Bonnycastle, Kevin, and George S. Rigakos, eds. *Unsettling Truths: Battered Women, Policy, Politics, and Contemporary Research in Canada*. Vancouver: Collective, 1998.

Brand, Pamela A., and Aline H. Kidd. "Frequency of Physical Aggression in Heterosexual and Female Homosexual Dyads." *Psychological Reports* 59 (1986): 1307–1313.

Brock, Debi. "Talkin' Bout a Revelation: Feminist Popular Discourse on Sexual Abuse." *Canadian Woman Studies* 12, no. 1 (1991): 12–16.

Brown, Laura S. "Not Outside the Range: One Feminist Perspective on Psychic Trauma." In *Trauma: Explorations in Memory*, edited by Cathy Caruth, 100–112. Baltimore, MD: Johns Hopkins University Press, 1995.

——. "Discomforts of the Powerless: Feminist Constructions of Distress." In *Constructions of Disorder: Meaning-Making Frameworks for Psychotherapy*, edited by Robert A. Neimeyer and Jonathan D. Raskin, 287–308. Washington, DC: American Psychological Association, 2000.

Burford, Gale, Joan Pennell, and Susan MacLeod. "Manual for Coordinators and Communities: The Organization and Practice of Family Group Decision Making." Rev. ed., 1995 [manual]. Available from <http://social.chass.ncsu.edu/jpennell/fgdm/>; Internet, accessed 10 January 2001.

Burman, Erica., ed. *Deconstructing Feminist Psychology*. London: Sage Publications, 1998.

Burton, Nadya. "Resistance to Prevention: Reconsidering Feminist Antiviolence Rhetoric." In *Violence Against Women: Philosophical Perspectives*, edited by Stanley G. French, Wanda Teays, and Laura M. Purdy, 182–200. Ithaca, NY: Cornell University Press, 1998.

Butler, Judith, and Joan Scott, eds. *Feminists Theorize the Political*. New York: Routledge, 1992.

Butler, Lola. "African American Lesbians Experiencing Partner Abuse." In *A Professional Guide to Practice Gay and Lesbian Domestic Violence: Understanding Practice Intervention*, edited by Joan C. McClennen and John Gunther, 181–206. Lewiston, NY: Edwin Mellen Press, 1999.

Canada. Solicitor-General. *The Four Circles of Hollow Water*. Ottawa, 1997.

Canadian Panel on Violence Against Women. *Changing the Landscape: Ending Violence-Achieving Equality. Final Report*, 4. Ottawa: Minister of Supply and Services Canada, 1993.

Card, Claudia. *Lesbian Choices*. New York: Columbia University Press, 1995.

_____. "Groping Through Gray Zones." In *On Feminist Ethics and Politics*, edited by Claudia Card, 3–26. Lawrence, KS: University of Kansas Press, 1999.

_____, ed. *On Feminist Ethics and Politics*. Lawrence, KS: University of Kansas Press, 1999.

Caruth, Cathy, ed. *Trauma: Explorations in Memory*. Baltimore, MD: Johns Hopkins University Press, 1995.

Causby, Vickie, Lettie Lockhart, Barbara White, and Kathryn Greene. "Fusion and Conflict Resolution in Lesbian Relationships." *Journal of Gay and Lesbian Social Services* 3 (1995): 67–82.

Cayouette, Susan. "Running Batterer Groups for Lesbians." In *Same-Sex Domestic Violence: Strategies for Change*, edited by Beth Leventhal and Sandra E. Lundy, 233–242. Thousand Oaks, CA: Sage Publications, 1999.

Champagne, Cheryl, Ruth Lapp, and Julie Lee. *Assisting Abused Lesbians: A Guide for Health Professionals and Service Providers*. London, ON: London Battered Women's Advocacy Centre, 1994.

Chesley, Laurie, Donna MacAulay, and Janice L. Ristock. *Abuse in Lesbian Relationships: Information and Resources*. Rev. ed. [Booklet]. Ottawa: Minister of Public Works and Government Services Canada, 1992. Distributed by The National Clearinghouse on Family Violence, Health Canada.

Chrisler, Joan C., and Alyce Huston Hemstreet, eds. *Variations on a Theme: Diversity and the Psychology of Women*. Albany, NY: State University of New York Press, 1995.

Chrystos. *Dream On*. Vancouver: Press Gang Publishers, 1991.

Coleman, Valerie E. *Violence Between Lesbian Couples: A Between-Groups Comparison*. Ph.D. dissertation: University Microfilms International, 9109022, 1990.

_____. "Lesbian Battering: The Relationship Between Personality and Perpetuation of Violence." *Violence and Victims* 9 (1994): 139–152.

Collins, Patricia Hill. "Learning From the Outsider Within: The Sociological Significance of Black Feminist Thought." *Social Problems* 33, no. 6 (1986): S14–S32.

_____. *Black Feminist Thought: Knowledge, Consciousness, and the Politics of Empowerment*. Boston: Unwin Hyman, 1990.

Comstock, Gary David. *Violence Against Lesbians and Gay Men*. New York: Columbia University Press, 1991.

Crenshaw, Kimberly W. "Mapping the Margins: Intersectionality, Identity Politics, and Violence Against Women of Color." *In The Public Nature of Private Violence: The Discovery of Domestic Abuse*, edited by Martha Albertson Fineman and Roxanne Mykitiuk, 93–118. New York: Routledge, 1994.

Currie, Dawn H. "Violent Men or Violent Women? Whose Definition Counts." In *Issues in Intimate Violence*, edited by Raquel Kennedy Bergen, 97-111. Thousand Oaks, CA: Sage Publications, 1998.

DeKeseredy, Walter S. "Tactics of the Antifeminist Backlash Against Canadian National Woman Abuse Surveys." *Violence Against Women* 5 (1999): 1258–1276.

De Vidas, Michael. "Childhood Sexual Abuse and Domestic Violence: A Support Group for Latino Gay Men and Lesbians." *Journal of Gay and Lesbian Social Services* 10, no. 2 (1999): 51–68.

Dobash, Rebecca Emerson, and Russell P. Dobash. "How Theoretical Definition and

Perspectives Affect Research and Policy." In *Research and Public Policy Issues*, edited by Douglas J. Besharov, 108–129. Washington, DC: AEI Press, 1990.

———. "Violence Against Women." In *Gender Violence: Interdisciplinary Perspectives*, edited by Laura L. O'Toole and Jessica R. Schiffmann, 266–278. New York: New York University Press, 1997.

———, eds. *Rethinking Violence Against Women*. Sage Series on Violence Against Women, vol. 9. Thousand Oaks, CA: Sage Publications, 1998.

Domestic Violence Prevention Act. Family Code. Division 10, sec. 6200§ (1994).

Domestic Violence Resource Centre. *'Out' of Sight* 7 (March 2000).

Duffy, Ann, and Julianne Momirov. *Family Violence: A Canadian Introduction*. Toronto: James Lorimer & Company, 1997.

Dutton, Donald G. "Patriarchy and Wife Assault: The Ecological Fallacy." *Violence and Victims* 9 (1994): 167–182.

Eaton, Mary. "Abuse by Any Other Name: Feminism, Difference, and Intralesbian Violence." In *The Public Nature of Private Violence: The Discovery of Domestic Abuse*, edited by Martha Albertson Fineman and Roxanne Mykitiuk, 195–224. New York: Routledge, 1994.

Elliott, Pam, ed. *Confronting Lesbian Battering: A Manual for the Battered Women's Movement*. St. Paul, MN: Minnesota Coalition for Battered Women, 1990.

———. "How Should Battered Lesbians Seek Help and Justice?" *Lesbian Battering Intervention Project Report*. St. Paul, MN, 1991, p. 3.

———. "Shattering Illusions: Same-Sex Domestic Violence." In *Violence in Gay and Lesbian Domestic Partnerships*, edited by Claire M. Renzetti and Charles Harvey Miley, 1–8. New York: Harrington Park Press, 1996.

Faulkner, Ellen. "Woman-to-Woman Abuse: Analyzing Extant Accounts of Lesbian Battering. In *Unsettling Truths: Battered Women, Policy, Politics, and Contemporary Research in Canada*, edited by Kevin Bonnycastle and George S. Rigakos, 52–62. Vancouver: Collective, 1998.

Fawcett, Barbara, Brid Featherstone, Jeff Hearn, and Christine Toft, eds. *Violence and Gender Relations: Theories and Interventions*. London: Sage Publications, 1996.

Featherstone, Brid. "Victims or Villains? Women Who Physically Abuse Their Children." In *Violence and Gender Relations: Theories and Interventions*, edited by Barbara Fawcett, Brid Featherstone, Jeff Hearn, and Christine Toft, 178–189. London: Sage Publications, 1996.

Fellows, Mary Louise, and Sherene Razack. "The Race to Innocence: Confronting Hierarchical Relations Among Women." *Iowa Journal of Race, Gender and Justice*, vol. 1, no. 2 (1998).

Felman, Shoshana. *Jacques Lacan and the Adventure of Insight: Psychoanalysis in Contemporary Culture*. Cambridge, MA: Harvard University Press, 1987.

Ferraro, Kathleen. "The Dance of Dependency: A Genealogy of Domestic Violence Discourse." *Hypatia* 11, no. 4 (1996): 77–91.

Fine, Michelle. *Disruptive Voices: The Possibilities of Feminist Research*. Ann Arbor, MI: University of Michigan Press, 1992.

Fineman, Martha Albertson, and Roxanne Mykitiuk, eds. *The Public Nature of*

Private Violence: The Discovery of Domestic Abuse. New York: Routledge, 1994.

Finn, Jerry. "Domestic Violence Organizations on the Web: A New Arena for Domestic Violence Services." *Violence Against Women* 6 (2000): 80–102.

Flax, Jane. "The End of Innocence." In *Feminists Theorize the Political*, edited by Judith Butler and Joan Scott. New York: Routledge, 1992.

———. *Disputed Subjects: Essays on Psychoanalysis, Politics and Philosophy*. New York: Routledge, 1993.

Foucault, Michel. *The Archeology of Knowledge and the Discourse on Language*. Translated by A. M. Sheridan Smith. New York: Pantheon Books, 1972.

———. *The History of Sexuality*. New York: Random House Books, 1978/1990.

———. *Discipline and Punish: The Birth of the Prison*. Translated by A. Sheridan Smith. London: Allen Lane, 1997.

Fox, Lisa J. "Couples Therapy for Gay and Lesbian Couples With a History of Domestic Violence," in *A Professional Guide to Understanding Gay and Lesbian Domestic Violence: Understanding Practice Interventions*, edited by Joan C. McClennen and John Gunther, 107–126. New York: Edwin Mellen Press, 1999.

Frankenburg, Ruth. *White Women, Race Matters: The Social Construction of Whiteness*. Minneapolis, MN: University of Minneapolis, 1993.

Fray-Witzer, Evan. "Twice-Abused: Same-Sex Domestic Violence and the Law." In *Same-Sex Domestic Violence: Strategies for Change*, edited by Beth Leventhal and Sandra E. Lundy, 19–42. Thousand Oaks, CA: Sage Publications, 1999.

French, Stanley G., Wanda Teays, and Laura M. Purdy, eds. *Violence Against Women: Philosophical Perspectives*. Ithaca, NY: Cornell University Press, 1998.

Garcia, Martha Lucia. "A 'New Kind' of Battered Woman: Challenges for the Movement." In *Same-Sex Domestic Violence: Strategies for Change*, edited by Beth Leventhal and Sandra E. Lundy, 165–172. Thousand Oaks, CA: Sage Publications, 1999.

Gates, Henry Louis Jr., ed. *Bearing Witness: Selections from African-American Autobiography in the Twentieth Century*. New York: Pantheon Books, 1991.

Gelles, Richard J., and Donileen R. Loseke, eds. *Current Controversies in Family Violence*. Newbury Park, CA: Sage Publications, 1993.

Gergen, Kenneth J., and Sheila McNamee. "From Disordering Discourse to Transformative Dialogue." In *Constructions of Disorder: Meaning-Making Frameworks for Psychotherapy*, edited by Robert A. Neimeyer and Jonathan D. Raskin, 347. Washington, DC: American Psychological Association, 2000.

Gilbert, L., P. B. Poorman, and S. Simmons. "Guidelines for Mental Health Systems Response to Lesbian Battering." In *Confronting Lesbian Battering: A Manual for the Battered Women's Movement*, edited by Pam Elliott, 105–117. St. Paul, MN: Minnesota Coalition for Battered Women, 1990.

Gilfus, Mary E. "The Price of the Ticket: A Survivor-Centered Appraisal of Trauma Theory." *Violence Against Women* 5, no. 11 (1999): 1238–1257.

Goddard, Alma Banda, and Tara Hardy. "Assessing the Lesbian Victim." In *Same-Sex Domestic Violence: Strategies for Change*, edited by Beth Leventhal and Sandra E. Lundy, 193–200. Thousand Oaks, CA: Sage Publications, 1999.

Gordon, Linda. *Heroes of Their Own Lives*. London: Virago, 1989.

Grant, Jennifer. "An Argument for Separate Services." In *Same-Sex Domestic Violence: Strategies for Change*, edited by Beth Leventhal and Sandra E. Lundy, 183-192. Thousand Oaks, CA: Sage Publications, 1999.

Greene, Kathryn, Vickie Causby, and Diane Helene Greene. "The Nature and Function of Fusion in the Dynamics of Lesbian Relationships." *Affilia* 14, no. 1 (Spring 1999): 78–97.

Grewal, Inderpal, Caren Kaplan. *Scattered Hegemonies: Postmodernity and Transnational Feminist Practices*. Minneapolis, MN: University of Minnesota Press, 1994.

Haaken, Janice. *Pillar of Salt: Gender, Memory, and the Perils of Looking Back*. London: Rutgers University Press, 1998.

_____. "Heretical Texts: 'The Courage to Heal' and the Incest Survivor Movement." In *New Versions of Victims: Feminists Struggle with the Concept*, edited by Sharon Lamb, 13–41. New York: New York University Press, 1999.

Hall, Alison. "Abuse by Lesbians." *Trouble and Strife* 23 (Spring 1992): 38–40.

Hamberger, L. Kevin, and Claire M. Renzetti, eds. *Domestic Partner Abuse*. New York: Springer, 1995.

Hammond, Nancy. "Lesbian Victims of Relationship Violence." *Women and Therapy* 8 (1989): 89–105.

Hanmer, Jalna, and Mary Maynard, eds. *Women, Violence and Social Control*. Atlantic Highlands, NJ: Humanities Press International, 1987.

Haraway, Donna J. "Situated Knowledge: The Science Question in Feminism and the Privilege of Partial Perspective." *Feminist Studies* 14 (1988): 575–599.

Hart, Barbara. "Lesbian Battering: An Examination." In *Naming the Violence: Speaking Out About Lesbian Battering*, edited by Kerry Lobel, 173–189. Seattle, WA: Seal Press, 1986.

Hekman, Susan. "Truth and Method: Feminist Standpoint Theory Revisited." *Signs* 22, no. 2 (1997): 341–63.

Herek, Gregory M., and Kevin T. Berrill, eds. *Hate Crimes: Confronting Violence Against Lesbians and Gay Men*. Newbury Park, CA: Sage Publications, 1992.

Herman, Judith. *Trauma and Recovery: The Aftermath of Violence from Domestic Abuse and Political Terror*. New York: Basic Books, 1992.

Holmes, Cindy. "The Politics of Naming the Violence: Examining Constructions of 'Lesbian Abuse' in Community-Based Educational Discourses." M.A. Thesis, Ontario Institute for Studies in Education at the University of Toronto, 2000.

hooks, bell. *Black Looks: Race and Representation*. Toronto: Between the Lines, 1992.

_____. "Violence in Intimate Relationships: A Feminist Perspective." In *Gender Violence: Interdisciplinary Perspectives*, edited by Laura L. O'Toole and Jessica R. Schiffmann, 279–284. New York: New York University Press, 1997.

Island, David, and Patrick Letellier. *Men Who Beat the Men Who Love Them*. New York: Harrington Park Press, 1991.

Istar, Arlene. "Couple Assessment: Identifying and Intervening in Domestic Violence in Lesbian Relationships." In *Violence in Gay and Lesbian Domestic Partnerships*, edited by Claire M. Renzetti and Charles Harvey Miley, 93-106. New York: Harrington Park Press, 1996.

Istar Lev, Arlene, and S. Sundance Lev. "Sexual Assault in the Lesbian, Gay, Bisexual and Transgendered Communities." In *A Professional Guide to Understanding Gay and Lesbian Domestic Violence: Understanding Practice Interventions*, edited by Joan C. McClennen and John Gunther, 35–62. New York: Edwin Mellen Press, 1999.

Jagose, Annamarie. *Queer Theory: An Introduction*. New York: New York University Press, 1996.

Jasinski, Jana L., and Linda M. Williams, eds. *Partner Violence: A Comprehensive Review of 20 Years of Research*. Thousand Oaks, CA: Sage Publications, 1998.

Johnson, Michael P. "Patriarchal Terrorism and Common Couple Violence: Two Forms of Violence Against Women." *Journal of Marriage and the Family* 57 (1995): 283–294.

Kanuha, Valli. "Compounding the Triple Jeopardy: Battering in Lesbian of Colour Relationships." *Women and Therapy* 9(1990): 169–184.

Kaye/Kantrowitz, Melanie. *The Issue is Power: Essays on Women, Jews, Violence and Resistance*. San Francisco: Aunt Lute Books, 1992.

Kelly, Carl E., and Lynn Warshafsky. "Partner Abuse in Gay Male and Lesbian Couples." Paper presented at the Third National Conference for Family Violence Researchers, Durham, NH, July 1987.

Kelly, Liz. "The Continuum of Sexual Violence," in *Women, Violence and Social Control*, edited by Jalna Hanmer and Mary Maynard. Atlantic Highlands, NJ: Humanities Press International, 1987.

———. *Surviving Sexual Violence*. Minneapolis, MN: University of Minnesota Press, 1988.

———. "Unspeakable Acts: Abuse By and Between Women." *Trouble and Strife* 21 (Summer 1991): 13-20.

Kelly, Liz, and Jill Radford. "Sexual Violence Against Women and Girls: An Approach to an International Overview." In *Rethinking Violence Against Women*, edited by Rebecca Emerson Dobash and Russell P. Dobash, 53–76. Sage Series on Violence Against Women, vol. 9. Thousand Oaks, CA: Sage Publications, 1998.

Kennedy, Elizabeth L., and Madeline D. Davis. *Boots of Leather, Slippers of Gold: The History of a Lesbian Community*. New York: Penguin Books, 1993.

Koss, Mary P., Lisa A. Goodman, Angela Browne, Louise F. Fitzgerald, Gwendolyn Puryear Ketia, and Nancy Felipe Russo. *No Safe Haven: Male Violence Against Women at Home, at Work, and in the Community*. Washington, DC: American Psychological Association, 1994.

Krestan, Jo-Ann, and Claudia S. Bepko. "The Problem of Fusion in the Lesbian Relationship." *Family Process* 19 (1980): 277–289.

Kurz, Demie. "Emergency Department Responses to Battered Women: Resistance to Medicalization." *Social Problems* 34 (1987): 69–81.

Laframboise, Donna. *The Princess at the Window: A New Gender Morality*. Toronto: Penguin Books, 1996.

Lakeman, Lee. "Why Law and Order Cannot End Violence Against Women and Why the Development of Women's (Social, Economic, Political, and Civil) Rights Might." *Canadian Woman Studies* 20, no. 3 (2000): 24–33.

Lamb, Sharon. *The Trouble With Blame: Victims, Perpetrators, and Responsibility*. Cambridge, MA: Harvard University Press, 1996.

_____. "Constructing the Victim: Popular Images and Lasting Labels." In *New Versions of Victims: Feminists Struggle with the Concept*, edited by Sharon Lamb, 108-138. New York: New York University Press, 1999.

_____, ed. In *New Versions of Victims: Feminists Struggle with the Concept*. New York: New York University Press, 1999.

Lather, Patti. *Getting Smart: Feminist Research and Pedagogy With/In the Postmodern*. New York: Routledge, 1991.

Lather, Patti, and Chris Smithies. *Troubling the Angels: Women Living with HIV/AIDS*. Boulder, CO: Westview Press, 1997.

Leeder, Elaine. "Enmeshed in Pain: Counselling the Lesbian Battering Couple." *Women and Therapy* 7 (1988): 81–99.

Letellier, Patrick. Gay and Bisexual Male Domestic Violence Victimization: Challenges to Feminist Theory and Responses to Violence." *Violence and Victims* 9 (1994): 95–106.

_____. "Twin Epidemics: Domestic Violence and HIV Infection Among Gay and Bisexual Men." In *Violence in Gay and Lesbian Domestic Partnerships*, edited by Claire M. Renzetti and Charles Harvey Miley, 69–82. New York: Harrington Park Press, 1996.

Leventhal, Beth, and Sandra E. Lundy, eds. *Same-Sex Domestic Violence: Strategies for Change*. Thousand Oaks, CA: Sage Publications, 1999.

Lie, Gwat-Yong, and Sabrina Gentlewarrier. "Intimate Violence in Lesbian Relationships: Discussion of Survey Findings and Practice Implications." *Journal of Social Service Research* 15, no. 1/2 (1991): 41–59.

Lie, Gwat-Yong, Rebecca Schilit, Judy Bush, Marilyn Montagne, and Lynn Reyes. "Lesbians in Currently Aggressive Relationships: How Frequently Do They Report Aggressive Past Relationships?" *Violence and Victims* 6 (1991): 121–135.

Lobel, Kerry, ed. *Naming the Violence: Speaking Out About Lesbian Battering*. Seattle, WA: Seal Press, 1986.

Lockhart, Lettie L., Barbara W. White, Vickie Causby, and Alicia Isaac. "Letting Out the Secret: Violence in Lesbian Relationships." *Journal of Interpersonal Violence* 9 (1994): 469–492.

Los Angeles Gay and Lesbian Center (LAGLC) [homepage]. Available from http://www.laglc.org; Internet, accessed 11 November 2000.

Loulan, Joann. *Lesbian Passion*. San Francisco, CA: Spinsters/Aunt Lute Books, 1987.

Maguire, Patricia. *Doing Participatory Research: A Feminist Approach*. Amherst: Center for International Education, School of Education, University of Massachusetts, 1987.

Malson, Helen. *The Thin Woman: Feminism, Post-Structuralism and the Social Psychology of Anorexia Nervosa*. London: Routledge, 1988.

Marcus, Sharon. "Fighting Bodies, Fighting Words: A Theory and Politics of Rape Prevention." In *Feminists Theorize the Political*, edited by Judith Butler and Joan Scott, 385–403. New York: Routledge, 1992.

Marecek, Jeanne. "Trauma Talk in Feminist Clinical Practice." In *New Versions of Victims: Feminists Struggle with the Concept*, edited by Sharon Lamb, 158–182.

New York: New York University Press, 1999.

Margulies, Jennifer. "Coalition Building 'Til it Hurts: Creating Safety Around S/M and Battering." In *Same-Sex Domestic Violence: Strategies for Change*, edited by Beth Leventhal and Sandra E. Lundy, 135-146. Thousand Oaks, CA: Sage Publications, 1999.

Marrujo, Becky, and Mary Kreger. "Definition of Roles in Abusive Lesbian Relationships." In *Violence in Gay and Lesbian Domestic Partnerships*, edited by Claire M. Renzetti and Charles Harvey Miley, 23–33. New York: Harrington Park Press, 1996.

McClennen, Joan C. "Partner Abuse Between Lesbian Couples: Toward a Better Understanding." In *A Professional Guide to Understanding Gay and Lesbian Domestic Violence: Understanding Practice Interventions*, edited by Joan C. McClennen and John Gunther, 77–94. New York: Edwin Mellen Press, 1999.

McClennen, Joan C., and John Gunther, eds. *A Professional Guide to Understanding Gay and Lesbian Domestic Violence: Understanding Practice Interventions*. New York: Edwin Mellen Press, 1999.

McGillivray, Anne, and Brenda Comaskey. *Black Eyes All of the Time: Intimate Violence, Aboriginal Women, and the Justice System*. Toronto: University of Toronto Press, 1999.

Mendez, Juan M. "Serving Gays and Lesbians of Color Who Are Survivors of Domestic Violence." *Journal of Gay and Lesbian Social Services* 4 (1996): 53–59.

Merrill, Gregory S. "Ruling the Exceptions: Same-Sex Battering and Domestic Violence Theory." In *Violence in Gay and Lesbian Domestic Partnerships*, edited by Claire M. Renzetti and Charles Harvey Miley, 9–22. New York: Harrington Park Press, 1996.

Morrow, Susan L., and Donna M. Hawxhurst. "Lesbian Partner Abuse: Implications for Therapists." *Journal of Counseling and Development* 68 (1989): 58–62.

Neimeyer, Robert A., and Jonathan D. Raskin, eds. *Constructions of Disorder: Meaning-Making Frameworks for Psychotherapy*. Washington, DC: American Psychological Association, 2000.

Network for Battered Lesbians and Bisexual Women [homepage]. Available from http://www.nblbw.org; Internet, accessed 11 November 2000.

New York City Gay and Lesbian Anti-Violence Project [homepage]. Available from http://www.avp.org; Internet, accessed 11 November 2000.

New York City Gay and Lesbian Anti-Violence Project (AVP), and the National Coalition of Anti-Violence Programs (NCAVP), "1998 Report on Lesbian, Gay, Bisexual and Transgender Domestic Violence." Available from http://www.avp.org; Internet, accessed 12 November 2000

NiCarthy, Ginny. *Getting Free: A Handbook for Women in Abusive Relationships*. Seattle: Seal Press, 1986.

Nickel, Robin S. "Children Witnessing Abuse Between Their Same-Gender Caregivers: Impact & Prevention." In *A Professional Guide to Understanding Gay and Lesbian Domestic Violence: Understanding Practice Interventions*, edited by Joan C. McClennen and John Gunther, 145–164. New York: Edwin Mellen Press, 1999.

Opie, Anne. "Qualitative Research, Appropriation of the 'Other' and Empower-
    ment," *Feminist Review* 40 (Spring 1992): 52–69.
O'Neill, Damian. "A Poststructuralist Review of the Theoretical Literature Sur-
    rounding Wife Abuse." *Violence Against Women* 4 (1998): 457–490.
O'Toole, Laura L., and Jessica R. Schiffman, eds. *Gender Violence: Interdisciplinary
    Perspectives*. New York: New York University Press, 1997.
Pearson, Patricia. *When She Was Bad: Violent Women and the Myth of Innocence*.
    Toronto: Random House, 1997.
Pence, Ellen. *In Our Best Interest: A Process for Personal and Social Change*. Du-
    luth, MN: Minnesota Program Development Fund, 1987.
Pharr, Suzanne. *Homophobia: A Weapon of Sexism*. Little Rock, AR: Chardon Press,
    1988.
_____. "Lesbian Battering: Social Change Urged." In *Confronting Lesbian Batter-
    ing: A Manual for the Battered Women's Movement*, edited by Pam Elliott,
    142–157. St. Paul, MN: Minnesota Coalition for Battered Women, 1990.
Plummer, Ken. *Telling Sexual Stories: Power, Change and Social Worlds*. London:
    Routledge, 1995.
Pratt, Mary Louise. *Imperial Eyes: Travel Writing and Transculturation*. New York:
    Routledge, 1992.
Price, Joshua M. "Spaces of Violence, Shades of Meaning: The Heterogeneity of Vio-
    lence Against Women in the United States." Ph.D. dissertation, University of
    Chicago, 1998.
Rabinow, Paul, ed. *The Foucault Reader*. New York: Pantheon Books, 1984.
Razack, Sherene H. *Looking White People in the Eye: Gender, Race, and Culture in
    Courtrooms and Classrooms*. Toronto: University of Toronto Press, 1998.
Reinharz, Shulamit. *Feminist Methods in Social Research*. New York: Oxford Uni-
    versity Press, 1992.
Renzetti, Claire M. "Violence in Lesbian Relationships: A Preliminary Analysis of
    Causal Factors." *Journal of Interpersonal Violence* 3 (1988): 381–399.
_____. "Building a 2nd Closet—3rd Party Responses to Victims of Lesbian Partner
    Abuse." *Family Relations* 38 (1989): 157–163.
_____. *Violent Betrayal: Partner Abuse in Lesbian Relationships*. Newbury Park,
    CA: Sage Publications, 1992.
_____. *Researching Sensitive Topics*. Newbury Park, CA: Sage Publications, 1993.
_____. "Violence in Lesbian Relationships." In *Battering and Family Therapy: A
    Feminist Perspective*, edited by Marsali Hansen and Michele Harway, 188–199.
    Newbury Park, CA: Sage Publications, 1993.
_____. "On Dancing with a Bear: Reflections on Some of the Current Debates
    Among Domestic Violence Theorists." *Violence and Victims* 9 (1994): 195–200.
_____. "Studying Partner Abuse in Lesbian Relationships: A Case for the Feminist
    Participatory Research Model." In *Lesbian Social Services: Research Issues*,
    edited by Carol Thorpe Tully, 29–42. New York: Haworth Press, 1995.
_____. "The Poverty of Services for Battered Lesbians." In *Violence in Gay and
    Lesbian Domestic Partnerships*, edited by Claire M. Renzetti and Charles Harvey
    Miley, 61–68. New York: Harrington Park Press, 1996.

_____. "Violence in Lesbian and Gay Relationships." In *Gender Violence: Interdisciplinary Perspectives*, edited by Laura L. O'Toole and Jessica R. Schiffmann, 285–293. New York: New York University Press, 1997.

_____. "Violence and Abuse in Lesbian Relationships: Theoretical and Empirical Issues." In *Issues in Intimate Violence*, edited by Raquel Kennedy Bergen, 117–128. Thousand Oaks, CA: Sage Publications, 1998.

_____. "The Challenge to Feminism Posed by Women's Use of Violence in Intimate Relationships." In *New Versions of Victims: Feminists Struggle with the Concept*, edited by Sharon Lamb, 42–56. New York: New York University Press, 1999.

Renzetti, Claire M. and Charles Harvey Miley, eds. *Violence in Gay and Lesbian Domestic Partnerships*. New York: Harrington Park Press, 1996.

Ristock, Janice L. "Beyond Ideologies: Understanding Violence in Lesbian Relationships." *Canadian Woman Studies* 12 (1991): 74–79.

_____. "'And Justice for All?'. . . The Social Context of Legal Responses to Abuse in Lesbian Relationships." *Canadian Journal of Women and the Law* 7 (1994): 415–430.

_____. "The Cultural Politics of Abuse in Lesbian Relationships: Challenges for Community Action." In *Subtle Sexism: Current Practice and Prospects for Change*, edited by Nijole Vaicaitis Benokraitis, 279–296. Thousand Oaks, CA: Sage Publications, 1997.

_____. "Community-Based Research: Lesbian Abuse and Other Telling Tales." In *Inside the Academy and Out: Lesbian/Gay/Queer Studies and Social Action*, edited by Janice L. Ristock and Catherine G. Taylor, 137–154. Toronto: University of Toronto Press, 1998.

_____. "Exploring Dynamics of Abusive Lesbian Relationships: Preliminary Analysis of a Multi-Site, Qualitative Study." *American Journal of Community Psychology*, in press.

_____. "Decentering Heterosexuality: Responses of Feminist Counselors to Abuse in Lesbian Relationships." *Women in Therapy*, in press.

Ristock, Janice L., and Joan Pennell. *Community Research as Empowerment: Feminist Links, Postmodern Interruptions*. Toronto: Oxford University Press, 1996.

Ristock, Janice L., and Catherine G. Taylor, eds. *Inside the Academy and Out: Lesbian/Gay/Queer Studies and Social Action*. Toronto: University of Toronto Press, 1998.

Robson, Ruthann. *Lesbian Outlaw: Survival Under the Rule of Law*. Ithaca, NY: Firebrand Books, 1992.

Russo, Ann. "Lesbians Organizing Lesbians Against Battering." In *Same-Sex Domestic Violence: Strategies for Change*, edited by Beth Leventhal and Sandra E. Lundy, 83–96. Thousand Oaks, CA: Sage Publications, 1999.

Santos, Tonja. "Woman-to-Woman Battering on College Campuses." In *Same-Sex Domestic Violence: Strategies for Change*, edited by Beth Leventhal and Sandra E. Lundy, 147–156. Thousand Oaks, CA: Sage Publications, 1999.

Scherzer, Teresa. "Domestic Violence in Lesbian Relationships: Findings of the Lesbian Relationships Research Project." *Journal of Lesbian Studies* 2 (1998): 29–47.

Schilit, Rebecca, Gwat-Yong Lie, and Marilyn Montagne. "Substance Use as a Corre-
    late of Violence in Intimate Lesbian Relationships." *Journal of Homosexuality*
    19, no. 3 (1990): 51–65.
Schilit, Rebecca, Gwat-Yong Lie, Judy Bush, Marilyn Montagne, and Lynn Reyes.
    "Intergenerational Transmission of Violence in Lesbian Relationships." *Affilia* 6
    (1991): 72–87.
Schur, Edwin M. *Labeling Women Deviant*. New York: Random House, 1984.
Scott, Joan. "Experience." In *Feminists Theorize the Political*, edited by Judith But-
    ler and Joan Scott, 22–40. New York: Routledge, 1992.
Simon, Roger I. "The Paradoxical Practice of Zakhor." In *Between Hope and De-
    spair*, edited by Roger I. Simon, Sharon Rosenberg, and Claudia Eppert, 18.
    Lanham, MD: Rowman and Littlefield Publishers, Inc., 2000.
Simon, Roger I., Sharon Rosenberg, and Claudia Eppert, eds. *Between Hope and
    Despair*. Lanham, MD: Rowman and Littlefield Publishers, Inc., 2000.
Sommers, Christina Hoff. *Who Stole Feminism: How Women Have Betrayed Women*.
    New York: Simon and Schuster, 1995.
Spivak, Gayatri Chakravorty. *In Other Worlds: Essays in Cultural Politics*. New
    York: Methuen, 1987.
Stahly, Geraldine Butts, and Gwat-Yong Lie. "Women and Violence: A Comparison of
    Lesbian and Heterosexual Battering Relationships." In *Variations on a Theme: Di-
    versity and the Psychology of Women*, edited by Joan C. Chrisler and Alyce Hus-
    ton Hemstreet, 51–78. Albany, NY: State University of New York Press, 1995.
Stoppard, Janet M. "Women's Bodies, Women's Lives and Depression: Towards a
    Reconciliation of Material and Discursive Accounts." In *Body Talk: The Material
    and Discursive Regulation of Sexuality, Madness and Reproduction*, edited by
    Jane M. Ussher, 10–32. New York: Routledge, 1997.
———. *Understanding Depression: Feminist Social Constructionist Approaches*.
    New York: Routledge, 2000.
Straus, Murray A. "The Conflict Tactics Scale and its Critics: An Evaluation and
    New Data on Validity and Reliability." In *Physical Violence in American Fami-
    lies: Risk Factors and Adaptations to Violence in 8,145 Families*, edited by Mur-
    ray A. Straus and Richard J. Gelles. New Brunswick, NJ: Transaction, 1990.
Straus, Murray A., and Richard Gelles, eds. *Physical Violence in American Families:
    Risk Factors and Adaptations to Violence in 8,145 Families*. New Brunswick, NJ:
    Transaction, 1990.
Straus, Murray A., Richard A. Gelles, and Suzanne K. Steinmetz. *Behind Closed
    Doors: Violence in the American Family*. New York: Doubleday, 1980.
Strauss, Anselm, and Juliet Corbin. *Basics of Qualitative Research: Grounded The-
    ory Procedures and Techniques*. Newbury Park, CA: Sage Publications, 1990.
Taylor, Joelle, and Tracey Chandler. *Lesbians Talk Violent Relationships*. London:
    Scarlet Press, 1995.
Tuel, Beverly D., and Richard K. Russell. "Self-esteem and Depression in Battered
    Women: A Comparison of Lesbian and Heterosexual Survivors." *Violence
    Against Women* 4 (1998): 344–362.

Tully, Carol Thorpe. "Hate Crimes, Domestic Violence, and the Lesbian and Gay Community." In *A Professional Guide to Understanding Gay and Lesbian Domestic Violence: Understanding Practice Interventions*, edited by Joan C. Mc-Clennen and John Gunther, 13–28. Lewsiston, NY: Edwin Mellen Press, 1999.

———. *Lesbians, Gays and the Empowerment Perspective*. New York: Columbia University Press, 2000.

Turell, Susan C. "Seeking Help for Same-Sex Relationship Abuses." *Journal of Gay and Lesbian Social Services* 10, no. 2 (1999): 35–50.

Ussher, Jane M. "Introduction: Towards a Material-Discursive Analysis of Madness, Sexuality and Reproduction." In *Body Talk: The Material and Discursive Regulation of Sexuality, Madness and Reproduction*, edited by Jane M. Ussher, 1–9. London: Routledge, 1997.

———, ed. *Body Talk: The Material and Discursive Regulation of Sexuality, Madness and Reproduction*. London: Routledge, 1997.

Waldner-Haugrud, Lisa K., Linda Vaden Gratch, and Brian Magruder. "Victimization and Perpetration Rates of Violence in Gay and Lesbian Relationships: Gender Issues Explored." *Violence and Victims* 12 (1997): 173–184.

Waldron, Charlene. "Lesbians of Colour and the Domestic Violence Movement." In *Violence in Gay and Lesbian Domestic Partnerships*, edited by Claire M. Renzetti and Charles Harvey Miley, 43–51. New York: Harrington Park Press, 1996.

Walker, Lenore E. *The Battered Woman*. New York: Harper & Row, 1979.

———. "Post-Traumatic Stress Disorder in Women: Diagnosis and Treatment of Battered Woman Syndrome." *Psychotherapy* 28 (1991): 21–29.

Walker, Lydia. "Battered Women's Shelters and Work with Battered Lesbians." In *Naming the Violence: Speaking Out About Lesbian Battering*, edited by Kerry Lobel, 73–76. Seattle: Seal Press, 1986.

Waterman, Caroline K., Lori J. Dawson, and Michael J. Bologna. "Sexual Coercion in Gay Male and Lesbian Relationships: Predictors and Implications for Support Services." *The Journal of Sex Research* 26 (1989): 118–124.

Weick, Ann, and Dennis Saleebey. "Postmodern Perspectives for Social Work." *Social Thought* 18, no. 3 (1998): 21–40.

Weiss, Robert Stuart. *Learning From Strangers: The Art and Method of Qualitative Interview Studies*. New York: Free Press, 1994.

Wilkinson, Sue, and Celia Kitzinger, eds. *Feminism and Discourse: Psychological Perspectives*. London: Sage Publications, 1995.

Wolf, Naomi. *Fire with Fire: The New Female Power and How it Will Change the Twenty-first Century*. London: Chatto and Windus, 1993.

Woman Organized to Make Abuse Nonexistent (W.O.M.A.N.) Inc. [homepage]. Available from http://www.norcov.com/womaninc; Internet, accessed 10 November 2000.

Yllo, Kersti A. "Through a Feminist Lens: Gender, Power and Violence." In *Current Controversies in Family Violence*, edited by Richard J. Gelles and Donileen R. Loseke, 47–62. Newbury Park, CA: Sage Publications, 1993.

Zemsky, Beth. "Lesbian Battering: Considerations for Intervention. In *Confronting*

Lesbian Battering: A Manual for the Battered Women's Movement, edited by Pam Elliott, 64–67. St. Paul, MN: Minnesota Coalition for Battered Women, 1990.

Ziegenmeyer, Nancy. *Taking Back My Life*. New York: Summit Books, 1992.

Zimmerman, Marc A., and Douglas D. Perkins, eds. *Empowerment Theory, Research, and Application*, special issue of *American Journal of Community Psychology* 23 (1995): 569–580.

INDEX

tionships, 56, 108, 175, 181, 185; of
sexual identity, 142, 155, 191; perpetrator, xi, 74, 122, 137; survivor,
122; victim, xi, 74, 101, 137; white
feminist heteronormative, 113
Causby, Vickie, 10
Central America, 156
Chandler, Tracey, 17
Chesley, Laurie, x, 141, 160
childhood sexual abuse. *See* abuse,
childhood; sexual abuse, childhood
children, 32, 50, 90, 144, 168; adop-
tion of, 90
Chrystos, 79
civil rights movement, 1
class, 7, 12, 22, 24, 34, 80, 116, 129,
131, 162, 180; differences, 129; issues, 130
classism, 17, 18, 162, 180, 184, 192
closet, the, 60–62, 94, 98; context of,
62
Coalition: Against Domestic Partner
Abuse, 167; of Lesbians on Support
and Education (CLOSE), x, 165
codependence, 89–91
coercive tactics, 9
Coleman, Valerie, 10, 14
collective consciousness work, 35–36,
139
colonization, 22, 43, 55, 179; context
of, 55, 69; effects of, 70
colonizers, 22
Comaskey, Brenda, 182
Community Holistic Healing Circle Program, 182–83
community(ies): -based innovations,
165–67; education, 156–57, 184;
ethnic, 192; First Nations, 55;
groups, 41; Indigenous, 22, 182–83
(*see also* aboriginal peoples); lesbian
(*see* lesbian, communities); Maori,
183; Ojibway, 182; organizations,
xiii; resource centers, 36, 189; response to relationship violence,
182–84

confidentiality, 33, 97–98, 152, 154,
155, 165, 182, 189, 191
conflict: model of, 12; tactics, 12
Conflict Tactics Scale, 11, 12
control, 51, 74, 76, 127, 150; economic, 8; homophobic, 9, 15; patterns of, 113–15, 127
coping strategies, 49, 75, 81, 93, 105,
179
Cossman, Brenda, 168
counseling, 97, 154, 157, 168, 169,
185, 186, 189; accessibility of, 103;
brief, 142; cost of, 103; couple, 34,
103, 106, 151, 154–55, 160, 163,
184, 192; group, 34, 105; individual, 34, 102–103, 105, 126, 155,
156, 159–60; peer, 189; services, 31,
36, 102
counselors, xi, 24, 31, 34, 82, 96–97,
102–105, 107–108, 155, 185–86,
188, 190, 192; addiction, 192; feminist, 102, 105, 131, 132, 136, 189;
in private practice, 36, 102, 106,
154; lesbian, 36, 102, 189, 192;
transgendered, 168
counterdiscourses, 132–33, 139, 180
criminal justice system, 96, 105, 143,
158, 159, 169, 170, 182; response to
lesbian relationship violence,
99–102, 163
crisis centers, 159, 169; drug, 103; hot-
lines, 97, 157, 189; rape, x, 168,
169–70
culture, 21, 112, 165, 182–83, 185,
191; dominant, 2, 74, 83, 180; heteronormative, 41; homophobic, xi,
60; oppressive, 115; patriarchal,
114–15; radical lesbian feminist, 3;
women's, 3
cycle of violence model, 72

Davis, Madeline, 3
Dawson, Lori, 52
De Vidas, Michael, 18
deconstruction: lens of, 38

institutionalization, 148, 156, 170, 181
interracial couples, 123–25
intersectionality, 17, 18, 22
interventions, 15, 34, 36, 165, 182–83;
     crisis, 166
interviews, xii, 27, 29, 38–39, 138,
     175; with lesbians about violence,
     30–34, 44, 59, 72, 81, 88, 92–93,
     107, 119, 123, 138, 186
intimidation, 112, 113–14
Isaac, Alicia, 10
Island, David, 13
isolation, 57, 87, 94–95, 151, 156, 177,
     187, 190

jealousy, 10, 57
Jhesekah, 167
Johnson, Michael, 56

Kanuha, Valli, 17
Kaye/Kantrowitz, Melanie, 16
Kelly, Liz, 17, 80
Kennedy, Elizabeth, 3
Kidd, Aline, 10
knowledge, 21, 39, 42, 44, 138, 141;
     production of, 19, 20, 42, 44; situ-
     ated, 29
Kreger, Mary, 74

L.A. Gay and Lesbian Center
     (LAGLC): website, 158, 160
Laframboise, Donna, 5, 6, 7
Lamb, Sharon, 21, 80, 81, 86, 94, 143
language, xi, 21, 108, 112, 131,
     137–39, 191, 192; about violence, x,
     2, 27–45, 111–12, 120, 163–64,
     171; exposing, 27–45; practices, 21,
     22, 137; systems, 20
Leeder, Elaine, 56
lesbian: -specfic theories, 13; abuse, xi,
     1–26, 28, 38, 40, 41, 42, 66, 106,
     113–14, 117–19, 121, 133, 137,
     142, 144, 148, 151, 153, 156,
     167–68, 180, 185; abusers, 148,
     153, 158, 161, 182; access to ser-

vices, 34, 129, 131, 142, 155, 166,
     170, 181; bars, 126, 167; battering,
     1–2, 6, 8, 10, 14, 15, 18, 41, 148,
     156; category of, xi, 23, 43; commu-
     nities, x, xi, 2, 3, 8, 30–31, 59, 63,
     95, 97, 107, 126, 131, 133, 137,
     154, 163, 165, 167, 175, 182–83,
     191, 192; couples, 1, 57, 89, 183,
     191; experiences, x, 192; experiences
     of relationship violence, 25, 49–78,
     141; feminist communities, 8, 35;
     health, 19; issues, 145; organiza-
     tions, 170; pride, 106; services, 145;
     sexuality, xii, 54–55, 83, 191;
     spaces, 3; stereotypes, 3, 86, 99,
     101, 184, 187, 190; violence, xii,
     16, 40, 56, 77, 83–84, 112
lesbian partner: abuse, 1–26, 27, 35,
     38, 40, 57, 80, 96, 99, 106, 118,
     131, 155, 168, 170, 181; butch, 50;
     femme, 50, 82; violence, 2, 8, 10,
     35, 39, 52, 72, 77, 82, 105, 108,
     113, 137, 151, 185
lesbian relationship violence, x, xi, 8,
     20, 22, 25, 27, 29, 39, 42–44,
     57–58, 63, 93, 99, 106, 111–12,
     129, 142–43, 145, 163, 180–81,
     184, 186, 191–93; as a cultural con-
     struct, 19; feminist analysis of, 131;
     feminist response to, 36; feminist
     service providers and, 34–37; getting
     help for, 186–93; heterogeneity of,
     22, 161–62; police and justice sys-
     tem responses to, 99–102, 163; poli-
     tics of responding to, 141–71;
     prevalence of, 6, 7, 10–13; research
     on, 42; responding to, 40, 77–78,
     161, 171, 181; situation-specific
     analysis of, 26; social context of, 22,
     118, 191; theories to explain, 13–20;
     websites and manuals on, 39–41,
     155–65, 186–93
lesbian relationships, xiii, 1, 3, 9, 23,
     43–44, 50, 70, 74, 84, 101, 103,
     106, 107, 117–18, 122, 130, 137,